WHAT IS
JEWISH
LITERATURE?

The publication of this book was made possible
through a generous grant from the
NATIONAL FOUNDATION FOR JEWISH CULTURE
through the
Joint Cultural Appeal

WHAT IS
JEWISH
LITERATURE?

Edited with an introduction by
Hana Wirth-Nesher

The Jewish Publication Society

Philadelphia   Jerusalem

5754 / 1994

Library of Congress Cataloging-in-Publication Data

What is Jewish literature? / edited with an introduction
by Hana Wirth-Nesher — 1st ed.

p.   cm.

Includes bibliographical references and index.

ISBN 0-8276-0513-7 (cloth)

ISBN 0-8276-0538-2 (paper)

1. Jewish literature—History and criticism.   2. Jews—Identity.
3. Jews—Intellectual life.   4. American literature—Jewish
authors—History and criticism.   5. Israeli literature—History
and criticism.   I. Wirth-Nesher, Hana, 1948–

PN842.W48   1994

809′.88924—dc20   94–2270

CIP

Designed by Edward D. King

Typeset in Stone Serif by The Composing Room
Printed by Edwards Brothers

To the memory of my father,
Samuel (Wroclawski) Wirth

and for my mother,
Berta Guttmann Wirth

Contents

Acknowledgments

I AM GRATEFUL TO Jacob Staub for being both catalyst and critic, and to Edward Alexander, Dan Miron, and Menakhem Perry for offering sound advice. In addition, I would like to thank Ellen Frankel and Brian McHale for careful readings and valuable suggestions, and David Roskies for all of the above, and for the encouragement that gave the book life. My thanks also to Tamara Adler and Gal Manor for research assistance, to Evelyne Goldblatt and Marie Burgin for technical help, to Diane Zuckerman and Alice Tufel for conscientious editing, and to the Cohen-Porter Fund for the Department of English at Tel Aviv University and to the U.S.-Israel Educational Foundation for financial support. Finally, special appreciation to Ellen Coin and Barry Fishkin for their generosity, and to Arie Nesher for encouragement, help, and a great deal of patience.

Reprint Acknowledgments

Alter, Robert. "Jewish Dreams and Nightmares." In *After the Tradition: Essays on Modern Jewish Writing*. New York: Dutton, 1969, 17–34. Reprinted from *Commentary* (January 1968): 48–54, by permission; all rights reserved.

Baal-Makhshoves [Israel Isidore Elyashev]. "Tsvey shprakhen: eyn eyntsiker literatur." In *Petrograder Tageblatt* [*One Literature in Two Languages*] (Petrograd, 1918). Reprinted in *Geklibene verk*. New York: Cyco-Bicher Farlag, 1953.

Bellow, Saul. "On Jewish Storytelling." In the introduction to *Great Jewish Stories*, edited by Saul Bellow. New York: Dell Publishing, 1963.

Harshav, Benjamin. "The Semiotics of Yiddish Communication." In *The Meaning of Yiddish*, by Benjamin Harshav. Berkeley: The University of California Press, 1990.

Hollander, John. "The Question of American Jewish Poetry." *Tikkun* 3 (May–June 1988): 33–37, 112–116. Copyright 1988 by John Hollander. Reprinted by permission of the author.

Kurzweil, Baruch. "Notes on Hebrew Literature: 1948–1958." *Judaism* 7 (Spring 1958): 121–129.

Markish, Simon. "The Example of Isaac Babel." *Commentary* 64 (November 1977): 36–45.

Miron, Dan. "Modern Hebrew Literature: Zionist Perspectives and Israeli Realities." *Prooftexts: A Journal of Jewish Literary History* 4 (1984): 49–69.

Ozick, Cynthia. "America: Toward Yavneh." *Judaism* 19 (Summer 1970): 264–282.

Ratosh, Yonatan [Uriel Halpern]. "Israeli or Jewish Literature?" Originally a radio lecture, subsequently published in *Machbarot lesifrut* 5 (April 1954), and collected as "Sifrut yehudit o klal-yehudit?" In *Sifruit yehudit be-lashon ha-ivrit* [*Jewish Literature in the Hebrew Language*]. Tel Aviv: Hadar Publishing Co., 1982.

Roskies, David. "The Story's the Thing." *Prooftexts: A Journal of Jewish Literary History* 5 (1985): 67–74.

Shaked, Gershon. "Shadows of Identity: A Comparative Study of German Jewish and American Jewish Literature." In *The Shadows Within: Essays on Modern Jewish Writers*, by Gershon Shaked. Philadelphia: The Jewish Publication Society, 1987, pp. 57–82.

Somekh, Sasson. "Lost Voices: Jewish Authors in Modern Arabic Literature." In *Jews Among Arabs: Contacts and Boundaries*, edited by Mark Cohen and Abraham Udovitch. Princeton: The Darwin Press, 1989.

Wirth-Nesher, Hana. "From Newark to Prague: Roth's Place in the American Jewish Literary Tradition." In *Reading Philip Roth*, edited by Asher Milbauer. London: Macmillan, 1988.

Wisse, Ruth. "Two Jews Talking: A View of Modern Yiddish Literature." *Prooftexts: A Journal of Jewish Literary History* 4 (1984): 35–48.

Introduction

HANA WIRTH-NESHER

Defining the Indefinable: What Is Jewish Literature?

WHILE THE last two decades have witnessed a steady increase in Jewish studies programs and Jewish literature courses throughout universities in the English-speaking world, there is no consensus nor is it likely that there ever will be one about defining the subject under study. This is not surprising in light of the impossibility of arriving at a universally acceptable definition of who is a Jew. The very enigmatic quality of the subject may account for some of its liveliness, but what has been missing for the English-speaking student of Jewish literature is access to the ongoing and often impassioned international debate on the subject of a common Jewish literature. This debate has been in progress since the Enlightenment, when every aspect of Jewish identity was called into question, and it has taken place in Hebrew, in Yiddish, and in the language of each country where Jews have attempted to distinguish a separate literary and cultural tradition, one that transcends linguistic and national boundaries.

The simplest formula for identifying Jewish literature is also the least satisfactory—literature written by Jews. Such a reductive approach, by its indiscriminate inclusiveness and its biological determinism, begs the question of what constitutes Jewish culture as a matrix for Jewish literary texts. Do Sholem Aleichem and Nathanael West really inhabit a shared universe in any respect? Is a writer steeped in Jewish liturgy and Hebrew texts, such as S.Y. Agnon, part of the same literary civilization as Arthur Miller or Bruno Schulz? The most forceful dismissal of the biographical condition is that of Itamar Even-Zohar: "Only a nationalistic Jewish approach, or a racist anti-Semitic one, or ignorance . . . would adopt the term 'Jewish literature' on the basis of origin of writers."[1] Some critics of Jewish literature have argued that theme determines Jewishness, and have then proposed that such universal topics as conflict between generations or ethical

3

commitment are signs of Jewish texts. The latent moral imperialism implied by such an approach is as dismaying as its intellectual shabbiness. Others have insisted that the text needs to be written in a Jewish language, as if that were a self-evident criterion. And even if we were to confine Jewish literature to specific languages, such as Yiddish, Hebrew, and Ladino to name a few obvious candidates, where would we place Kafka? Primo Levi? Elie Wiesel? Saul Bellow? Nelly Sachs? Paul Celan? And would the works of Israeli Arab writers such as Anton Shamas be labeled Jewish literature simply because they were written in Hebrew? This criterion is altogether too tidy, as it ignores cultural affiliations that are not always consistent with language choices.

Some have claimed that Jewishness is measured by religiosity, by what one critic called the "conversion into the essential Jew, achieved by acts of striving, sacrificing, and suffering for the sake of some fundamental goodness . . . that has been lost and buried."[2] Thus, once more, the "essential Jew" is indistinguishable from the essential Christian, or any human victim ennobled by suffering. Others still have argued that Jewish literature is always short-lived, a symptom of incomplete assimilation in the case of immigrant literature or a lack of self-sufficiency in one language and culture. Transient and anomalous, it is always aiming for its own extinction.

Biographical or linguistic definitions aim for limited claims and precision, eschewing the more ambitious attempts to identify a Jewish imagination or a Jewish orientation toward texts. The contrast of Hebraism and Hellenism, going back to the previous century, underscores Judaism's aversion to the pictorial and the aesthetic and its valorization of the abstract. In an essay that eloquently reviews some of the long-standing tenets of a Jewish imagination, Geoffrey Hartman singles out the domination of the written word (a text-dependency), a poetics of imitation where forgetfulness is sinfulness, fantasy always shadowed by profanation because of the absence of a split between letter and spirit, a distinctive humor that assuages the anguish of profanation, an anti-apocalyptic tendency, and a communicative bond strengthened by a hermeneutic tradition in which the imaginative center is not a Person.[3] While any one of these factors may be challenged with counterexamples, this list is a classic case of the whole being greater than the sum of its parts. The composite of these traits approaches a contour of a Jewish imagination that is more problematic than the sharper line drawn by the minimal claims of birth and speech, but it is also a far more compelling picture. Working with the same large canvas, Yossi Yzraely has suggested that Jewish drama is antithetical to the entire tradition of Western theater, which is an art form of the "here and now," propelled by conflict and dependent on action. Yzraely's Jewish drama, in contrast, is based upon a Jewish notion of time that eclipses the present in a vast temporal frame, upon longing and storytelling replacing action and resolution, and upon the repudiation of beginning, middle, and end for a theater where "the beginning is not a beginning and the end is not an end."[4] Finally, in this very brief and sketchy survey, some have suggested that Jewish literature is marked by a profound consciousness of Jewish history, or, in Robert Alter's terms, of drawing upon "literary traditions that are recognizably Jewish."[5] As this formula contains the definition within the bounds of literariness, it is attractive and deceptively neat. Yet it poses intriguing questions: Is Agnon's evocation of the Bible similar to, say, Philip Roth's drawing on Kafka, and in turn, Kafka's drawing on the Yiddish theater? Benjamin Harshav has suggested a provocative reverse case—that the work of New York Yiddish poets such as Moyshe Leib Halpern is actually a lost branch of American literature despite the fact that it is not written in English, because these poets drew on the texts of Whitman and other American writers and self-consciously placed themselves within an American literary tradition.[6]

None of this precludes the possibility that a work can inhabit several literary traditions simultaneously. Its characterization as Jewish will depend upon the reader and all of the circumstances of its reception. Bellow's novel *Mr. Sammler's Planet*, for example, could be comfortably discussed as American fiction, as a Jewish novel, as Holocaust literature. The reader who will recognize that the character of Lionel Feffer, Bellow's caricature of a 1960s radical, is derived in part from Sholem Aleichem's Feffer (Peppercorn) in *Tevye the Dairyman* will be aware of the book's connections to a Jewish literary tradition. But to appreciate it as American literature, such associations are not necessary. The point is, we simply cannot read outside a framework of expectations dictated by familiar categories. While the categories themselves may be unstable and problematic, they are an inherent part of the reading process.

The essays collected in this volume all address the same question—What is Jewish literature?—but each does so in a different voice and from a different perspective. As Jewish civilization has always been an international phenomenon, this volume is an international collection, presenting literary scholars from different countries, writing in different languages and from within different literary frames of reference. It does not attempt to be comprehensive; it does not presume to give voice to all of the literary traditions and languages in this century that have in some fashion participated in the debate. It attempts rather to offer a wide range of positions, of impassioned stands, of rich speculation. Pieces were selected for their location in the controversy, for the way in which they enter into a dialogue with others.

The book is divided into four parts. The first—Jewish Literature in

"Exile"?—takes up the question that has shadowed Jewish writers for cen-turies: How can we sing our songs in a foreign land? And if the Jews sing, what characterizes those songs? Saul Bellow, a Jewish storyteller himself, has identified Jewish literature by its tone, by its blend of laughter and trembling. He makes a plea for accepting what he calls the accidents of history, the Jewish writers who accept the mixture and impurity of their cultural makeup, and inscribe it into their art. One of the most outspoken of the writers in the English-speaking Jewish community, the largest in the world today, has been Cynthia Ozick, who recently claimed that the very phrase "Jewish writer" may be an oxymoron. If paganism is the ultimate ground for all poetry, she argues, literature itself commits the sin of idol worship. In her renewal of what she calls the central quarrel of the West, Hellenism versus Hebraism, she identifies art with anti-Judaism, a recogni-tion that has not interfered with her own writing of fictional works that embody that paradox. In her essay reprinted in this volume, she denies the staying power of any Jewish literature written in the Diaspora that is not "centrally Jewish," that does not draw on liturgy, Torah, Talmud, or any of the traditional religious texts that she identifies as Jewish civilization. Al-though she has subsequently called her plea for a New Yiddish in English merely "a literary conceit calculated to dispel pessimism,"[7] she continues to require a theological underpinning for any Jewish literature, paradoxi-cal though it is, that will last beyond its own generation.

For John Hollander, the very opposite is true. Poetry is not anti-Jewish; on the contrary, poetry is like Jewishness itself in that "both know very well what they are, and though with a lot to say on nearly everything, they cannot explain THAT." Moreover, if the condition of the Jew has been exile, and the condition of the poet is to be exiled from language, then, perhaps, "all poets are Yids," an assertion he quotes from the Russian symbolist poet Marina Tsvetayeva. In that case, the Jewish poet in English, or any other language but Hebrew, is exiled twice from the irrecoverability of an original language. Aware of the dangers of writing in English, a literary tradition encompassing the King James Bible with its distortions of Judaism, Hollander also recognizes the "dangerous iconicity" in a poet's devotion to language. His essay traces the complex and ambivalent path of the Jewish poet in English, sensitive to the interlacing of exile, sacredness, religion, language, and art.

As writers of poems and novels as well as critical essays, Hollander and Ozick both treat the subject of Jewish literature in the language of mystery, of the ineffable, suggesting parallels between the essence of Jewishness and the essence of writing. What Ozick terms mutually exclusive (but fructify-ing nonetheless), Hollander perceives to be more than compatible, to be inextricable. Both write out of some sense of exile, out of their problematic location as self-consciously Jewish poets creating in the English language.

But "exile meant different things to different Jews at various times and places," argues Robert Alter, in an essay that challenges the archetypal reading of Jewish literature, such as that of the dreamer in Exile identified by Leslie Fiedler.[8] By historicizing the Jewish element in a given text, as he does for Kafka, Alter invokes "the bone and blood of Jewish memories" without resorting to mythic archetypes that would be just as applicable to other literatures as to Jewish texts.

Parts II and III—Jewish, Hebrew, or Israeli Literature? and Yiddish Language, Jewish Culture?—deal with debates within the Hebrew and Yiddish literary communities, first concerning the relationship between nationality and Jewishness, primarily as it affects Hebrew literature, and second on the place of talmudic, liturgical, or textual sources for secular Jewish culture and literature. Part IV—Individual Voices, A Common Tradition?— offers case studies of authors from four different traditions whose works— composed in German, Arabic, Russian, and English—have been discussed as instructive examples of major contributions to two literary streams, Jewish and non-Jewish.

The essay by Baal-Makhshoves, which appeared in Yiddish in 1918, must be understood in the context of the heated debate between Yiddishists and Hebraists over the determination of a national language for the Jewish people. Appearing after the Czernowitz conference, which was the arena for empassioned competing claims for Yiddish and Hebrew as authentic languages of the Jewish people, the essay derides what Baal-Makhshoves terms a false polarity, for, according to him, what has characterized Jewish literature going back to biblical times is not one language or the other, but the very fact of bilingualism. "Jewish writers," he claims, "live and breathe between two languages, even as a bridegroom is escorted to the bridal canopy between two parents." The centrality of multilingualism and diglossia in Jewish civilization was later to be explored in the studies of scholars such as Max Weinreich, Joshua Fishman, Itamar Even-Zohar, and Benjamin Harshav, among others.[9] Imbued with nineteenth century romantic nationalism and influenced by Herder's celebration of the folk spirit (*volksgeist*) inherent in every people, Baal-Makhshoves's essay equates the bilingualism of Jewish civilization with its democratic spirit, as it rejects the elitism of only one intellectual language for cultural expression. This essay bristles with the names, movements, and concerns of the author's time, all highly charged ideologically. Finally, in the spirit theorists about the subject, primarily Ahad Ha'am and Dov Sadan. He can recognize Kurzweil's view of Jewish culture as "a myth of a lost paradise," that of traditional Judaism, and he can expose Ratosh's disdain for what he termed immigrant literature, handicapped by its dependence on that same traditional Judaism: "Theories that predicate the existence of a single, all-encompassing Jewish literature are bound to remain ingenious tours de force, which fail to carry conviction." Miron's skepticism and academic precision offer an antidote to the boldly partisan theories of the preceding essays, but the reader will have to decide whether these "ingenious tours de force . . . fail to carry conviction."

In the section on Yiddish literature, three scholars bring a strictly secular approach to questions of Jewishness, locating the literary texts within the broader communication system of the entire culture. These essays are analyses of and elegies for a lost civilization. In the section's first essay, David G. Roskies concisely and provocatively traces the transformation of oral folklore into the modern story in Yiddish and argues that "storytelling was the path of most resistance. To be a professional writer meant to master European forms, to cultivate a 'literary' style, to cater to a differentiated audience. For moderns to choose storytelling was an ideological statement in and of itself." Roskies suggests the role that literature has played in the shaping of modern Jewish collective myth.

Ruth Wisse, in her essay, isolates what she considers to be a distinctive feature of modern Yiddish literature, the conversation among Jews, which "proved an ideal vehicle for exploring and assessing the process of secularization." Tracing this structure in the works of several central figures in Yiddish literature, she identifies the "pitched argument" as an indigenous Jewish form, "evoking generations of student-scholars, the Jewish equivalent of duelers or knights-errant." In an essay on the semiotics of Yiddish communication, Benjamin Harshav proposes a conversational model as well, but one that is derived from talmudic discourse. According to Harshav, no language carries with it an inherent nature; therefore, no language can be inherently Jewish. But at the second level of language—that is, "the 'language' of communication accepted by the speakers of a community"—Yiddish language and culture "internalized and schematized some essential characteristics of 'talmudic' dialectical argument and questioning, combined with typical communicative patterns evolved in the precarious, marginal, Diaspora existence." These characteristics, according to Harshav, are also prevalent in Jewish literature and Jewish "behavior," although he never claims that these are exclusive to Jews. Harshav demonstrates how questioning, with its source in talmudic study, shapes the themes and the structures of Jewish literature.

Each contributor in Part IV, the last section, analyzes one or two major Jewish writers in the context of the author's cultural background. In comparing works of German Jewish and American Jewish literature, Gershon Shaked concludes that the former "took their identity as imposed and absolute, a cruel fate against which they all rebelled," whereas the latter "place less emphasis on pressure from the outside" because "they choose it [their Jewish identity] even though all gates seem to be open." In an earlier study of the Austrian novelist Joseph Roth, Shaked had described the "Jewish" [*sic*] characteristics of a German Jewish novel in the distance between the language of its composition and the language of its fictive world, so that readers experience a type of translation, although they are actually reading the "original."[10] Sasson Somekh, in his essay on Jewish authors in modern Arabic literature, charts the contribution of Jewish writings to the national literatures of both Egypt and Iraq, and he compares the reception of Jewish authors in each of these countries. Despite the differences between the two countries' attitudes toward Jewish culture in their midst, the fate of major Jewish writers working in Arabic, such as Mourad Farag in Egypt and Anwar Sha'ul in Iraq, has been that of "lost voices," and Somekh's essay raises questions about the role of the national literatures of Jewish writers in the formation and recognition of Jewish literature in the Diaspora.

To be a Jewish writer in another language and culture, according to Simon Markish, is "to find harmony in dichotomy." This is what he sees in the case of Isaac Babel, who could describe a pogrom "with a clear, calm, and at times even admiring gaze," who could remain loyal to the Soviet regime while pleading with his wife to give their daughter a Jewish name, unsuccessfully. For Markish, Babel is "the most important figure in Russian Jewish literature of the Soviet period, the model of the writer in Soviet-Russian culture." Moreover, that "calm gaze" at two cultures, both of which formed his identity, constitutes "an innovation of the greatest significance for the modern Jewish literatures of the Diaspora."

Finally, my own discussion of Philip Roth in the American Jewish literary tradition focuses on two main issues: the place of the Holocaust in the self-definition of American Jewish writers and the need for a writer like Roth to construct a dual literary heritage for himself, American and Jewish. Roth's repeated and ironic invocation of both Henry James and Franz Kafka (among others) as literary precursors marks his self-conscious participation in two literary cultures. Like many other American Jewish writers, Roth is haunted by the "counterlife," the road not taken, the fate of European Jewry, the alter ego, and even more specifically, the Jewish writers silenced in the Holocaust. In his epilogue to the trilogy *Zuckerman Bound*, Roth invents yet another significant literary precursor, Sisovsky, a fictional author said to have been shot by the Gestapo, whose lost manuscripts the American Jewish writer Zuckerman has come to Prague to recover from oblivion. From the thinly veiled biographical details and from the knowledge of Roth's own mission to publish the works of Eastern European writers in his Other Europe series, it is clear that the inspiration for Sisovsky was the Polish Jewish writer Bruno Schulz, murdered in the street before he could finish his work-in-progress, *The Messiah*, a much sought-after but as yet unretrieved manuscript.

In her novel *The Messiah of Stockholm*, Cynthia Ozick made Bruno Schulz the obsession of her central protagonist, a man convinced that he is Schulz's child and driven to find the lost manuscript. One of the most exciting Israeli books to appear in recent years, David Grossman's *See Under: Love*, exposes the traumatized collective memory of Israeli society through the metaphor of a character's obsession with Bruno Schulz and the same lost manuscript. Across national and linguistic boundaries, these authors are all in quest of the *same* literary parent. A sign of the multinational novel, common to post-modernism? A sign of yet another form of Jewish literature?

While my essay on Philip Roth contains the last words in this collection, they are, of course, not the final words. It would be foolhardy to choose any position or to force a conclusion. Recently it has been suggested that an entire genre has been overlooked in English literary history, the novel of Jewish identity. Written by non-Jews, these novels—such as Maria Edgeworth's *Harrington* or George Eliot's *Daniel Deronda*—all attempt to exorcise the powerful figure of Shylock from the English imagination.[11] Is this yet another branch of Jewish literature? The debate goes on. This volume is offered to the reader not for its comprehensiveness, but rather for its provocation to enter into the debate. The contributors themselves reflect the multilingual and international nature of any discussion about Jewish culture. Some are affiliated with Israeli universities, others with universities in Europe or the United States. The countries of origin range from Germany and Poland, to Iraq, Israel, and the United States. Some are poets and fiction writers themselves, as well as critics, scholars, and teachers. The voices range from the polemical to the speculative, from the scientific to the lyrical. Several sadly note the passing of the Jewish literature they describe; others celebrate continuities in Jewish culture. Some quote or argue with the other contributors in this volume. They were all collected in the spirit of contemporary discussions about the cultural constructedness of collective identities, whether they be ethnic, national, racial, or other.[12] By placing such divergent concepts of Jewish literature between the covers of one book, I have aimed to undermine any one essentialist view of Jewish culture, while at the same time tracing the distinctive features of the act of self-definition in recent Jewish literary history. Each of these definitions is an invention that answers specific needs of time and place. What *is* Jewish literature? Why do you want to know? Who said such a thing exists anyway? And why not ask?

Notes

1. Itamar Even-Zohar, "Israeli Hebrew Literature: A Model," *Papers in Historical Poetics* (Tel Aviv: The Porter Institute for Poetics and Semiotics, 1978), 80. See also "Aspects of the Hebrew-Yiddish Polysystem," *Poetics Today*, 11 (Spring 1990): 121–131.

2. Theodore Solotareff, "Philip Roth and the Jewish Moralists," *Chicago Review* 8 (1959).

3. Geoffrey Hartman, "On the Jewish Imagination," *Prooftexts: A Journal of Jewish Literary History* 5 (1985): 201–220. Reprinted in *Contemporary Jewish Religious Thought*, ed. Arthur A. Cohen and Paul Mendes-Flohr (New York: Charles Scribner's Sons, 1987).

4. Interview with Yossi Yzraely, Tel Aviv, August 1991.

5. Robert Alter, "Jewish Dreams and Nightmares," *Commentary* 45 (January 1968): 48. Reprinted in this volume.

6. Benjamin Harshav and Barbara Harshav, "Introduction," in *American Yiddish Poetry: A Bilingual Anthology* (Berkeley: University of California Press, 1988).

7. Cynthia Ozick, Introductory Note to "Toward a New Yiddish," in *Art and Ardor* (New York: E.P. Dutton, 1984), 152.

8. Leslie Fiedler, "The Jew in American Literature," in *The Collected Essays of Leslie Fiedler* (New York: Stein and Day, 1970).

9. See Joshua Fishman, *Sociolinguistics: A Brief Introduction* (Rowley, Mass.: Newbury House Publishers, 1972); Max Weinreich, *History of the Yiddish Language* (Chicago: University of Chicago Press, 1980); Uriel Weinreich, *Languages in Contact: Findings and Problems* (New York: Publications of the Linguistic Circle of New York, 1953); Itamar Even-Zohar, "The Nature and Functionalization of the Language of Literature Under Diglossia," *Hasifrut* 2, no. 2 (1970): 286–303 [in Hebrew; English summary, pp. 443–446]; id., "Aspects of the Hebrew-Yiddish Polysystem," in *Poetics Today*; Harshav and Harshav, "Introduction," in *American Yiddish Poetry*.

10. Gershon Shaked, "How Jewish is a German Jewish Novel? Joseph Roth's *Hiob, Roman eines einfachen Mannes*," originally published as "Wie Judisch ist ein Judisch-Deutscher Roman? Uber Joseph Roth's *Hiob, Roman eines einfachen Mannes*, in *Bulletin des Leo Baeck Instituts* (Judischer Verlag, vol. 73, 1986).

11. See Michael Ragussis, "Representation, Conversion, and Literary Form: *Harrington* and the Novel of Jewish Identity," *Critical Inquiry* 16 (Autumn 1989): 113–144.

12. Among the studies addressing this subject are Homi K. Bhabha, ed., *Nation and Narration* (New York: Routledge, 1990); Benedict Anderson, *Imagined Communities* (London: Verso, 1983); Werner Sollors, ed., *The Invention of Ethnicity* (New York: Oxford, 1989).

I.
Jewish Literature in "Exile"?

SAUL BELLOW

On Jewish Storytelling

THE RELIGION of the Jews has appeared to the world as divinely inspired history. The message of the Old Testament, however, cannot be easily separated
from its stories and metaphors. Various commentators, unrestrained by
orthodoxy and looking at the Bible with the clear or cold eye of the twentieth century, have spoken of the books of both testaments as novels.

The late Ernest Sutherland Bates edited a Bible "to read as living literature" and D.H. Lawrence spoke of the patriarchs and King David as though
they were fictional characters. Thomas Mann, in one of his Joseph novels,
suggests that in having a story to tell, the nearly tragic account of the envy
of his brethren (how he was given a coat of many colors; how his brothers
were angry; how he was sold into Egypt by them; how his father mourned
him; how he was molested by Potiphar's wife and imprisoned; how he
interpreted dreams and rose to greatness; how there was a famine in the
land and his brothers came to buy grain; how he revealed himself at last to
them)—that in having such a story to tell Joseph may have been a greater
man than the Pharaoh, his master.

For there is power in a story. It testifies to the worth, the significance of
an individual. For a short while all the strength and all the radiance of the
world are brought to bear upon a few human figures.

Hamlet, dying, says to his friend:

O God, Horatio, what a wounded name,
Things standing thus unknown, shall live behind me!
If thou didst ever hold me in thy heart,
Absent thee from felicity awhile,
And in this harsh world draw thy breath in pain,
To tell my story.

(Act V, scene ii)

In defeat, a story contains the hope of vindication, of justice. The storyteller is able to make others accept his version of things. And in the stories

15

of the Jewish tradition the world, and even the universe, have a human meaning. Indeed, the Jewish imagination has sometimes been found guilty of overhumanizing everything, of making too much of a case for us, for mankind, and of investing externals with too many meanings. To certain writers, Christianity itself has appeared to be an invention of Jewish storytellers whose purpose has been to obtain victory for the weak and the few over the strong and the numerous. To such accusations Jews would apply the term *bilbul*. A *bilbul* is a false charge; literally, a confusion.

For the last generation of East European Jews, daily life without stories would have been inconceivable. My father would say, whenever I asked him to explain any matter, "The thing is like this. There was a man who lived . . ." "There was once a scholar . . ." "There was a widow with a son . . ." "A teamster was driving on a lonely road. . . ."

An old man lived all alone in the forest. He was the last of his family and he was so sick and feeble that he could hardly cook his gruel. Well, one cold day he had no more firewood and he went out to gather some. He was stooped and old and he carried a rope. In the woods he spread the rope on the snow and laid his fuel on it and tied a knot but he was too weak to lift the bundle. This was too much for him.

He lifted his eyes and called to Heaven. "Gott meiner. Send me Death." At once he saw the Angel of Death coming toward him. And the Angel said to him, "You sent for me, what do you want?" And the old man thought quickly and said, "Yes, as a matter of fact I did. I can't get these sticks up on my back and wonder if you'd mind giving me a hand."

"So, you see, when it comes to dying," my father said, "nobody is really ready."

Three Jews were boasting of their rabbis, and one said, "My rabbi's faith is so great and he fears the Lord so much that he trembles day and night, and he has to be belted into his bed at night with straps so that he doesn't fall out."

The second said, "Yes, you have a marvelous rabbi, but he really can't be compared to my rabbi. Mine is so holy and so just that he makes God tremble. God is afraid of displeasing him. And if the world has not been going so well lately, you can figure it out for yourselves. God is trembling."

The third Jew said, "Your rabbis are both great men. No doubt about it. But my rabbi passed through both stages. For a long time he trembled, too, and in the second stage, he made God tremble. But then he thought it over very carefully and finally he said to God, 'Look—why should we both tremble?'"

I would call the attitudes of these stories characteristically Jewish. In them, laughter and trembling are so curiously mingled that it is not easy to of the People of the Book, he identifies Jewish literature itself with its inherent bilingualism as the genuine Jewish homeland.

The next two essays, which first appeared nearly forty years ago, take controversial and opposing positions regarding the relationship among Jewish, Hebrew, and Israeli literature. While their diagnosis of the cultural situation in Israel during the early years of statehood is similar, namely that the emerging indigenous Israeli literature was separating itself from its Jewish sources and traditions, their prescriptions for that emergent nation could not have been more different. Baruch Kurzweil lamented the rupture with the Jewish past and predicted that secular Zionism, in its zeal to create a wholly new Hebrew national culture, would become "a generation without books," naked in its "renunciation of Judaism." Yonatan Ratosh, on the other hand, advocated a strict severance from Hebrew literature in the Diaspora, and from Jewish literature generally. Calling Kurzweil "that great devotee of a universal Jewish literature," Ratosh warned that an Israeli literature based on "pipe dreams and yearnings for the banks of the Rhine and the Vistula" would only result in a "disconnected literature" not of "the motherland, but at best the literature of the provinces." A leading figure among the Young Hebrews, coined "the Canaanites" by their opponents, Ratosh aimed for a national identity rooted in the Middle East and predating Judaism. The national Hebrew literature, Ratosh argued, would no longer be Jewish literature. Kurzweil called Ratosh "the aesthetic and ideological firebrand of the opposition movement." At stake in this debate is the formation of national character as it separated itself from its parent culture. What Ratosh envisioned as healthy self-sufficiency and rootedness, Kurzweil diagnosed as spiritually crippling. Kurzweil's plea for a return to the spiritual sources of Jewish life, on the other hand, were dismissed by Ratosh, in his zealous nationalism, as provincial and stultifying.

In contrast to both Ratosh and Kurzweil, who believed in the existence of a universal, multilingual Jewish literature but differed in their attitudes toward it, Dan Miron repudiates this notion entirely: "There is no such thing as a unified Jewish literature, and there has not been one since the fragmentation of our national culture at the end of the eighteenth and beginning of the nineteenth centuries." Out of this insistence on the arbitrariness of all formulations about Jewish literature, Miron is able to place both Kurzweil and Ratosh ideologically, to explain how and why they reached their conclusions, and to view them in the context of other major determine the relations of the two. At times the laughter seems simply to restore the equilibrium of sanity; at times the figures of the story, or parable, appear to invite or encourage trembling with the secret aim of overcoming it by means of laughter. Aristophanes and Lucian do not hesitate to involve the Olympian gods in their fun, and Rabelais's humor does not spare the heavens either. But these are different kinds of comic genius. Jewish humor is mysterious and eludes our efforts—even, in my opinion, the efforts of Sigmund Freud—to analyze it.

Recently, one Jewish writer (Hyman Slate in *The Noble Savage*) has argued that laughter, the comic sense of life, may be offered as proof of the existence of God. Existence, he says, is too funny to be uncaused. The real secret, the ultimate mystery, may never reveal itself to the earnest thought of a Spinoza, but when we laugh (the idea is remotely Hasidic), our minds refer us to God's existence. Chaos is exposed. . . .

Quite understandably, to the writer in the Russian Pale it seemed most important to present Jewish life as sympathetically as possible. Because the Jews were remorselessly oppressed, all the good qualities of Jewish life were heaped up in the foreground of their stories. Raw things—jealousies, ambitions, hatreds—were frequently withheld.

The Jewish slums of Montreal during my childhood, just after the First World War, were not too far removed from the ghettos of Poland and Russia. Life in such places of exile and suffering was anything but ordinary. But whatever it was, ordinary or extraordinary, harsh or sweet, it was difficult to recognize it in the work of most modern Jewish writers. These writers generally tended to idealize it, to cover it up, in prayer shawls and phylacteries and Sabbath sentiment, the Seder, the matchmaking, the marriage canopy; for sadness the Kaddish, for amusement the *schnorrer*, for admiration the bearded scholar. Jewish literature and art have sentimentalized and sweetened the ghetto; their "pleasing" pictures are far less interesting than the real things.

In this century, so agonizing to the Jews, some people think it wrong to object to such lack of realism, to insist on maintaining the distinction between public relations and art. It may appear that the survivors of Hitler's terror in Europe and Israel will benefit more from good publicity than from realistic representation, or that posters are needed more urgently than masterpieces. Admittedly, say some people, *Exodus* was not much of a novel, but it was extraordinarily effective as a document and we need such documents now. We do not need stories like Philip Roth's which expose unpleasant Jewish traits.

The Jews are much slandered, much threatened, greatly sinned against—should they for these reasons be unfairly represented in literature, to their alleged advantage? The question is a very ticklish one. It could be shown, I think, that the argument based on need is also the one used by Khrushchev. The Russian oligarchy approves only of what it quaintly calls "socialist realism." It would prefer to have us read Simonov rather than Pasternak. Paradoxically, therefore, the American Jewish public buys Uris and Pasternak for entirely different reasons—*Exodus* because it is good for us, and *Doctor Zhivago* because it is bad for them.

In literature we cannot accept a political standard. We can only have a literary one. But in all the free countries of the world, Jewish writers are able to write exactly as they please, in French (André Schwartz-Bart), in Italian (Italo Svevo), in English, or in Yiddish and Hebrew.

In Jerusalem several years ago I had an amusing and enlightening conversation with the dean of Hebrew writers, S.Y. Agnon. This spare old man, whose face has a remarkably youthful color, received me in his house, not far from the barbed wire entanglements that divide the city, and while we were drinking tea, he asked me if any of my books had been translated into Hebrew. If they had not been, I had better see to it immediately, because, he said, they would survive only in the Holy Tongue. His advice, I assume, was only half serious. This was his witty way of calling my attention to a curious situation. I cited Heinrich Heine as an example of a poet who had done rather well in German.

"Ah," said Mr. Agnon, "we have him beautifully translated into Hebrew. He is safe."

Mr. Agnon feels secure in his ancient tradition. But Jews have been writing in languages other than Hebrew for more than two thousand years. The New Testament scholar Hugh J. Schonfield asserts that parts of the Gospels were composed in a sort of Yiddish Greek, "as colorful in imagery and metaphor as it is often careless in grammatical construction."

With less wit and subtlety than Mr. Agnon, other Jewish writers worry about using the languages of the Diaspora. They sometimes feel like borrowers, compelled by strange circumstances to use a tongue of which their ancestors were ignorant. I cannot recall that Joseph Conrad, a Pole, ever felt this to be an intolerable difficulty. He loved England and the English language. I do remember that James Joyce, an Irishman, did feel such a difficulty. Stephen Dedalus in *A Portrait of the Artist* somewhat envies an old English Jesuit, perfectly at home in his own language. But then, young Dedalus was at this period of his life still rather parochial. In a story by Meyer Levin, one character exclaims:

> I was a foreigner, writing in a foreign language . . . What am I? Native, certainly. My parents came to this country . . . they were the true immigrants, the actual foreigners. . . . But I, American-born, raised on hot dogs,

I am out of place in America. Remember this: art to be universal must be narrowly confined. An artist must be a perfect unit of time and place, at home with himself, unextraneous. Who am I? Where do I come from? I am an accident. What right have I to scribble in this American language that comes no more naturally to me than it does to the laundry Chinaman?

Theories like those expressed by Mr. Levin's character, as Mr. Levin is at pains to show, about the "perfect unit of time and place," seldom bring any art into the world. Art appears, and then theory contemplates it; that is the usual order in the relations between art and theory. It cannot be argued that the stories of Isaac Babel are not characteristically Jewish. And they were written in Russian by a man who knew Yiddish well enough to have written them in that language. Before he disappeared from view during one of Stalin's purges, Babel had been put in charge of publishing the works of Sholem Aleichem in Yiddish. Why should he have chosen, therefore, to write his own stories in Russian, the language of the oppressors, of Pobodonostev and the Black Hundreds? If, before writing, he had taken his bearings, he could not have found himself to be "a perfect unit of time and place." He wrote in Russian from motives we can never expect to understand fully. These stories have about them something that justifies them to the most grudging inquiry—they have spirit, originality, beauty. Who was Babel? Where did he come from? He was an accident. We are all such accidents. We do not make up history and culture. We simply appear, not by our own choice. We make what we can of our condition with the means available. We must accept the mixture as we find it—the impurity of it, the tragedy of it, the hope of it.

America: Toward Yavneh

Two years ago an illustrious man of letters came out of Diaspora to this place [Israel] and offered Exile as a metaphor for the Essential Jew, and himself as a metaphor of Exile. He came, he said, as a visitor. Now immediately I would distinguish between a visitor and a pilgrim: both will come to a place and go away again, but a visitor arrives, a pilgrim is restored. A visitor passes through a place; the place passes through the pilgrim. A visitor comes either to teach or learn or perhaps simply and neutrally to observe; but a pilgrim comes on purpose to be taught renewal. And so, as self-defined "guest" and ideological outsider, this visitor I speak of designated, with all authenticity, his personal mode, mien, and consciousness as exilic; then, less authentically, he characterized Exile as an arena for humankind's finest perceptions, free of "lunatic parochialism"; and finally —questionably—he concluded that to be most exiled is to be most exalted, that a sensibility most outside the commonality of Jews is most within the "genius of Judaism." "Yes," he said, "I *am* a wanderer, a *Luftmensch*. . . . But I have made of my harrying . . . a creative impulse so strong that it has recast much of the politics, art, and intellectual constructs of the age." Far from being cultural disaster, outsideness becomes cultural opportunity. "Marx lies in Highgate and Freud in Golders Green . . . Einstein's ashes were scattered off New Jersey." Think also of Trotsky, Kafka, Levi-Strauss, Chomsky, Spinoza, Heine. Homelessness is the virtue of being disarmed, and powerlessness has at least the power to slay without weaponry the serpent Nationalism, whose secret name is Atavistic Tribalism. By declaring himself marginal man, wanderer, and guest, the visitor pronounced himself "unto the elements . . . free." Impressively in command of the lyrical and the moral imagination, he put both at the service of his percep-

---

This talk was delivered at the Weizmann Institute in Rehovoth, Israel, in the summer of 1970.

tion of universalism, and called this the genius of Judaism. Diaspora, then, is the rootless though paradoxically fruitful soil of the Essential Jew (explained the visitor), and my own envisioning sensibility, born of my precarious tenure there (explained the visitor), is the genius of Judaism. Diaspora, *c'est moi*: what I am, he in effect told us, is what a Jew ought to be—thereby elevating his individual and personal satisfactions to a general theory in fact to a behavioral ideal.

Now my intention here is not to fall into a polemical struggle with an absent luminary. I am on another line, and am lured by a seizure of history more deeply ancient than any local debate in a corner of our current Dispersion. George Steiner justifies his vision of Diaspora partly by his own achievements and reputation, partly through contemplation of the achievements and reputation of other Jews. What I want to question—the vocation and leash of these speculations—is whether the accomplishments of Jews in Diaspora are in fact *Jewish* accomplishments; and further, whether it matters that they are or are not. When George Steiner speaks of universalism and calls it Jewish, for instance, I agree that universalism is of course a Jewish impulse—but not as he conceives it. Jewish universalism emphasizes that the God of Israel is also the God of mankind-in-general. It does not claim that the God of mankind-in-general must be the God of Israel. To celebrate what the "harrying" of Diaspora does for the Jew is somehow also to celebrate the harrying. You cannot praise the consequence without some of your praise sticking to its brute instrumentality. An idol is a-thing-that-subsists-for-its-own-sake-without-a-history; significantly, that is also what a poem is; and even universalism can become tainted if it is turned into an idol or a poem. In short, even if Diaspora is credited with begetting, or reinforcing, the universalist mentality, it remains a perverse criterion.

By contrast, then, I come to this place as a pilgrim, to speak in dispraise of Diaspora: I include specifically the Diaspora of freedom. Now, it is well-known that dispraise of Diaspora is an obvious and popular stance among some Israelis. And indeed it could not be otherwise, since Zionism is an inspiration with two parents: the memory of home, its warm mother; revulsion against Exile, its stern father. But lately we have seen—particularly at the time of the Eichmann trial we saw—how Israeli rejection of Diaspora becomes not a revulsion against the millennial victimization of *galut* experience, but a revulsion against the victimized Jew himself—his preoccupations, his manners and mores, the very shape of his body. The distastefulness of the portrait, its emphasis on pettiness and cowardice, coincides remarkably with that of the classical anti-Semite—also, more pathetically, with that of the classical Jewish anti-Semite. It is a description frequently in the mouths of some English and American Jews as well, and it might have been partly to counteract such unhappy distortions that George Steiner drew his opposite portrait of the Jew as *Luftmensch*, ennobled by otherness, universalized through wandering, gifted in his homelessness by exceptional sight and judgment, made free by unbelonging. If George Steiner has special praise for the human consequences of the two thousand years between Israel and Israel, some Israelis would negate and disvalue that same period as if it never was. Both the praise and the dispraise are partial renderings of root situations—but they are superficial because they are largely social responses; they are told in the language of a kind of rhetoricized sociology. My dispraise of Diaspora means to take another direction; it is centered on a revulsion against the values—very plainly I mean the beliefs—of the surrounding culture itself; a revulsion against Greek and pagan modes, whether in their Christian or post-Christian vessels, whether in their purely literary vessels, or whether in their vessels of *Kulturgeschichte*. It is a revulsion—I want to state it even more plainly— against what is called, strangely, Western Civilization.

I have this in common with Steiner: like him, I want to offer myself as a metaphor of Diaspora. Steiner finds his construct of Diaspora appropriate to some aspects of himself; so do I. I say with him, Diaspora, *c'est moi*; only the view darkly differs. For one thing, I am the ordinary Diaspora animal, and this makes me a better, or at least a more useful, because worse, example. Let me tell you what I do and how I live. I am a writer, slow and unprolific, largely unknown. Obscurity is here doubly and triply pertinent, for to be a writer is to be almost nothing; the writer is not a religious thinker, or a philosopher, or a political scientist, or a historian, or a sociologist, or a philologist. To be a writer is to be an autodidact, with all the limitations, gaps, and gaucheries typical of the autodidact, who belabors clichés as though they were sacral revelations. Especially as a Jew I am an autodidact; the synagogue at present does not speak to me, and I have no divine shelter other than reading; at the moment print is all my Judaism, and I crawl through print besotted with avaricious ignorance, happening here and there upon a valley of light. My reading has become more and more urgent, though in narrower and narrower channels. I no longer read much "literature." I read mainly to find out not what it is to be a Jew—my own life in its quotidian particulars tells me that—but to find out what it is to *think* as a Jew. Novels and poems no longer appear to address me; even our celebrated Jewish novelists, though I read them all, appear to be in the grip of a sociology more or less gross, more or less revealing; the only Jewish novelist who seems to me purely and profoundly ideational is Saul Bellow—so I sit alone in a wastepile of discarded artists, reading one novelist. But one is not enough to make what we always hear called a Literary Renaissance among American Jews. Until very recently, my whole life was given over to the religion of Art, which is the religion of the Gentile nations—I had no other aspiration, no other commitment, was zealous for no other creed. In my twenties I lived for the life of the elderly Henry James. In my thirties I worshipped E. M. Forster for the lure of his English paganism. Fifteen years went into a silent and shadowed apprenticeship of craft and vision. When at last I wrote a huge novel I meant it to be a Work of Art—but as the years ground through that labor, it turned, amazingly and horribly, into a curse. I discovered at the end that I had cursed the world I lived in, grain by grain. And I did not know why. Furthermore, that immense and silent and obscure labor had little response—my work did not speak to the Gentiles, for whom it had been begun, nor to the Jews, for whom it had been finished. And I did not know why. Though I had yearned to be famous in the religion of Art, to become so to speak a saint of Art, I remained obscure. —Diaspora, *c'est moi*: remember that I speak of myself metaphorically only, and so I do not use the word "obscurity" as having anything to do with personal reputation, but with shadow, with futility, with vanity, frivolity, and waste. I include in this hopeless destiny of obscurity persons of splendid achievement, eminent writers who have performed brilliant summarizing work. I include George Steiner, and Walter Kaufmann who spoke here last year in impassioned disparagement of nationalism; I include the spectacular Leslie Fiedler and the marvelously gifted Philip Roth who said: "I am not a Jewish writer; I am a writer who is a Jew." I do not know whether he would hold this view today. Nevertheless, Philip Roth's words do not represent a credo; they speak for a doom. I will come back to them shortly.

Thirty years ago, literary idealism was captured by the band styled as New Critics. These were largely Christian Karaites who would allow no tradition to be attached to a text. The history, psychology, and even the opinions of a writer were declared irrelevant to the work and its word. A ritual called *explication du texte* was the sacrament of this movement. It died out, killed by the power and persuasiveness of biography, but also because of the rivalry and exhaustion of its priests. For the priests of that sect, the text had become an idol: humanity was left out. (Some of the best critics of that time and afterward, Lionel Trilling, Philip Rahv, Alfred Kazin and Irving Howe, were Jews; they did not conform, and put humanity back in.) Now again, after a period of vagueness and confusion following the dissolution of the New Criticism, the text has become an idol, though in another form.

Now it is the novel that has been aestheticized, poeticized, and thereby paganized. I will try to seize these complexities in the briefest way, by grabbing hold only of the points that stick out the most. The most flagrant point is this: the nineteenth-century novel has been pronounced dead. Since the nineteenth-century novel is essentially *the* novel, some conclude that the novel itself is dead. Critics now talk of "exhausted forms"— narrative is played out, psychology is played out, and so forth. So what is left? Two possibilities: parody of the old forms, Tolstoyan mockeries such as Nabokov's; and a new "form" called language, involving not only parody, but game, play, and rite. The novel is now said to be "about itself," a ceremony of language. This is currently the only sort of fiction receiving the practical attention of serious literary intellectuals in America. How to describe the genesis of this new breed of novel? Its father is the Frenchman Robbe-Grillet, its mother is the de-Judaized American aesthetician Susan Sontag; its diligent foster-uncles are two de-Judaized American critics, Kostelanetz and Gilman. Its practitioners are by and large not Jews. Where so many Jews are writers of fiction, this has a certain significance as to temperament. Roth, Bellow, and Malamud, the most celebrated of the Jewish writers, are all accused of continuing to work in "exhausted forms."

But this is not the real burden of the accusation; modes of technique are not the real issue. What is regarded as exhausted in nineteenth-century fiction is not simply the worked-out vein of characterization and story-telling, but something beyond mere devices: call it History, call it Idea. The novel at its nineteenth-century pinnacle was a Judaized novel. George Eliot and Dickens and Tolstoy were all touched by the Jewish covenant; they wrote of conduct and of the consequences of conduct; they were concerned with a society of will and commandment. At bottom it is not the old novel as "form" that is being rejected, but the novel as a Jewish force. The "new" novel, by contrast, is to be taken like a sacrament. It is to be a poem without a history—which is to say an idol. It is not to judge or interpret. It is to *be*; it is not to allow anything to *happen* or *become*. "Happen" implies history, "becomes" implies idea; both imply *teshuvah*, a turning. But the new fiction is to be the literary equivalent of the drug culture, or of Christianity. It is to be self-sustaining, enclosed, lyrical, and magical—like the eucharistic moment, wherein the word makes flesh. "Life," writes one of the most praised of these practitioners, "is not the subject of fiction."[1] Fiction, he says, "is where characters, unlike ourselves, freed from existence, can shine like essence, and purely Be"—and he quotes from Ortega y Gasset in a passage despising those who will not "adjust their attention . . . to the work of art; instead they penetrate through it to passionately wallow in the human reality which the work of art refers to." But it is above all the Jewish sense-of-things to "passionately wallow in the human reality." Covenant and conduct are above decoration. The commandment against idols, it seems to me, is overwhelmingly pertinent to the position of the Jewish fiction writer in America today. If he feels separate from the religion of Art in the streets, he can stay out of the streets. But if the religion of Art is to dominate imaginative literature entirely, and I believe it will in America for a very long time, can he stay out of American literature?

If he wants to stay Jewish, I think he will have to. Even as a writer, especially as a writer, he will have to acknowledge exile. If what I have called aesthetic paganism is to be a long-range thesis of American culture, then it is not the kind of literary or social culture he can be at home in. The problem of Diaspora in its most crucial essence is the problem of aesthetics. This no doubt sounds very abstract, despite those social particulars I have tried to illustrate with. But it is not abstract. The German Final Solution was an aesthetic solution: it was a job of editing, it was the artist's finger removing a smudge, it simply annihilated what was considered not harmonious. In daily life the morality of Germans continued as before, neighbors were kindly—who can deny it? From the German point of view, getting rid of the Jew had nothing to do with conduct and everything to do with art. The religion of Art isolates the Jew—only the Jew is indifferent to aesthetics, only the Jew wants to "passionately wallow in the human reality." Among the ancients it was the Greeks, not the Jews, who contemplated pure form. Even now, in the whole planet of diverse cultures, the Jew is the only one who stands there naked without art. The Jewish writer, if he intends himself really to be a *Jewish* writer, is all alone, judging culture like mad, while the rest of the culture just goes on *being* culture. Earlier I quoted George Steiner's view that the Jew has "recast much of the politics, art and intellectual constructs of the age." No. He has recast nothing, least of all arts. He has judged what he found. If he does not judge what he finds, if he joins it instead, he disappears. Those Diaspora Jews who survive and transcend alien cultures—Steiner cites, among others, Freud and Kafka—are precisely those who judge it. Critics, interpreters, summarizers of culture who are Jews can at least breathe, if only transiently, in Diaspora. If they are giants, like Freud and Kafka, they may endure, though one becomes less and less assured of the long-term survival, even of Freud.

But for those who are less than giants—and culture is what happens every day, culture is normality, culture is dependent for its sustenance not on its major but on its minor figures—for those Jewish summarizers and literary and cultural critics and observers who do not tower over but rather hope merely to sustain, history promises little. The culture they buzz round like honeybees drops them. They become non-existent. This is not because they are minor figures to begin with; as I have said, a culture is fed chiefly by its diligent second-rank. But the diligent second-rank, when it is Jewish, does not survive even as minor. Compare Chesterton and Israel

Zangwill. Both were of what we now call a "minority faith," one a Catholic, one a Jew; born ten years apart, they had, in a literary way, similar careers. But everybody knows that Chesterton is an English writer and that Zangwill is not. Chesterton is not much read, except in school assignments. Zangwill is not read at all, and the last place you would expect to find him is in a textbook. Chesterton is a minor English literary figure and is noted as such among specialists. Zangwill is only a Jew who lived in England. For some Jewish historians he survives as a producer of documents, or as himself a document. For English culture he does not survive at all.

But go further and consider those who do *not* intend to be Jewish. Consider Isaac D'Israeli and his contemporary, Charles Lamb. Each is a gifted minor writer of rather similar charm. But everyone knows Charles Lamb, and if anyone has ever heard of Isaac D'Israeli it is because he is the father of a Jewish Prime Minister. Yet Isaac D'Israeli was the perfect English man-of-letters, easily comparable to, in America now, Lionel Trilling. He was not notably Jewish in his concerns, as, of course, Zangwill was. In literature his fate is the same as Zangwill's—no, worse. Even Jewish specialists find him uninteresting. He does not exist, even as a document. Lamb survives, Hazlitt survives, De Quincy survives, Leslie Stephen survives, George Saintsbury survives—all minor. But Isaac D'Israeli is wiped out of the only culture he was able to breathe in, as if he never breathed at all.

One can move through history from culture to culture and discover equal dooms. In the Italy of the Renaissance, cultivated Jews, like others, wrote sonnets in Italian in imitation of Petrarch. They did not endure even in a minor way—not as a minor note in Jewish culture, not as a minor note in Italian culture. In the so-called Golden Age of Spain, which—as Richard Rubenstein has pointed out—is considered Golden only by Jews, was there not some gifted Jew of Toledo who wrote verses in Spanish? If so, try to find his name. So if Philip Roth still wants to say "I am not a Jewish writer; I am a writer who is a Jew," the distinction turns out to be wind; it is precisely those who make this distinction whom Diaspora most determinedly wipes out.

And it is especially to the point that one has to look to minor writers for historical examples. There are no major Jewish writers, unless you insist on including two French half-Jews, Montaigne and Proust. The novel at its height in the last century was Judaizing in that it could not have been written without the Jewish Bible; in America especially, Hawthorne and Melville and Whitman are biblically indebted, but there never yet lived a Jewish Dickens. There have been no Jewish literary giants in Diaspora.

Marx and Freud are vast presences, but they are, as I observed earlier, analyzers and judges of culture—they belong to that awkward category known as "the social sciences." Imaginative writers, by contrast, are compelled to swim in the medium of culture; literature is an instrument of a culture, not a summary of it. Consequently, there are no major works of Jewish imaginative genius written in any Gentile language, sprung out of any Gentile culture. Talmud speculates that when the Jew went into exile, God too was exiled. Is this a metaphor of incapacity? The literature of the Bible—very nearly our only major literature—issued from out of the Land. When we went into exile, did our capacity for literature abandon us also? Why have our various Diasporas spilled out no Jewish Dante, or Shakespeare, or Tolstoy, or Yeats? Why have we not had equal powers of hugeness of vision? These visions, these powers, were not hugely conceived. Dante made literature out of an urban vernacular, Shakespeare spoke to a small island people, Tolstoy brooded on upper-class Russians, Yeats was the kindling for a Dublin-confined renascence. They did not intend to address the principle of Mankind; each was, if you will allow the infamous word, tribal. Literature does not spring from the urge to Esperanto but from the tribe. When Carl Sandburg writes in a poem "There is only one man, and his name is Mankind," he is unwittingly calling for the end of culture. The annihilation of idiosyncrasy assures the annihilation of culture. It *is* possible to write "There is one ant, and its name is Antkind"; anthood is praised thereby. The ants are blessed with the universal brotherhood of instinct. But they have no literature. Whenever we in Diaspora make a literature that is of-the-nations, relying on what we have in common with all men, what we fashion turns out to be a culture of instinct, not of singularity of culture; it does not deserve perpetuation. What is there of culture in Shylock's cry "Hath not a Jew hands, organs, dimensions, senses, passions?" Very liberal of Shakespeare to grant this, very Socialist of him, and humanitarian, and modern, and priest/minister/rabbi-American of him—nevertheless, what Shylock's formulation signifies is that Shakespeare, even at his moral pinnacle, does not see the Jew as *a man*, but only as Mankind—which is to say as Ant, natural creature rather than culture-making creature. In our modern Diasporas we have consistently followed Shakespeare in this diminution of our civilizing qualities; as makers-of-literature we have by and large been possessed of organs and dimensions rather than of culture. We are all Shylocks proclaiming our resemblances; "allee samee," we say, insuring the obliteration of our progeny.

The fact is that nothing thought or written in Diaspora has ever been able to last unless it has been centrally Jewish. If it is centrally Jewish it will last for Jews; if it is not centrally Jewish it will last neither for Jews nor for the host-nations. Rashi lasts and Yehudah Halevi lasts—one, so to speak, a social thinker, the other a poet; they last for Jews. Leivik will last, and Sholem Aleichem: for Jews. Isaac D'Israeli did not last for Jews or for anyone; neither did that putative Jew of Toledo who wrote good Spanish poetry; neither will Norman Mailer. "Our cultural account in the Diaspora," Bialik said, "is all debit and no credit." Even a Heine does not right the balance. After so long a sojourn among Germans, didn't the Jews owe Germany at least a poet? For a while Heine pretended he was a German poet, though his private letters repeatedly said something else. But Germany would not keep him; Hitler struck him from the ledger and returned Heine permanently to the Jewish people. If he lasts, he lasts for us.

By "centrally Jewish" I mean, for literature, whatever touches on the liturgical. Obviously this does not refer only to prayer. It refers to a type of literature and to a type of perception. There is a critical difference between liturgy and a poem. Liturgy is in command of the reciprocal moral imagination rather than of the isolated lyrical imagination. A poem is a private flattery; it moves the private heart, but to no end other than being moved. A poem is a decoration of the heart, the art of the instant. It is what Yehudah Halevi called flowers without fruit. Liturgy is also a poem, but it means not to have only a private voice. Liturgy has a choral voice, a communal voice, the echo of the voice of the Lord of History. Poetry shuns judgment and memory and seizes the moment. In all of history the literature that has lasted for Jews has been liturgical. The secular Jew is a figment; when a Jew becomes a secular person he is no longer a Jew. This is especially true for makers of literature. It was not only an injunction that Moses uttered when he said we would be a people attentive to holiness, it was a description and a destiny.

When a Jew in Diaspora leaves liturgy—I am speaking now of the possibilities of a Diaspora literature—literary history drops him and he does not last.

By "last" I mean, very plainly, *sub specia aeternitatis*. If it is enough for any novelist or poet to have the attention of three decades and then to be forgotten, I am not speaking to him. But no committed writer seriously aims to be minor or obscure. I offer a tragic American exemplar of wasted powers and large-scale denial. Why, for instance, does Norman Mailer, born in the *shtetl* called Brooklyn, so strenuously and with little irony turn himself into Esau? Because he supposes that in the land of Esau the means to glory is Esau's means. Having failed through inadequate self-persuasion to write the novels of Esau, Mailer now swings round to interpretative journalism, a minor liturgical art; with old Jacob's eye he begins to judge

Gentile culture. But even while judging he is allured, and his lust to be Esau grows. One day he will become a small Gentile footnote, about the size of H.L. Mencken. And the House of Israel will not know him. And he will have had his three decades of Diaspora flattery. Esau gains the short run, but the long run belongs to Jacob.

How do these admittedly merciless reflections—history confers realism, not consolation—affect the position of Jewish culture in the American Diaspora?

I spoke earlier, in that sociological hump I had to get over, of fear of an American abattoir. This may stem from the paranoia of alienation, or from a Realpolitik grasp of scary historical parallels. Never mind. Let us say it will never happen, or not for a long time. And that despite every other kind of domestic upheaval, the Jews of America have a good space of future laid out before them. What then? Will cultural news come out of American Jewry?

I have a curious vision, transient but joyous. It has to do with two deeply obvious circumstances. The first is that of all Jews alive today, 45 percent live in America, and perhaps 50 percent have English for their mother-tongue. This is not so much a datum as an opportunity, and I will return to it. The second is that there has been, from America, no Ingathering of Jews into the Land of Israel. But why not? What are our reasons, our actual and truthful reasons? Is it that we don't want to leave our houses, jobs, cars, yards, fences, language, fleshpots? Yes. Is it that despite occasional dark frights we are in love with the American idea, and trust it after all? Also yes. "This is a good Diaspora," I heard someone say the other day, "as Diasporas go." So is it that in the meantime we are nevertheless living spectacularly productive and reasonably happy lives? Also yes. These are all our true reasons, reasons in praise of the American Diaspora, reasons of antlike instinct rather than culture. But sometimes I wonder whether there is not another reason, too—not *our* reasons, but history's. The Nazi period teaches us how not to be disposed of; also how not to dispose of ourselves. We always note how in Germany we wanted to be German. In America something else is happening. By now I have probably uttered the word "history" a hundred times; it is a Jewish word. But turn now to Joseph Brenner, who in a furious essay called "Self-Criticism" spits it out like a demon-shriek:

> History! History! [he cries.] But what has history to tell? It can tell that wherever the majority population, by some fluke, did not hate the Jews among them, the Jews immediately started aping them in everything, gave in on everything, and mustered the last of their meager strength to be like everyone else. Even when the yoke of ghetto weighed most heavily

upon them—how many broke through the walls? How many lost all self-respect in the face of the culture and beautiful way of life of the others! How many envied the others! How many yearned to be like them!

All this is of course applicable to numbers of American Jews behind their silken walls. Diaspora-flattery is our pustule, culture-envy our infection. Not only do we flatter Gentiles, we crave the flattery of Gentiles. Often in America we receive it. We have produced a religious philosopher who can define himself as Jew only by means of the pressure of Christian philosophies—he cannot figure out how to be Jewish without the rivalry of polemics, because polemics produce concern and attention, and attention flatters. Our indifferent, disaffected, de-Judaized novelists are finally given the ultimate flattery of mimicry: a celebrated Gentile novelist writes a novel about an indifferent, disaffected, de-Judaized Jewish novelist. Our rabbis no longer learn or teach; they have become pastors, ersatz ministers who are flattered by invitations to serve at the White House. Jews who yearn faintly after Judaism come to Martin Buber only by way of Christian theologians; they do not start with *Shema yisrael*,[2] and Buber without *Shema yisrael* as a premise is likely to be peculiarly misleading. We are interested in Buber because we are flattered by the interest of Gentiles in him: the pangs of flattery throb even in our self-discoveries. In America, Exile has become a flatterer; the fleshpots are spiritual. The reason we do not Ingather is not because of our material comforts, but because of our spiritual self-centeredness. Craving flattery, we explore how to merit it, how to commit ourselves more responsively. The Jewish community in America is obviously undistinguished, so far, in its religious achievements; but the astounding fact is that we *define ourselves as a religious community*. This we do ourselves; Gentiles of good will want to receive us mainly as representatives of Mankind, not as a peculiar people. The sociological explanations for our willingness to think of ourselves as a religious community, though most of us profess to be agnostics at least, are multiple, common-place, accurate, well-known—but irrelevant. Our synagogues are empty; this too is irrelevant, because nowadays they are only cathedrals, and we have always done without cathedrals. But our conversations have become liturgical. Even our professions of agnosticism take a liturgical turn. Our sociologists measure not only our communal safety but our communal commitment, the degree of our dedication or falling away. We talk to each other unremittingly, querulously, feverishly, constantly, forever, stream after stream of Jewish investigation. We translate Yiddish with the fury of lost love, we publish translations of medieval Hebrew documents. We pour *piyyutim*[3] into the air of every household. Even the enviers brood on the propriety of their envy. Even those who crave flattery are disposed to examine their lust. We have a fascination not with what we are, but with what we might become. We are not like Germany; we are a good deal like an incipient Spain. Both ended in abattoir, but Germany was nearly in vain. Germany and its language gave us Moses Hess, Heine, Buber, Rosenzweig, Baeck—individuals, not a culture or a willed people-hood; and no literature. Spain was for a time Jerusalem Displaced; psalms and songs came out of it. And Jerusalem Displaced is what we mean when we say Yavneh.[4]

So we are not yet Ingathered; and perhaps our destiny in another place is history's reason: that America shall, for a while, become Yavneh. For a while, while the State consolidates itself against savagery. We in Diaspora are not meant by this to be insulated from the savagery; we are one people, and what happens in one part of our body is suffered in another part: when the temple is wounded, the heart slows. I do not mean that Jews in America are intended to be preserved while Jews in Israel bleed. What I mean is this: that for the moment our two parts, Diaspora Israel and Jerusalem Israel, have between us the responsibility of a double reconstruction—the healers, the health-bringers, the safekeepers, in Jerusalem; the Aggadists,[5] the makers-of-literature, just now gathering strength in America. This is not to deny culture-making to the Land of Israel! The orchestras go forth; Agnon was and is and will be; painters proliferate; a poet of genius resides in the Land. Torah continues to come out of Zion, and what immensities of literary vision lie ahead is an enigma that dazzles; one does not preclude even a new Psalmist. All this is, for Israel, corollary to restoration.

For us in Diaspora cultural regeneration must be more modest, as Yiddish with all its glories, for instance, is nevertheless second to Hebrew. "Yavneh" is of course an impressionistic term, a metaphor suggesting renewal. The original Academy at Yavneh was founded after the destruction of the Temple; the new one in prospect coincides with the restoration of Zion. We are, after all, the first Diaspora in two millennia to exist simultaneously with the homeland; we are not used to it yet, we have not really taken it in, neither in America nor in Russia, and we do not yet know what the full consequence of this simultaneity can be. The informal liturgical culture rapidly burgeoning among American Jews is as much the result of the restoration of Israel as it is of the Holocaust. And yet it appears to have its own life; it is not merely an aftermath or backwash; it has an urge not to repeat or recapitulate, but to go forward—as, at an earlier Yavneh, Yohanan ben Zakkai plunged into the elaboration of Aggadah and preserved Torah by augmenting it. It seems to me we are ready to re-think ourselves in America now, to preserve ourselves by a new culture-making.

Now, you will say that this is a vast and stupid contradiction following all I have noted so far about the historic hopelessness of Diaspora culture. I have already remarked that "there are no major works of Jewish imaginative genius written in any Gentile language, sprung out of any Gentile culture." Then how, you will object, can there be a Yavneh in America, where all the Jews speak a Gentile language and breathe a Gentile culture? My answer is this: it can happen if the Jews of America learn to speak a new language appropriate to the task of a Yavneh.

This new language I will call, for shorthand purposes, New Yiddish. (If you stem from the Sephardic tradition, New Ladino will serve just as well.) Like old Yiddish, New Yiddish will be the language of a culture which is centrally Jewish in its concerns and thereby liturgical in nature. Like old Yiddish before its massacre by Hitler, New Yiddish will be the language of multitudes of Jews, spoken to Jews by Jews, written by Jews for Jews. And most necessary of all, New Yiddish, like old Yiddish, will be in possession of a significant literature capable of every conceivable resonance. But since New Yiddish will be a Jewish language, the resonances will be mainly liturgical. This does not mean that all kinds of linguistic devices and techniques will not be applicable; a liturgical literature is as free as any other to develop in any mode. To speak for the moment only of the experience of old Yiddish: the Yiddish writer A. Tabatchnik reveals in an important essay that the opening up of Yiddish poetry to modernist devices such as symbolism and impressionism not only did not obliterate the liturgical qualities of Yiddish, but in fact heightened them remarkably. There is nothing artistically confining about a liturgical literature; on the contrary, to include history is to include everything. It is the non-liturgical literatures which leave things out, which narrow themselves to minute sensuous perceptions, and commit huge indifferences. A liturgical literature has the configuration of the ram's horn: you give your strength to the inch-hole and the splendor spreads wide. A Jewish liturgical literature gives its strength to its peoplehood and the whole human note is heard everywhere, enlarged. The liturgical literature produced by New Yiddish may include a religious consciousness, but it will not generally be religious in any explicit sense; it will without question "passionately wallow in the human reality"; it will be touched by the covenant. The human reality will ring through its novels and poems, though for a long time it will not be ripe enough for poetry; its first achievements will be mainly novels. These novels, the product of richly conscious literary artists, will utilize every innovative device, not excluding those now being tested in the novels of aesthetic paganism; but device will not be a self-rubbing Romantic end in itself—verbal experiment and permutation will be organic, as fingers are to the principle of the hand. Above all, the liturgical mode will itself induce new forms, will in fact *be* a new form; and beyond that, given the nature of liturgy, a *public* rather than a coterie form. Unlike the novels of aesthetic paganism, liturgical novels will be capable of genuine comic perception in contrast to the grotesqueries of despair that pass for jokes among our current Gnostics and aestheticians. Compare, to see the point, the celestial Joseph comedies of a freely Judaized Thomas Mann with the narrow and precious whinnies of much of Barth, Barthelme, and Nabokov. Here I insert a warning to the trigger-happy: it is important not to confuse the liturgical novel with the catechismic novel which is so delightful to both the Vatican and the lords of Soviet socialist realism. The liturgical novel, because of its special view of history, will hardly be able to avoid the dark side of the earth, or the knife of irony; the liturgical novel will not be didactic or prescriptive: on the contrary, it will be aggadic, utterly freed to invention, discourse, parable, experiment, enlightenment, profundity, humanity. All this will be characteristic of the literature of New Yiddish. And it will characterize a new Yavneh preoccupied not by Talmud proper, but by fresh talmudic modes which, in our age, take the urgent forms of imaginative literature.

You will say: how can you command such a fantasy? How can you demand such a language? True, you might concede, if there *were* such a language it might produce such a literature. But who will invent this language, where will it be born? My answer is that I am speaking it now, you are hearing it now, this is the sound of its spoken prose. Furthermore, half the Jews alive today already speak it. Only 20 percent of us are Hebrew-speaking, but it is centuries now since Hebrew was anything other than the possession of a blessed minority. In the Diaspora we are condemned to our various vernaculars; even Rashi referred to French as *bilshonenu*, "in our language." The example of Yiddish is predominant. After all, it was not philological permutations that changed a fifteenth-century German dialect into Yiddish—the German that became Yiddish became *Jewish*; it became the instrument of our peoplehood on the European continent, and when a spectacular body of literature at last sprang out of it, it fulfilled itself as a Jewish language. I envision the same for the English of English-speaking Jews. Already English merits every condition of New Yiddish, with the vital exception of having a mature literature. But even now for Jews the English vernacular is on its way toward becoming Jewish; already there are traces (in the form of novels)[6] of a Jewish liturgical literature written in English. As for essays, there are dozens, and several actually contain, as in old Yiddish, numerous Hebrew words essential to their intent. And there already exists an adversary movement hostile to the language and culture of this incipient Yavneh; eminent Gentile intellectuals complain in print of "the rabbinical mind," "minority-group self-pity," "the New York intellectuals." Opposition is at least proof of reality.

When Jews poured Jewish ideas into the vessel of German they invented Yiddish. As we more and more pour not merely the Jewish sensibility, but the Jewish vision, into the vessel of English, we achieve the profoundest invention of all: a language for our need, our possibility, our overwhelming *idea*. If out of this new language we can produce a Yavneh for our generation within an alien culture, we will have made something worthwhile out of the American Diaspora, however long or short its duration. Besides, New Yiddish has a startling linguistic advantage over Old Yiddish, which persecution pushed far from its geographic starting-point. New Yiddish can be understood by the Gentile culture around us. So we have a clear choice, to take up an opportunity or to reject it. We can do what the German Jews did, and what Isaac D'Israeli did—we can give ourselves over altogether to Gentile culture and be lost to history, becoming a vestige-nation without a literature; or we can do what we have never before dared to do in a Diaspora language: make it our own, our own necessary instrument, understanding ourselves in it while being understood by everyone who cares to listen or read. If we make out of English a New Yiddish, then we can fashion a Yavneh not only for our own renewal but as a demonstration for our compatriots. From being envious apes we can become masters of our own civilization—and let those who want to call this "re-ghettoization," or similar pejoratives, look to their own destiny. We need not live like ants on the spine of the earth. In the conflict between the illuminations of liturgy and the occult darknesses of random aesthetic we need not go under. By bursting forth with a literature attentive to the implications of covenant and commandment—to the human reality—we can, even in America, try to be a holy people, and let the holiness shine for others in a Jewish language which is nevertheless generally accessible. We will not have to flatter or parody; we will not require flattery; we will develop Aggadah *bilshonenu*, in our own language, and build in Diaspora a permanent body of Jewish literature.

If we blow into the narrow end of the shofar, we will be heard far. But if we choose to be Mankind rather than Jewish and blow into the wider part, we will not be heard at all; for us America will have been in vain.

Notes

1. William H. Gass, "The Concept of Character in Fiction," in *Fiction and the Figures of Life* (New York: Vintage, 1958), pp. 34–55.
2. "Hear, O Israel," the Unitary Credo [editor's note].
3. Liturgical poetry of chiefly medieval composition [editor's note].

4. Yavneh was a small town where, with Roman permission after the fall of Jerusalem and the destruction of the Temple, Rabbi Yohanan ben Zakkai and his students established an academy. It was out of Yavneh that the definition of Jewish life as a community in exile was derived; learning as a substitute for homeland; learning as the instrument of redemption and restoration [editor's note].

5. *Aggadah* comprises the storytelling, imaginative elements in Talmud [editor's note].

6. Among them, Saul Bellow's *Mr. Sammler's Planet* (New York: Viking, 1970).

JOHN HOLLANDER

The Question of
American Jewish Poetry

W<small>HEN</small> I <small>CONFRONT</small> the question of what American Jewish poetry is, I find
myself asking many other questions—questions about what such a ques-
tion might mean. My colleague Harold Bloom, when asked once to discourse on American Jewish culture, said that the phrase reminded him of
the history teacher's line about the Holy Roman Empire: that it was neither holy, nor Roman, nor an empire. What most people mean by American Jewish culture is just as peculiar. Certainly for all serious scholars, the
very idea of *culture* is as problematic as the idea of Jewishness. And the
ambiguities in both terms generate even more problems when they are
conjoined. If by *culture* is meant something like what an American Jewish
disciple of Matthew Arnold, such as Lionel Trilling, would have meant by
it, then it involves a relation among texts, moral ideas, and the way in
which they affect institutions. For most people it would mean, perhaps,
Judaized versions of Balto-Slavic or Austro-Hungarian peasant cooking.
For anthropologists and sociologists, for fund-raisers and political an-
alysts, "culture" would comprise very different areas of behavior, or as I
should prefer to say, of life.

I would leave this discussion to social scientists and theorists of tradition were I not unsure how closely related my questions about American
Jewish culture and American Jewish poetry might turn out to be. How
poetry stands in relation to culture generally is itself a complex matter, and
one not to be debated here. But in any case, were I not a poet and scholar, I
should find this question far easier to contemplate. For example, in his
remarkable book *Alone with America*, the poet and translator Richard Howard selected (in 1969) forty-one of his contemporaries—then roughly between thirty and forty-five years of age—and wrote extensive essays on

their poetical works. (His judgments seem to have borne up well under time, and nobody now would claim that, even with so considerable a number of poets, Howard had dipped very deeply into mediocrity.) Of his forty-one poets, eleven were Jewish—at least as far as the Law of Return would define them—and two more had Jewish fathers. Howard, himself a poet of considerable distinction, also is a Jew.

I am by no means sure that a selection of forty-one American poets of the previous generation would have avoided so much mediocrity. But the list would have included poets ten or fifteen years older than those How-ard selected—poets such as Elizabeth Bishop, Robert Lowell, Theodore Roethke, only two or three of whom would likely have been Jewish (Del-more Schwartz, Karl Shapiro, perhaps Muriel Rukeyser). It may be that historians some years hence will look back on the last thirty-five years as a time in which American Jewish poetry flourished exceptionally.

But I am burdened by the American imaginative restraint that demands what Emerson called speaking in "hard words." The first hard question is: "Well, do these American Jewish poets write American Jewish poetry?" But that question is itself misleading. And matters are not made clearer by rephrasing it in the apparently sophisticated literary language: "Which of these poets write poems with Jewish *content*?" or "Which poems reflect Jewish experience?" Such terms as these mean little to poets, and perhaps even less to serious and inquiring literary critics. After all, can anything a Jew experiences—even apostasy—*not* be "Jewish experience"? In any case, the notion of "content" in poetry, the strangely Marxist concept of litera-ture "reflecting" conditions of society, is a rather fumbling notion as far as the teaching and interpretation of literature are concerned. Moreover, po-etry always takes concepts such as these and reinterprets them: If some-thing serious and complex is meant by a poem "reflecting" world events, a true poet will reinvent that concept of reflection in each poem he or she writes, will create a new and unique form of distorting mirror. So, too, with the notion of 'content': It usually is invoked only in contrast to a notion like 'form.' Can there be Jewish form and Gentile content? Or vice versa? The notion that *form* is what makes a text a poem is a little more adequate than the one that claims that content makes it so, but not much more.

Consider a poem by Moses Ibn Ezra, written in Hebrew, in Spain around the year 1100. It is "about"—its content concerns, if one must—an apple. A contemporary American poet translates and adapts it—makes a new English poem of it. The poet is Jewish, yet there must be hundreds of Gentile scholars who know more Hebrew than he does. He grafts his own epigram on to the original one. Is the fact that he writes a new poem by interpreting a traditional text a Jewish act? A Judaistic one? The original says something like this:

> The Apple, in truth, God created only for the pleasure
> of those who smell and touch it. I see how green and
> red are conjoined in it: I see there the face of the
> wan lover and the blushing beloved.

The modern poet takes only the conceit of the red and green from the Hebrew and, instead of the medieval Spanish Jewish poet, who substituted his power of poetic meditation for any fool's ability to take a bite out of the fruit, he imagines an interpreter fully conscious of apples as symbolic and literal fruit at once:

> O apple with which—as first fruit of desire—
> Our hunger for significance is fed:
> Around your globe pale grass borders on fire,
> The lovesick green pursues the blushing red.

What is it that makes either of these two texts a poem? Is content a kind of liquor poured into a bottle called 'form'? Is a Gentile thought embodied, in the first instance, in the Hebrew language, the literary tongue but not the vernacular of medieval Jews? Modern criticism is properly unhappy with the notion of poetry's having themes or subjects, conceptions derived from composition classes and, when purportedly embraced by poems, only done so in a deep and systematic travesty of thematic discourse. A poem might be Christian, English romantic, or Emersonian American. I could imagine in the last instance, for example, identical stances being taken in the poem by an American Jewish and a Gentile writer. Would only the former be writing a Jewish poem, with Jewish content?

It is clear why it might be better to ask, with respect, say, to the American Jewish poets in Howard's collection, "Can you tell from their poems that these poets are Jews? And, when you can, how does each poet's work reveal or conceal or ignore that fact in its own way?" For the essence of true poetry is originality of a mode of expression; that is, poets will express or figure forth in language not only something totally unique in themselves, but, as a kind of general metaphor for the holiness of human individuality, will thus reinvent expressing, or poetic telling. Now, many of the poets Howard discusses—Howard Nemerov, Theodore Weiss, Howard Moss, Kenneth Koch (save in what must be one of his more inspired moments in a long comic poem, in which specially prepared *matzot* are employed in a visionary South American city as screens in windows against killer bees)— do not reveal much Jewish identity in their work. For some of them, the modernist stance of impersonality was so central to their notion of poetic

writing that anything as intimate as their particular sense of "Jewish identity" was irrelevant to what they had to say—as irrelevant, for example, as
their blood pressure. Of course, the intimacy associated with Jewish identity would seem to be a condition of certain kinds of exilic assimilation; but,
in any case, poetic consciousness always internalizes, makes a peculiar
kind of private matter, questions that ordinary language and political life
hold to be public.

Of course, Irving Feldman—whose recent work has become stronger
than ever—and Edward Field both reconsider and work over some of the
ambience of urban American *Yiddishkeit* with irony and with warmth, but
their ways of doing so are original and widely different from each other's.
Allen Ginsberg's long—to me, I must confess, turgid—wail about the mad-
ness of his poor mother is called *Kaddish*. Whether or not one admires this
poem, one must recognize that it ignores the meaning—the nature, structure, liturgical function—of the prayer after which it takes its title. The
litany of Aramaic predicates of sanctification, conjoined with Hebrew
afterthoughts; the fact that its recitation by mourners is only one special
occasion of its frequent reappearance throughout the synagogue service;
the fact that the text on that occasion does not refer to its use as a prayer
for mourners—as if *thereby* (that is, by having those mourners, instead of
lamenting in public, intone sanctifications of God's name) it were being
deeply, rather than trivially, appropriate: Of none of these facts is the
poem's allusion in the title aware. It is as if the poem thought that "kaddish" meant only a public plaint or dirge of the bereaved. Furthermore,
there is nothing in Ginsberg's *Kaddish* to suggest that he somehow knows
all this and is deliberately making his "kaddish"—his poetic revision of the
prose, as it were, of public ritual—into a metaphoric antisanctification: No
matter how blasphemous that may sound, it might have made a true
poem, and more truly interestingly Jewish in an antinomian way.
    It certainly is true that, from the point of view of a naive notion of
content, some writer who puts into rhyme sentimental childhood memories of Friday night kiddush, say, ending with a cry of self-rebuke for
having lapsed from the old ways, would be expressing Jewish content or
whatever. But it wouldn't be poetry, and this is the heart of the problem.
Most people think that a poem is anything printed with a jagged right-
hand edge. (The technical term for this style, pregnant with appropriate
moral overtones, is an "unjustified" right-hand margin, and although obviously no Calvinist, I relish it.) But that is just like saying, fifty years ago,
that a poem is anything that rhymes. Free verse has replaced certain kinds
of jingling rhymed verse as the mode in which amateurs write what they

think are poems. What is Jewish or not Jewish about certain American poems is all tied up in the vexing problem of what is poetic or not poetic about them.

And so I would prefer to draw back for a moment and approach the question from another direction. Let me do so by citing a strange remark by one poet that is quoted as an epigraph to a poem by another one. Neither of the two poets was American. The remark is by the Russian symbolist, Marina Tsvetayeva: *Vcye payeti zhyidi,* "All poets are Yids." The poet was not Jewish, and we may surmise that she meant by it that all poets are like Jews in the Diaspora, alienated and in exile from something perhaps irrecoverable, nevertheless having to live with and in and among the rest of society. That is a touching and characteristically modern idea, although hardly as suggestive as the metaphoric extension of Jewish identity to stand for the condition of imaginative fullness and modified incapacity that Joyce or Proust, in very different ways, could evoke. What is interesting for me about her remark is that it is quoted as an epigraph to a profound and difficult poem by the great contemporary poet Paul Celan. (Born in Bukovina, Celan wrote in German, survived the Holocaust, and lived in Paris, where he taught at the École Normale Supérieure until his death in 1970.) Celan is possibly the greatest poet since Rilke to write in German and he is probably also the major Jewish poet of his generation anywhere. As a Jewish poet, Celan takes back the phrase for the sake of a deeper Jewish significance. It is not merely that modern poets and Jews are outsiders, by nature itinerant no matter how locally rooted. It is more that both—and a Gentile poet might be less likely to perceive this point—carry the burden of an absolutely inexplicable sense of their own identity and history. Jewish identity is not so much a mystery as a problem: "People," religion, nationality, linguistic culture—to know anything of these terms, and of Jewish history, is to know how limited their conceptual usefulness really is. If poetry is like Jewishness, it is that both know very well what they are, and though with a lot to say on nearly everything, they cannot easily explain *that.* Both poetry and Jewish identity are forever condemned to being misunderstood, to being wrongly interpreted. Clear, effective writing—whether reporting of facts, classifying and interpreting them, making suggestions, giving orders, framing instructions, making laws— aims at being understood. But "to be great," said Emerson, "is to be misunderstood," and even merely very good poetry shares this with greatness.

Poetry always seems to know that it cannot ever fully be understood. It certainly is possible to put a set of instructions for assembling something into rhyme (viz. "Turn part B the other way / And into it insert flap A"), but that will not make it poetry. Or, in a contemporary equivalent of rhyming jingle, we could write out those instructions in short lines that do not come to the end of the page. Or, if one believes that poetry is not verse, but the expression of sincere feelings, one could drop upon one's toe a very heavy weight or a quantity of boiling water and become—without knowing how to write—a great poet. The major American poet of our age, Wallace Stevens, observed both that "[s]entimentality is a failure of feeling" and that "[r]ealism is a corruption of reality." Poetry is neither of these, but rather a matter of intense meaning, of having so much significance with respect to its own local and the most general parts of life that it breeds rereading and further rereading over the years. True poetry—rather than what I might call literature in verse—partakes of what Rabbi Ben Bag Bag said of Torah itself: "Turn it and turn it over again, for everything is in it."

But if intensity of meaning can lead to difficulty of reading, the openness of poetry to easy misconstrual has perhaps another source. Dante, in that remarkable little book about the dawning of his imaginative existence called *The New Life*, talks of what he calls *un schermo della veritade*, "a screen for the truth." He is referring to an unnamed lady past whom he was looking, in a church full of people, at his secret muse, Beatrice d'Este. This lady sat in his line of sight. Everyone else believed him to have been looking at her, and he half-collaborated with this misprision of his intentions. He thought to make of the noble lady a screen for the truth, he says, and he thereafter wrote poems "to" and "about" her, all the while thinking of Beatrice. This story is about all poetry, really, which always uses its "subject" or "occasion" as *un schermo della veritade*, a screen. And this screen may be very clouded, or very ornate; and each poet will not only construct his or her own screen, but virtually invent the materials and the mode of construction. Yet the result will always be that the *subjects* of poems are no more what they are "about" than their verse-forms are. This fact, too, makes difficult any discussion of Jewish subjects or contents in poetry. A remarkable comment on this question is made in a beautiful poem of Paul Celan's that anyone but a rabid Satmar Hasid or ultra-Orthodox rejectionist would call Jewish. It is titled "Hawdalah" and starts out with a meditation on the braided, twisted candle used in the havdalah service, which ushers out the Sabbath on Saturday evenings. In an inadequate translation, it begins:

> On the one, the
> only
> thread, on it
> you spin—by it
> spun about, into the free, there,
> into the bound . . .

[*An dem einen, dem
einzigen
Faden, an ihm
spinnst du—von ihm
Umsponnener, ins Freihe, dahin,
ins Gebundne*]

This is a strange love poem reminding itself that the literal root meaning of the word *havdalah* is "division" or "separation," and that the spinning around of the twisted strand of light is of the essence of the kinds of twisting of literal meaning (the Greek word for it is *trope*, or *turning*) that is itself of the essence of poetry. This is hardly a traditional Judaistic observation to make, although in a general sense it is a sort of midrash on the text, as it were, of the candle's braided structure, and of how this twisting bears light aloft.

One other way of reading the relation between the condition of being Jewish and that of being a poet has to do with a misunderstanding by others of one's own sense of history. As Yosef Hayim Yerushalmi has shown in his fine study, *Zahor: Jewish History and Jewish Memory*, the very notion of Jewish historiography is more or less a modern German one, whereas the internalization of the memory of a people in any individual's consciousness is very traditional indeed. The central metaphor of the Pesakh Haggadah might be said to reside in the notion that "I was there at the Exodus from Egypt." But such a trope is hardly historiographic. (It is not even used, for example, to create a first-person narrative of What Happened That Night, etc.) Similarly, poetic history is *not* the literary history or the history of ideas that so many people think it must be. The stuff of tradition is braided into poetry with the stuff of what is often called 'experience', and every true poet has very complex relations with those who have preceded him or her. In one account of poetic tradition, the poets who have gone before are ancestors, direct family forebears. (Should one think of them now as one's people?) But more and more for me, the account in *Bereshit* about Jacob's wrestling match seems a central fable of poetry.

The man with whom Jacob wrestles by the ford of the river Jabbok (the text designates him merely as *ish*, "some man"); who cripples Jacob's thigh in order to win; who asks to be released from Jacob's lock on him because day is about to dawn (shades of Dracula!—even if, Rashi so anxiously hastens to assure us, because whoever or whatever it was had to go to his morning prayers); who, in exchange for being released, blesses him by giving him a new name—Israel (meaning "one who has struggled with

'El'"); and who, when asked *his* name, says that one must not ask such a question—this presence is, for any poet, a figure of his major precursors in poetic history, those great figures who have told all the great and important stories, who have been there first. The only strength with which one has to wrestle is the power of one's own language. One always comes away from such a struggle with emotional sciatica from which one suffers until the end of one's days. And one is blessed to receive a new name if one comes away victorious from any part of the struggle, but unlike our father Jacob's, it is a name that can be uttered no more than that of the ineffable 'El' with whom the struggle has occurred.

The matter of a poet's language is very important. In the first place, it is very private: Stevens once wrote that "every poet's language is his own distinct tongue. He cannot speak the common language and continue to write poetry any more than he can think the common thought and continue to be a poet." How, then, could Jewish poetry be Judaistic in a common way? And how could a poet speak in a common Jewish language, even if his uncommon one, his own poetic word-hoard, were based on a tongue thought of as commonly Jewish? Part of what Stevens meant by the uncommonness of poetic language reflects another aspect of a matter considered earlier. Paul Celan's deeper understanding of Tsvetayeva's comparison of all poets to Jews would seem to say that all poets are in a kind of linguistic *galut*—they are members of a people dispersed and wandering in a realm of ordinary language, a world of the literal. But poets also are, in a way, an interpretive community, internally and externally expounding and revising, individually working out a *gemara* or completion of the argument about what poetry really must be: a working out given to none of them truly to complete, but from which they are not free to desist.

But Jewish Diaspora has always had the Hebrew language—or perhaps, as with the Alexandrians, just the memory of a Hebrew language—as a clew or thread to hold on to amid the mazes of exile. In medieval Spanish and German its constant seraphic presence lurked always in the spirit of the Hebrew letters, the adapted means of writing, as well as in significant parts of the vocabulary. The poetic diaspora which affects all poets, though, has only an imaginary idea of a language of its own, and each poet must forge it anew from the common metal, or spin its new thread from the fibers picked out of common speech. Thus it is that the Jewish exilic poet can be seen to exhibit two modes of longing for estranged, original language.

For American poetry, in its way a kind of *gemara* of the history of poetry in the English language, there are other problems. The contemporary Israeli poets—Yehuda Amichai, or the late Dan Pagis, for example—can write in a modern Hebrew that is still the biblical language. A poet whose language is English, whose wrestling grips are English hammerlocks and chanceries, has the English Bible built into the heart not only of the diction and syntax, but also the poetics of his language. The English Bible is a polemically Protestant translation of an orthodox Christian book called the Old Testament, which is itself a Christian interpretative translation of the Torah. A modern poet—and by this I suppose that I mean any poet from Alexandrian times on—is, if Greek, a wrestler with the shade of that fictional but very great author, Homer; if Jewish, with Homer's analogue, Moses, who figures as the author of the Pentateuch, and not merely as a character in Exodus.

Thus there is a profound and ever-present irony in a poet's writing "in" (would "out of" be better?) a language from whose literary tradition Torah is not, in fact, merely absent but rather present in such fascinatingly distorted form. The cadences and grammatical constructions of the King James version, the shadows of misunderstanding lurking in the archaic meanings of words that have since undergone semantic change, are always singing an undersong in our language, from Milton through Whitman and in subsequent re-echoings. A British or American poet can engage the fabric of scripture in English or even in Latin and still be working in commonly uncommon ways. And to intensify the Latin presence in English by allusion or quotation has the same touch of the natural that moving into extended Hebrew phrases or clauses does in Yiddish. In any case, the English Bible has a strange power for the poet. For example, the way in which the King James Bible translates the grammar of the construct state of the Hebrew tends to create, in the language of the translation, metaphors and even allegorical personifications, traces of fable and parable, which are absent from the original. The dark or shadowed valley—the *gei tsalmavet*—of Psalm 23 becomes that allegorical region, "the valley of the shadow of death," only in translation. But what *is*, for a poet, "the valley *of* the shadow of death"? Does some heroic figure called the Shadow of Death live there? Rule it? Did he, or she, or it move hills about to create it and then desert it? Did Death leave its shadow there for eternity? Or are the hills that cast the shadow themselves embodiments of death? Or what? This kind of prepositional phrase—the common form "the X of Y," ordinarily transparent—becomes complex, opaque, and problematic in the language of poetry. The language of the King James Bible is poetic primarily because it is so richly ambiguous, forcing listeners and readers to interpret in order simply to construe. For a Jewish poet writing in English, then, the resonances of the English Bible are already full of complex fables.

But if poets are in some way exiled from some irrecoverable original language, and if diasporic Jewish poets are so in at least two ways, it must be said that all poets devote to the matter of their personal uncommon languages a most profound and absorbed attention. It is more than the care of a workman for his tools; for language is both material and implement at once. There is a dangerous power, close to magic, by which it molds its fictions, and, as an object of such devotion and attention, a dangerous iconicity, or image-like quality to it. Particularly for Judaic tradition, this creates additional complications.

Poetry, as has been observed, lives in remarkably, almost supernaturally, meaningful language, gaining intensity of significance by consciously working with its own structure. Because of this fact, it can always seem poised on the brink of image-making, in the proscribed Judaic sense— though the figures here are of speech and thought rather than of clay or brass. But for the modern poet, older, previously employed poetic images and fictions have indeed become silent, impotent idols of mental brass. Modern poetry will not be content with the tropes and fables that long usage has turned to clarity. The poet must, if invoking them at all, twist them about into originality and thereby into poetic truth. First Isaiah's (2:4) trope for peace following war is one that almost every literate person used to know: "And they shall beat their swords into ploughshares, and their spears into pruninghooks." The poetic quality here—the way of being poetic peculiar to ancient Semitic literature—comes from its figures and from the way in which one serves to gloss, or revise, the preceding one (in this case, it is not only a matter of intensification). But let us consider a more modern poet, using the same image. The Roman Virgil, talking of the twisting of peaceful civilization into the strict violence of warfare, writes (in the *Georgics*, I, 508) that unbending blades are forged from curved sickles; but as this works in the peculiar way of Latin poetry, certain words are pushed up syntactically against others in the line to make an additional point. Virgil's *et curvae rigidum falces conflantur in esenem*—or, as I'll try to make it work in English, "From sickles curved unbending blades are formed"—says in effect that the curvature of sickles that causes the grain to bend as well during the mowing of peacetime is as nothing to the rigid inflexibilities of the straight swords of battle. The spirit of the Latin language itself makes the metaphor more than another instance of what may have been a Roman commonplace. It is this way of revising an old figure and making metaphor with it as if it had itself been a literal meaning that in part makes for poetic originality.

At this point, one thinks once again of what Tsvetayeva's remark must have meant to Paul Celan: that, among other things, every true poet is in a kind of diaspora in his own language. Celan, who in his later poetry had to invent new German words out of purely German materials, and based on analogies of purely German grammatical structure, probably grew up in a German rather than a Yiddish-speaking home. But he was keenly aware of a poet's distance even from the language with which he thinks to gauge all sorts of other distances. *Sprachgitter,* meaning "the grid of language," is the title of one of his books, and it evokes images of an infinite regress of Dantean poetic screens, and screens of screens. But all poets, even those without Celan's sense of living and writing in a postapocalyptic time and space, know what exile inside one's own language might mean. For poetry doesn't *use* words in the way ordinary discourse does; rather, it stands back from them, misuses them, plays with them as no grown-up who really *knew* the language would, notices funny things about them that only a non-native speaker would. Poets know, with Emerson, that every word is a fossil poem, that the history of its meanings, changing over millennia by means of the tropes of metaphor and metonymy which characterize the stuff of poetry, is a kind of fable of transformation. For poetry, etymology is one of the great primal stories, to be told and retold on the occasion of a fresh look at any word. As a Jewish poet, I suppose that *haggadah* rather than *halakha*, fable and fiction rather than law, is most important to me in Judaic tradition. But as a poet I also note that the word *halakha* means "a way," "a going," "a walking"; and that, as in so many other languages, including English and Chinese, the basic word for ethical procedures on life's journey literally evokes a footpath. I suppose that a scholar might point out that the concern for the interpretative play of etymologies is rooted deeply in Judaic tradition; certainly, portions of the Pentateuch are studded with etymological wordplay, false etymologies invoked as narrative devices, mysterious and unavowed puns, and so forth. But the poet of a passage in the Pentateuch had more wonder at his own language than did all his commentators.

Hebrew, some dialects of Aramaic, some of Alexandrian Greek, some versions of medieval Spanish and German—these have been the languages of Jewish literature. One might argue that modern German, the language of Kafka, Celan, Freud, Gershom Scholem, Martin Buber, Walter Benjamin, and Leo Strauss, must be added to these. But we have as yet had no great Jewish literary culture in English. An American Jewish poet must make his or her own way, making American English his or her own. The first steps of this process always involve, for a young writer, purging one's style of cliché, of empty public gesture; and this entails, of course, the impossibility of, say, versifying rabbinically ordained sentiments. As a matter of fact, the poet's almost idolatrous relation to language cooperates with another more profound Judaic danger. For if Jewishness is to be identified solely with normative rabbinic religion—particularly as it has become sectarian since European modernity—then the poet's path is the road to *kherem*, religious destruction.

Consider in this light the stern rabbinic admonition in one of my favorite midrashim on *Bereshit*, Genesis 1:1, which appears to have been directed against a Jewish Gnostic and poetic spirit. It starts out by pondering the significance of the fact that the story of the origination of everything and anything, the opening words of the Torah, begins not with *aleph*, the first letter of the alphabet, but with *bet*, the second one, in the word *bereshit*. It asks:

> Why was the world created with a *bet*? Just as the *bet* is closed at the sides but open in front, so you are not permitted to investigate what is above and what is below, what is before and what is behind.

One of the amusing things about this passage is that it gives what literary scholars would call an emblematic reading of the image of the letter *bet*, treating it momentarily as a hieroglyph or picture—not a picture of its original pictographic value (*bet*, of course, means "house," and the original Phoenician syllabic sign was derived from such a pictogram), but of an abstract picture of openness and closure. This reading in itself comes dangerously close to being an iconic pun, and therefore open to the charge of image-making. And yet, the forms and numerical values of the letters of the Hebrew alphabet were always exempted from such a prohibition. It is as if all the impulses that, in Greek, Roman, and Christian tradition, went toward the production of significant visual images of the human body, of symbolic objects and eventually landscapes, were, in Judaic tradition, reserved for the imagery of alphabetic letters. But my personal delight at this midrash quite apart, the rabbinic injunction not to inquire about what is above, what is beneath, what was before time, and what will come hereafter is a *kherem*, a destructive ban, against the Imagination itself. For it is precisely these forbidden questions that the poet will always be asking and whose answers he or she must continually supply in the form of fable.

I suppose that what I have been saying implies that all poetry is in some way or another unofficial midrash, a revisionist commentary upon some kind of canonical text. At the very beginning of Western literary tradition those texts were Homer and Torah, but the great poetry that followed them became part of the canon as well. It is not that great poetry is purely original and minor poetry derivative or allusive to prior poetry. Rather, it is, as all true poets and critics have always known, that great poetry is more original in its way of being derivative. Modernism in poetry—by which, in this instance, I mean romanticism—creates the great fiction that there is a fresh, unopened book called "Experience" that all genuine poetry will henceforth proceed to copy. But that book has itself become worn and dog-eared, and people who today ask honestly but naively to hear of how, say, American Jewish poetry reflects American Jewish experience are simply talking about an old book (dating back to the 1790s in English) without knowing it. The true text of the world is always fresh and always renewing itself. But its pages are as full of poems, pictures, stories, philosophies, laws, and songs as they are of mountains, rivers, railroads, cities, and histories. And all poetry is in some way a continuing midrash on such a book.

The great poet of the English language who almost literally avowed this point was the radical Protestant John Milton, himself enough of a Hebraist to know some midrash in the original. *Paradise Lost* is so great a midrash on *Bereshit*, and so great a poem, that it remains authoritative whether one is Milton's kind of Protestant or not, and it remains as much a part of nature for any true poet writing in English as the Sahara desert or the Mississippi. This is a truth that I myself came to see only in my mid-thirties, when, after having published three books of verse, I began to understand what poetry really was. But to extend this notion further, I would also suggest that a poet's work—and this may be the hardest notion to grasp—is also a midrash upon his or her language itself.

As long as that tongue is Hebrew, or even Yiddish or Ladino, there is nothing problematic about this assertion: Major Yiddish poetry, for example, will frequently call implicit attention to the various Hebraic, Germanic, or Slavic origins of the words in daily use by means of ironies implicit in deeply significant rhyming patterns. But what is an American poet to do? The English language itself, partly Germanic, partly Romance, veined with Latin and Greek special vocabularies, its writing system and early literature shaped by Christendom, its poetic history shaped by the gradual unfolding of the Protestant Reformation first in England and then in America, its great "rabbis" being Spenser and Shakespeare and Milton and Wordsworth and Emerson and Whitman, its character partaking for the Jewish poet of Hebrew and Aramaic and the Yiddish or Spanish or Arabic of daily life over the centuries all at once—the English language itself is as much the language of *Galut*, but no more so, than the Greek *koine* of two thousand years ago, or the medieval French in which Rashi also wrote. I also should add modern Hebrew to this list: If it were not one of the languages of *Galut*, of the Diaspora, it would have undergone the same kind of linguistic change that all languages do over two and a half millennia, and could be almost unrecognizably related to the Hebrew of the Pentateuch. The very fact of its having been so successfully but artificially resuscitated as a living vernacular has itself attested to the fact of diaspora, to the interruption of its vernacular history by wave upon wave of conquest and exile. If this is tantamount to saying that modern Israel is still part of *Galut*, then I am afraid it must be so. But it is, after all, diasporic language in which all modern poetry—whatever its linguistic or cultural environment—is written. That is why any American—or German, or Russian, or Israeli—Jewish poet must make his or her language his or her own by wandering into it while quite young, and perhaps getting lost in the forest of that language for many years.

It may be, then, that an American Jewish poet has to spend years becoming an American poet and learning what that can mean before being able, perhaps, to cope poetically with his or her own Jewishness, however problematic a notion *that* might be. This uncertain venture may even give the appearance of wandering away from Jewish identity—at least, as other people construe it—when for the poet it is evidence of just the opposite. For in a temporary or apprentice devotion to impersonality, the young poet learns how to be truthful about self in the only way that poetry can be, by being figurative, rather than shallowly literal about it. One must learn to construct and, what is just as hard, to believe in the good of those Dantean screens. So, if an American poet's Jewishness—whatever that might be—is somehow temporarily shelved, this shelving is done as part of something so deep and so intimate that it cannot pause to explain itself.

Thus, one cannot escape the fact that the history of great American poetry up through the present generation has been intimately involved with the history of revisionist American Protestantism; and the question of how Judaistic notions might be woven into such a tradition is profoundly difficult. The touching paradox inadvertently invoked by Emma Lazarus, the first American poet some of whose poems would reveal her to be Jewish, is interesting in this regard. Writing in 1882, she compared Jewish identity in diasporic nations to the *pi'el* form of the Hebrew verb:

> Every student of the Hebrew language is aware that we have in the conjugation of our verbs a mode known as the *intensive voice*, which by means of an almost imperceptible modification of vowel points, intensifies the meaning of any primitive root. A similar significance seems to attach to the Jews themselves in connection with the people among whom they dwell. They are the intensive form of any nationality whose language and customs they adopt. . . . Influenced by the same causes, they represent the same results. . . .[1]

But alas, students of Jewish history will feel that this is a German Jew, and not an American one, talking. Emma Lazarus speaks more for the Sephardic and German immigrants of the 1840s and after than she does for the millions who came from Eastern Europe and whose families led the ways of life that would become the stuff of American Jewish cliché. Also, Jews were no more the *pi'el* of American identity than were the immigrant Irish, or Italians, or Caribbeans, or West Africans, or Norwegians, or Poles. Her final sentence sounds more like Disraeli than anything else: " . . . but the deeper lights and shadows of their Oriental temperament throw their failings, as well as their virtues, into more prominent relief."

Still, I would adapt Emma Lazarus's remark by saying that poetry is, among other things, the *pi'el* of ordinary discourse. As for the rest of the matter, let it go. In any case, I don't think that an American Jewish poet can write Jewish poetry without thereby writing American poetry. And since, with regard to consciousness of being Jewish, it is useful to know what a commentator as well as a poet had in mind, I will end by quoting and briefly discussing a poem I wrote when some of these puzzles were especially vivid to me. To frame this ending, I can offer only a final word about beginnings.

My first book of poems, published when I was twenty-eight, had nothing of what normative Judaism would want to call Jewish content—save, perhaps, for a poem that took off from an aphorism of Martin Buber, and save for a sort of Yeatsian dramatic lyric, written for Orpah, Naomi's other daughter-in-law in the Book of Ruth, who goes home to her own people and chooses not to enter biblical history. But when it finally came time to give the book a title, I felt the need for some kind of avowal of my ambivalence about publishing a book—that mixture of ambition and reticence that comes from having at least glimpsed what real poetry truly is, and wondering about one's chutzpah in trying to write it, while at the same time knowing that aiming lower wouldn't make the cost of the arrow worthwhile. A text from *Ecclesiastes* that I had always liked—"As the crackling of thorns under a pot, so is the laughter of a fool"—seemed appropriate here, but only through a midrash on it saying that "when all other woods are kindled, their sound does not travel far; but when thorns are kindled, their sound travels far," as though to say: We too are wood. With that epigraph, the book was entitled *A Crackling of Thorns*. But in another sense, midrash came through to me in my childhood, not from formal study (I was never anywhere near a yeshiva), but from the Pesakh Seder. Even in early childhood, I was made to grasp the fact that the annual scene of rejoicing and remembering was also the scene of interpretation. For me, that may have been an important poetic scene of instruction as well. Over the years I've returned to both the rhetorical form and the interpretative strategy of midrash from time to time.

I suppose that the American Jewish poet can be either blessed or cursed by whatever knowledge he or she has of Jewish history and tradition. I obviously believe in the power of the blessing, but it would be easy for any writer to be trapped in a slough of sentimentality or a homiletic bog. Literalness is the death of poetic imagination, and all groups in the cultural community that speak for Jewishness will always be very literal about what "Jewish experience" is, as will all groups that want to speak for "American experience." Both kinds of experience are for the poet momentary aspects of the protean body of being who one is, and the analogues between American and modern Jewish identity are interesting apart from the almost exponential complications resulting from a combination of the two. These complications of the varieties of experience remain to be explored by practical criticism and cultural history. Being no sort of historian, I have had to invent figures for the kind of Marrano existence that modern poets lead even when they do not seem to. Since such figures are borrowed and reinterpreted from the text of Jewish history, I cannot be sure whether any such figure makes a parable of modern poetic or modern Jewish existence. The invention below will have to speak and withhold, for itself. Some years ago I read of how Cecil Roth, studying the history of the Marranos in Spain, had earlier in this century encountered some ordinary Christian families in part of northern Portugal who burned a candle inside a crock or pitcher on Friday evenings. When he inquired about the significance of this act, he was told that nobody knew why, but that it had always been done in their families. Years later, at the end of a long, avowedly Judaic and American poem—an allegorical quest that meditates on the colors of the spectrum and, at the same time, the seven lights of the lost menorah carried from Jerusalem to Rome—this same figure returned to me, and I to it. I was writing "Violet" (the color on my allegorical spectrum closest to black, to darkness, and to death), and thinking of the poet's eternal task of telling a certain kind of truth, at a time too late for such kinds of truth-telling:

How then can we now shape
Our last stanza, furnish
This chamber of codas?

Here in the pale tan of
The yet ungathered grain
There may be time to chant

The epic of whispers
In the light of a last
Candle that may be made

To outlast its waning
Wax, a frail flame shaking
In a simulacrum

Of respiration. Oh,
We shall carry it set
Down inside a pitcher

Out into the field, late
Wonderers errant in
Among the rich flowers.

Like a star reflected
In a cup of water,
It will light up no path:

Neither will it go out . . .[2]

Notes

1. Emma Lazarus, *Epistle to the Hebrews* (New York: Federation of American Zionists, 1900), 21 [editor's note].

2. From *Spectral Emanations* (New York: Atheneum Publishers, 1979).

ROBERT ALTER

Jewish Dreams and Nightmares

What have I in common with Jews? I have hardly anything in common with
myself and should stand very quietly in a corner, content that I can breathe.
—Franz Kafka, *Diaries*

THERE IS something presumptuously proprietary about the whole idea of
sorting out writers according to national, ethnic, or religious origins, like
so many potatoes whose essential characteristics can be determined by
whether they come from Idaho or Maine. Obviously enough, the primary
focus for useful criticism of any original writer must be on the stubbornly
individual imagination that has sought to articulate a personal sense of
self and world through the literary medium, and this attention to individual peculiarities rather than shared characteristics is especially necessary in
understanding serious writers since the middle of the last century, so many
of whom have been alienated in one way or another from their native
social groups. Indeed, as Kafka's chilling confession of self-estrangement
reminds us, some of the most troubled, and therefore representative, modern writers have been alienated from themselves as well, haunted by the
fear that every affirmation or act of communication was a falsification, a
betrayal.

Nevertheless, the onerous question of the writer's background persists.
One justifiably speaks of Melville, Hawthorne, even Poe, as essentially
American writers, for their achievement cannot be intelligently grasped
without an awareness of its intimate relationship to the common social
and cultural experience of nineteenth-century America. Even more strikingly, the Jewishness of writers like Mendele, Peretz, and Sholem Aleichem
obviously has the greatest relevance to any serious assessment of their
literary enterprise because their fictional worlds are shaped out of the stuff
of East-European Jewish life, its language, its folklore, its religious traditions, its social realia. With Jewish writers, however, the attempt to attribute literary qualities to ethnic origins is in many instances acutely problematic. The Jews, in any case a perplexing group to define, become almost
perversely elusive as the process of modernization spreads after the French

Revolution. It is by no means clear what sense is to be made of the Jewishness of a writer who neither uses a uniquely Jewish language, nor describes a distinctively Jewish milieu, nor draws upon literary traditions that are recognizably Jewish. If one were to compile an anthology of all the unabashed nonsense written by literary critics over the past fifty years, a good many pages would have to be devoted to what has been advanced about the Jewish values, vision, and worldview of a wide variety of apostates, supposed descendants of Jews, offspring of mixed marriages, or merely assimilated Jews, from St. Theresa and Heine down to Proust and even J.D. Salinger.

One cannot, however, simply discount the possibility that some essentially Jewish qualities may adhere to the writing of the most thoroughly acculturated Jews. Most readers have sensed in at least some of these "posttraditional" or "transitional" Jewish writers certain modes of imagination or general orientations towards art and experience that seem characteristically Jewish, even where the writer scrupulously avoids all references to his [or her] ethnic origins. The difficulty, of course, is to translate such vague intuitions into clear descriptive statements about what actually goes on in the literary works.

I was led to ponder again this intriguing but treacherous question of Jewish literary identity by an essay of Leslie Fiedler's, "Master of Dreams."[1] What Fiedler sketches out in his essay might be described as a single grand mythic plot which, in sundry variations, modifications, and reversals, is presumed to underlie all Jewish literature, and, apparently, all Jewish cultural activity as well. Fiedler's point of departure is the Joseph story in Genesis, which he interestingly characterizes as a "dream of the dreamer, a myth of myth itself." Joseph, whose troubles begin because of his own seemingly grandiose dream, makes his way to power by interpreting the dreams of others and so translates his original dream into dazzling fact, his fathers and brothers—and virtually the whole world besides—bowing down to him as viceroy of the mightiest king on earth. In the light of this communal dream of the Joseph story, Fiedler sees the Jew's characteristic cultural role as a vendor of dreams and an interpreter of dreams to the world—that is, as poet and therapist (in Fiedler's anecdotal English, "My Son the Artist" and "My Son the Doctor"). The Jewish sons who become poets, according to this account, continue to pursue the original myth of myth: their fictions are about the attempt—what some of them now recognize as a doomed attempt—to make the splendid dream literal fact, and their fictional surrogates are even frequently called upon to resist the temptations of a Potiphar's wife in order to remain faithful to the dream they bear within them. Fiedler concedes that there are wide differences in the literary forms adopted by Jewish writers, but he suggests that they all belong to a single tradition both because they all participate in a Joseph-like myth of myth, and because they share a distinctive purpose, which, in keeping with the double role of the biblical master of dreams, is "therapeutic and prophetic."

The treatment of the biblical subject in "Master of Dreams" suggests a useful analogue for Fiedler's criticism—Midrash, the early rabbinic method of homiletic exegesis. One possible way of describing Midrash is as the art of imaginatively connecting things intrinsically unconnected, and the same could be said of much that Fiedler has written. Since for the creators of the Midrash the entire Bible, together with the Oral Law, exists in one eternal, divinely revealed present, everything is potentially an intricate commentary on everything else. One needs only the recurrence of, say, a verb-root in a verse in Genesis, in Isaiah, and in Psalms, to see the later statements as explications, developments, fuller revelations of the earlier one. When, for example, the Midrash *Bereshit rabba* tells us that Abraham's "splitting" of wood for the sacrifice of Isaac was answered on a grand scale by God's "splitting" of the Red Sea for his descendants, our real knowledge of the relevant verses in Genesis and Exodus has not been augmented, but what we may enjoy is following the trajectory of the interpretative imagination from point to point, not unlike the delight we take in the linking of ostensible disparates that is effected through poetic metaphor. This procedure is not so far removed from that of modern archetypal criticism, which in just such an instance might easily speak not of verbal continuities but of "the recurrence of the cleavage motif," with or without Freudian innuendos.

Fiedler is more subtle and inventive than most mythopoeic critics in his articulation of archetypes, but he clearly shares with the medieval Midrash an indifference to historical perspective which allows him to speak of the varied literary productions of far-flung times and places as one eternal system, and he is thoroughly midrashic in his readiness to establish through the merest hint of an association a "real" connection between things. Thus, there is actually not the faintest suggestion in the biblical story that Joseph is either a poet or a therapist. He interprets dreams for purposes at once practical and divine, but surely not to cure anyone, while the common association between dreamer and poet which Fiedler invokes is not even vaguely intimated in the biblical account. Though Fiedler would have us think of Joseph as a prototype of both Freud and Kafka, it makes better sense on the grounds of the text itself to imagine Joseph rather as a sort of ancient Near Eastern RAND Corporation figure—the Jewish intellectual as government planner, manipulating that great Pharaonic power structure from the top, managing, through his two Seven-Year Plans, to centralize control of land and economic resources to a degree unprecedented in Egyptian history. If Fiedler's own bold anachronisms invite anachronistic response, this, too, is in the ahistorical spirit of midrashic interpretation: The rabbis did not hesitate to represent Joseph as an earlocked talmudist applying himself to the subtleties of the Law in the study house of Shem, and by the same logic he can be given a Viennese beard, a passion for literary self-expression, or a knowledge of computer mathematics.

There is, then, a special fascination in Fiedler's criticism, but as in the case of the ancient midrashim, we may sometimes want to qualify that fascination with an adjective like "quaint." The real question raised by his whole scheme of an archetypal Jewish myth of myth is not whether it is firmly anchored in the biblical story but whether it is really helpful in locating and identifying a distinctive Jewish movement in Western culture, and in this essential regard I cannot see that it has any utility at all. On the contrary, it seems to me to encourage a common error much in need of correction. For there has been a tacit conspiracy afoot in recent years to foist on the American public as peculiarly Jewish various admired characteristics which in fact belong to the common humanity of us all. The Jewish folk is imagined as possessing a kind of monopoly on vividness, compassion, humor, pathos, and the like; Jewish critics and novelists are thought to be unique in their preoccupation with questions of morality; and now we are asked to believe that the Jews have all along exercised a privileged control over the cultural market on dreams.

When Fiedler characterizes the Joseph story as "the dreamer's own dream of how, dreaming, he makes it in the waking world," and then goes on to represent modern Jewish writing as a varying account of the difficulties of "making it" through dreams in actuality, he is describing not a distinctively Jewish imaginative mode but the central tradition of the novel, from *Don Quixote* to *Lolita*. Cervantes had hit on a new set of literary terms to encompass a new, radically disorienting world (the one we still inhabit) by inventing a dreamer who madly and persistently tried to live out his shining dream in a gray existence stolidly resistant to dreams and intolerant of their perpetrators. The model of the heroically unhinged Don, progenitor of a genre, is followed by Stendhal's Julien Sorel, Flaubert's Emma Bovary, Dostoyevski's Prince Mishkin and his Raskolnikov, Melville's Ahab, George Eliot's Dorothea Brooke, Gide's Lafcadio, Joyce's Stephen Daedalus as well as his Leopold Bloom—in fact, by the protagonists of most of the substantial novels written over the past two centuries. One might, of course, seize on the conjecture of some literary historians that Cervantes himself was a Marrano or the descendant of converts from Judaism, but this would be to succumb to a kind of philosemitic version of the *Protocols of the Elders of Zion* as an explanation of Western culture. According to such a theory, which seems to be tacitly assumed by many critics, the main currents at least of modern culture all derive from subterranean Jewish sources: a tenuous connection through three Christian generations with Jewish forebears is supposedly enough to infect the writer with a uniquely Jewish imagination, and this in turn he passes on to the surrounding Gentile world around him. (Fiedler applies much the same logic to fictional characters in describing the hero of *An American Dream* as an "essentially" Jewish figure by arbitrarily identifying him as a compound of two projected characters in Mailer's unwritten long novel, one Gentile and the other one-quarter Jewish, which then enables him blithely to assert that "Stephen Rojack . . . is half-Jewish, since in the world of myth a quarter-Jew plus a full Gentile equals a half-Jew.") All this is undoubtedly somewhat less incredible than the obverse theory that the Jews have secretly seized control of Western civilization in order to destroy it from within, but it resembles the *Protocols* myth in reshaping observable realities to fit the contours of collective fantasy.

It is not the Jewish dreamer in Exile but the writer at large who, "thinking only of making his own dreams come true, ends by deciphering the alien dreams of that world as well," and the "prophetic" and "therapeutic" ends which Fiedler assigns to Jewish writers are in fact the general aims of most serious European and American writers, at least since the middle of the nineteenth century. The Joseph scheme works all too well in too many cases, whether we apply it to the writer's life or to his literary creations. Who, for example, could be closer to the archetype of Joseph than Charles Dickens, a master of dreams who determined from early youth to realize a great dream of worldly success and achieved it by creating and selling dreams to the millions—"the artist as tycoon," in F.W. Dupee's telling phrase—even to acquiring the very Gads Hill mansion he had envisaged from afar as a boy? The prophetic and therapeutic impulse in Dickens's novels hardly needs comment at this point in time, and it is equally clear that in the works of his maturity, by bodying forth in fiction his own dreams, he was interpreting the collective dreams of a culture to which part of him remained permanently alien, from his descent into the pit of the blacking warehouse as a child to his glorious assumption into the palaces of the great.

Or, using this same mythic touchstone to identify characteristically Jewish literary inventions, one might justifiably conclude that the most remarkable American Jewish novel is neither *Call It Sleep* nor *Herzog* but Ralph Ellison's *Invisible Man*. Ellison prefaces his book with a dedication to Morteza Sprague, "a dedicated dreamer in a land most strange," which is a

neat description of the archetypal Joseph himself and also accurately characterizes Ellison's protagonist. The novel begins and ends with a dream
and many of the intervening episodes are strikingly dreamlike, for the
protagonist is at once attempting to escape a nightmare and realize a
dream of worldly success, on the world's own meretricious terms. His slow
recognition of who he really is—"I am your brother Joseph," one almost
hears him saying in the poignant scene where he realizes his deep kinship
with an evicted Harlem couple—involves a rejection of the false dream, a
perception of the extent to which the nightmare is reality. In this version,
it is at the end of his long journey from home that he is cast into a dark pit,
Joseph-like, by those who should be his brothers, and he promises us that
he will emerge from these depths with a new, unillusioned strength. There
are even Potiphar's wives to mislead this young man with a vision on his
progress through a land most strange. In contrast to the three sexual
partners of Steve Rojack—that highly supposititious "mythical" Jew—
who are improbably seen by Fiedler as Potiphar's wives, the two white
seductresses in *Invisible Man* are really imagined as alien women who, by
using the hero for their own gratification, would thrust him into a false
role, would unwittingly involve him in a symbolic betrayal of himself and
his people. It is difficult, finally, to think of a novel written by a Jew that is
as intent as this one to enunciate a prophecy and effect a kind of therapy.
The young Negro, by working out the visions that haunt him, ends up
deciphering the darker dreams of American society as well. It is entirely
appropriate that the novel should conclude with a long dream-like se-
quence charged with intimations of apocalypse, the nightmare now gal-
loping across the waking world, and that this episode in turn should be
followed by a formal, allegorical dream of apocalypse, prophesying doom
to America if it does not act quickly to redeem its own humanity.

   The tracing of archetypes is a pleasant enough pastime, but its value as a
means of making useful literary identifications is dubious. Ellison himself
has stated the matter succinctly in objecting to another archetypal interpretation of his novel: "Archetypes are timeless, novels are time-haunted."
If we are to discover any clue to the connection between a writer's origins
in a particular group and the nature of his work, we must begin in time,
which is to say, we must take history seriously into account. The case of
Kafka, whom Fiedler cites as the great modern paradigm of Joseph as artist,
the Jewish son as dreamer, takes us to the heart of this whole issue. No
other Jew who has contributed significantly to European literature appears
so intensely, perhaps disturbingly, Jewish in the quality of his imagination
as Kafka. Though he never introduces explicitly Jewish materials into his
work, though he never really writes "about" Jews (even symbolically, I

would argue), most readers of *The Trial, The Castle, Amerika*, and the short-
er parables and fables, have sensed that this peculiar mode of fiction would
never have occurred to a Christian imagination. One is struck by the
emphatic difference of Kafka's work from the various kinds of fiction that
have been predominant in the European novel, but it is not so easy to
determine whether or how that difference is Jewish.

To think of Kafka as a Joseph-figure will not really help us, for reasons
which I hope I have already made clear. The invocation of that archetype
does not, for example, enable us to distinguish between Kafka and Dickens, a writer whom he admired and imitated, and who shared with him a
"Jewish" preoccupation with failed relationships between fathers and
sons. Critics have made a variety of other suggestions about the Jewishness
of Kafka's fiction, some of them comical, some interesting, some perhaps
even credible. To begin with, there has been a general rush to align Kafka
with various Jewish cultural traditions, without regard to the degree of
familiarity he may actually have had with them. The fact that Kafka is
both a Jewish writer and an arcane one has invited a certain degree of loose
talk about the "kabbalistic" elements in his work, though he had no direct
knowledge of the Kabbalah, and the Germanized home in which he grew
up was hardly the sort where he could have picked up very much of it
through oral tradition. More plausibly, comparisons have been drawn between the Hasidic folktale and the parable form Kafka favored in which
the order of action is so often inscrutably miraculous. The biographical
evidence, however, suggests affinity rather than influence. Kafka was fasci-
nated by whatever he learned of Hasidic lore, but the better part of his
acquaintance with it took place toward the end of his life, through his
friendship with Georg Langer and then from his reading of Buber's early
compilations, especially *Der grosse Maggid*, which did not appear until
1922. Again, a good many critics who have never studied a page of the
Talmud have not hesitated to describe the peculiar questioning movement
of Kafka's prose as "talmudic," but there is virtually no real similarity, and
in any case Kafka's knowledge of the Talmud, until his last years, was
confined to quotations passed on to him by those of his friends who had
once studied in the East-European yeshivot. One is free to suppose, of
course, that Westernized Jews as a rule simply continue to talk and think
in talmudic fashion, but such a supposition can be made only out of
ignorance of both the Talmud itself and the way modern Jews actually talk
and think.

Heinz Politzer, in his book *Franz Kafka: Parable and Paradox*, links Kafka's fiction somewhat more probably with a still older mode of Jewish
literature. Politzer compares Kafka's spare, taut tales, which repeatedly

generate a sense of fatal significance in the events narrated, to the narrative method of the Hebrew Bible. Picking up the notion developed by
Erich Auerbach of the biblical story as a tale "fraught with background,"
Politzer argues that in Kafka's enigmatic fictions one can observe this same
general effect of starkly drawn surfaces, which suggest a heavy pressure of
dark meanings behind them that are never spelled out by the narrator. In
Kafka, he goes on to say, as in the ancient Hebrew stories, the characters
are at once impersonal and more than personal, uncannily representative
in their very distance and peculiarity, inviting multiple interpretation by
leading us to think of them as our surrogates in a cosmic drama. Kafka
certainly read the Hebrew Bible in translation intently, occasionally even
alluded to aspects of his own experience in biblical terms, and at the end of
his life he was learning to read it in its original language. It is at least
plausible that his familiarity with the Bible helped him work out his own
characteristic narrative art; in any case, he must have discovered in it a
compelling imaginative kinship. Such notions of kinship, however, can be
adopted for the needs of precise literary analysis only with great caution,
for they are but a step away from assuming a Hebrew Imagination over
and against a Greek Imagination as timeless categories, which, of course,
would bring us back through another door into the wide-and-woolly
realm of myths of culture.

Critics less interested in Kafka's treatment of literary form than in his
moral, philosophical, and theological concerns have associated him not
with Jewish literary traditions but with the distinctive values and assumptions of historical Judaism. Thus, the absence of any radical disjuncture in
Kafka between spirit and flesh, this world and the next, even between the
prosaic and the miraculous, has been attributed to his Jewish background,
which, it must be admitted, is a suggestive idea if not altogether a demon-
strable one. The fact, on the other hand, that moral or spiritual obligations
in Kafka so often take the form of commandments from an unreachable
authority and frequently necessitate tortuous interpretation, can obviously be connected with Kafka's personal awareness of rabbinic Judaism,
and represents a particularly Jewish formulation of a general spiritual predicament. Still clearer is the condition of exile—for Jews, a theological
category as well as a historical experience—which underlies all of Kafka's
major fiction. It is this, above all else, that commentators have quite properly stressed in identifying the distinctively Jewish note in Kafka: If modern literature in general is a literature that adopts the viewpoint of the
outsider, Kafka, as the alienated member of an exiled people, is the paradigmatic modernist precisely because he is a paradigmatic Jew.

The general validity of this familiar idea is, I suppose, unassailable, but
its usefulness is limited because of the very fact that in its usual formula-

tion it remains so general. "Exile" tends to be applied to Kafka and to other Jewish writers as an evocative but unexamined abstraction with a supposedly fixed meaning, when in fact "exile" meant different things to different Jews at various times and places, and for most of them, at least until fairly recently, it was quite distinct from alienation, a concept with which many literary critics automatically identify it. It makes sense, therefore, to try to state in concrete terms how this particular writer seems to have encountered the experience of exile and then how that encounter enters into the substance of his imaginative work.

Living in Prague, Kafka of course belonged to a very special kind of double-exile—a Jew in the Austro-Hungarian Empire and a German writer in a Czech city. His position, moreover, as an employee in a state-sponsored insurance agency extended his initial sense of himself as a suspect intruder: at his office he was, as he pointedly phrased it, the single "display-Jew" in a "dark nest of bureaucrats," and so every workday forced upon him at least the negative awareness of Jewishness as a condition of being unwanted, mistrusted, transparently dependent on the favor of others. At the same time, Kafka was acutely conscious of Jewish history and Jewish peoplehood, even without any deep knowledge of the former or very much external involvement in the latter, until the Zionism of his last years. He was inclined to view the Jews of his own generation as in fact transitional, standing uncertainly at the irrevocable end of a long process of Jewish history, but his sense of belonging to a twilight period seems to have had the effect of sharpening his interest in the history and culture of his people. The Yiddish theater in Prague, for example, held a fascination for Kafka out of all proportion to the artistic merit of the plays it presented because he saw in it the living manifestation of an uninhibited, self-sufficient folk culture, unlike anything he had known personally. The very idea of Yiddish literature continued to attract him—he carefully read and took notes in his diary on Pines's *Histoire de la litterature Judeo-Allemande*—because with its obvious stress on "an uninterrupted tradition of national struggle that determines every work," he envisaged it as an alluring antithesis to that anguished exploration of a private world which writing inevitably was for him.

The case of Kafka, the acculturated Jew, shows how a man may feel his way into a body of collective history through his very consciousness of being outside it: Kafka brooded over the experience of the people from whom he derived, and I would argue that certain key images and states of awareness that were the product of European Jewish history exerted continual pressure on his imagination as he wrote. In this connection, there is one passage in his recorded conversations with the Czech writer Gustav Janouch that is especially revealing. Janouch had asked him if he still remembered the old Jewish quarter of Prague, largely destroyed before Kafka could have known it; this, according to Janouch, is the reply he received:

> In us it still lives—the dark corners, the secret alleys, shuttered windows, squalid courtyards, rowdy pubs, and sinister inns. We walk through the broad streets of the newly built town. But our steps and our glances are uncertain. Inside we tremble just as before in the ancient streets of our misery. Our heart knows nothing of the slum clearance that has been achieved. The unhealthy old Jewish town within us is far more real than the new hygienic town around us. With our eyes open we walk through a dream: ourselves only a ghost of a vanished age.[2]

This remarkable statement is a kind of spiritual autobiography, a summary of what the awareness of being a Jew meant in Kafka's inner life; at the same time, it might be observed that what he has in effect described here is the imaginative landscape of all three of his novels—the hidden alleys and sinister attics of *The Trial*, the medieval squalor and confusion of the courtyards, the dubious inns and devious byways in *The Castle*, and even the new-world landscape of *Amerika*, which begins with skyscrapers but breaks off in a dark and filthy garret where the protagonist is held prisoner. The world of Kafka's novels incorporates the maddening impersonality and inscrutability of modern bureaucracy in an image of an insecure medieval community derived from a ghetto Kafka remembered obsessively without ever having known.

Let me emphasize that the recognition of such a connection may tell us something about the genesis of Kafka's enigmatic fictions but it is by no means a key to their meaning. What Kafka's imaginative intimacy with the Jewish past did was to give a special shape to the imagery and a particular sharpness to the edge of feeling in his work, but the work is surely not intended as a representation of Jewish experience. It is, for example, a serious misplacement of emphasis to describe *The Castle*, as a few critics have done, as a Zionist myth of an outcast in search of a land, though the novel would not have been conceived in the terms it was and would not carry the conviction it does without Kafka's concrete imagination of uncertain steps and glances along the ancient streets of Jewish misery. Or again, to insist that the eternally exiled hero of "The Hunter Gracchus" is an avatar of the Wandering Jew would be to force a hauntingly elusive tale into the predictable contours of allegory. It seems wiser to say that Kafka's general and untranslatable fable of a wanderer through awesome eternity is imagined with such disturbing intensity because of the presence in the writer of Jewish memories, personal and collective, out of which he could create this particular "ghost of a vanished age" walking open-eyed through a dream of damnation. It is not as an archetypal Jew that Gracchus speaks at the end of the story, but the words and images his inventor chooses for him resonate with the experience of rejection and exclusion of many generations: "Nobody will read what I say here, no one will come to help me; even if all the people were commanded to help me, every door and window would remain shut, everybody would take to bed and draw the bedclothes over his head, the whole earth would become an inn for a night." It is one of those unsettling moments in Kafka when, in the retrospectively ironic light of history, we see the recollection of the past as a grimly accurate prophecy of the future, too.

Another major theme of Kafka's, which he often connects with the situation of the outsider or pariah, is the irruption of the inhuman into the human, or more generally, the radical ambiguity of what seems to be human. While this movement of his imagination was obviously energized by the tensions and fears of his own private neuroses, it seems to me that his notion of a convergence of inhuman and human frequently draws on his hallucinated memory of the Jewish past. Even in a bizarre story like "A Report to an Academy," which is so far removed from any overt reference to Jews, I would contend that Kafka's fictional invention is formed on a kind of "analogical matrix" of his experience as a transitional Jew. The scientific report, one recalls, is that of a gifted ape who has managed "with an effort which up till now has never been repeated . . . to reach the cultural level of an average European."[3] In the torturous confinement of a cage so small that he could neither stand nor sit in it, the idea had dawned on the ape of getting out by imitating his captors, and he began, most appropriately, by learning to spit, and then to drink schnapps by the bottle, an act which at first violently repelled him. In retrospect, the ape stresses again and again that he finds no intrinsic advantage in being human: "There was no attraction for me in imitating human beings; I imitated them because I needed a way out, and for no other reason . . . ah, one learns when one has to; one learns when one needs a way out" (257). Conversely, the ape makes no special plea for apehood; there may be nothing especially admirable in being an ape rather than a human, but, if one begins as an ape, it is at least an authentic condition, what one would naturally prefer to remain, other things being equal. When at the end of the report the ape adjures his audience, "Do not tell me that it was not worth the trouble," there is a quaver of doubt in his voice: cages are admittedly maddening to live in, but has he not lost a great deal by betraying his native self for a way out, selling his birthright, so to speak, for a mess of lentils?

Now, one of the distinctive qualities of a Kafka parable is that it has no paraphrasable "moral," and I would not want to transform "A Report to an Academy" into an allegory of assimilation. I suspect, however, that this

fable, which calls into question the whole status of humanity, was initially
shaped around Kafka's awareness of himself as part of the modern movement of Jews who had emerged from the confinement of ghetto life to join
European culture, and that the ape's disquieting ambiguity about his own
achievement flows from Kafka's insight into how much of themselves Jews
had left behind in their former existence without even the compensation
of genuine acceptance in the "human" world outside the cage. The very
contrast between human and Jew was one that modernizing Jews themselves implicitly accepted in their desperation for a way out. The poet Y.L.
Gordon's famous line, "Be a man outside and a Jew at home," summed up
this whole self-negating mentality as it was articulated in the Hebrew
Enlightenment, and Kafka himself must have been particularly struck by
Gordon's formulation, for he copied it into his diary when he ran across it
in Pines's history.

Typically, however, confusions between human and inhuman in Kafka
terrify more than they perplex, and the imaginative core of that terror is
often Jewish for this writer who lived so intensely with the fear and trembling of a vanished ghetto. The nightmarish little tale entitled "An Old
Manuscript" is paradigmatic in this respect. Again, the terms of reference
of the story are as universal as those of some ancient myth. A nameless
town in a nameless empire has been taken over by fierce, implacable nomads who speak no recognizably human tongue. The Emperor remains a
powerless spectator, shut up in his palace, a little like the symbolic King of
banished sons in many of the midrashic parables, while the townspeople,
in the person of the cobbler who is the narrator, confess their incapacity to
cope with the terrible strangers:

> From my stock, too, they have taken many good articles. But I cannot
> complain when I see how the butcher, for instance, suffers across the
> street. As soon as he brings in any meat the nomads snatch it all from him
> and gobble it up. Even their horses devour flesh; often enough a horseman
> and his horse are lying side by side, both of them gnawing at the same
> joint, one at either end. The butcher is nervous and does not dare to stop
> his deliveries of meat. We understand that, however, and subscribe money
> to keep him going. If the nomads got no meat, who knows what they
> might think of doing; who knows anyhow what they may think of, even
> though they get meat every day.
>
> Kafka, *The Complete Stories*, 416–417.

One does not have to invoke mythic archetypes to feel the bone and
blood of Jewish memories in these ghastly images. Behind the nameless
nomadic horsemen are dark hordes of Cossacks, Haidameks, pogromists of
every breed—the alien and menacing *goy* in his most violent embodiments, speaking no intelligible language, obeying no human laws, even

eagerly violating, as we learn in the next paragraph, the Noahide injunction against consuming the flesh of an animal while it is still alive. To the Jew trembling before the torch and ax and sword of the attacker, it seemed that the enemy quite literally could not belong to the same species, and so here the ironic displacement of inhuman and human of "A Report to an Academy" is reversed—the Jew, in the analogical matrix of this story, associated with vulnerable humanity, and the Gentile with inhuman otherness.

What should also be noted is that the story pronounces judgment on the passivity of the townspeople as well as on the stark bestiality of the nomads. Edmund Wilson has accused Kafka of "meaching compliance" with the brutal and unreasonable forces he means to expose in his fiction,[4] but I think this misses the point, for the object of Kafka's "satire" (the term is applied by Wilson) is not only the inhuman powers but also man's pathetic inadequacy of response to them. To put this in terms of the ethnic background of Kafka's imaginings, he never sentimentalized Jewish history; though he was intrigued by the lore of his forebears and their unusual sense of community, he remained ruthlessly honest about the way Jews were. In the passage quoted, one can see a distinctly familiar response of Jews to violence and impending disaster—the attempt to buy off calamity, to temporize with it. (How sadly characteristic that the tradesmen of the community should answer the terrible challenge only by pooling resources to subsidize the principal victim of the invaders!) The story makes clear that this response represents a failure of courage and of imagination as well: In the face of imminent and hideous destruction, where bold, perhaps violent, action is required, the townspeople can muster no more than a piously impotent wringing of hands, a collection of donations, and the grotesquely timid understatement that "This is a misunderstanding of some kind; and it will be the ruin of us."

Kafka, in sum, addressed himself to the broadest questions of human nature and spiritual existence, working with images, actions, and situations that were by design universal in character; but his self-awareness as a Jew and his consciousness of Jewish history impelled his imagination in a particular direction and imparted a peculiar intensity to much of what he wrote, where the abstractness or generality of the parable is strangely wedded to the most concrete sense of actual experience felt and recollected. He could envision the ultimate ambiguities of human life in general with a hyperlucidity because he had experienced them in poignant particularity as a Jew. Out of the stuff of a Jewish experience which he himself thought of as marginal, he was able to create fiction at once universal and hauntingly Jewish.

All this is far from exhausting the question of how Kafka's antecedents enter into his writing, but it should at least suggest that there is no simple formulaic key for identifying the Jewish character of all Jewish writers. As I have tried to illustrate in the case of Kafka, one must always attend to the particular ways in which Jewish experience impinges on the individual, and this impingement is bound to differ in small things and large from one writer to the next. The varied materials of art itself, with their confusingly various connections with reality, are more recalcitrant, less pleasingly symmetrical, than the neat designs of archetypal criticism, but, in the final analysis, they are a good deal more interesting.

Editor's Notes

1. Leslie Fiedler, "Master of Dreams, *Partisan Review* 34 (Summer 1967): 339–56.

2. Gustav Janouch, *Conversations with Kafka*, tr. Goronwy Rees (New York: New Directions, 1971), 80.

3. Franz Kafka, *The Complete Stories* (New York: Schocken, 1946) p. 258.

4. Edmund Wilson, "A Dissenting Opinion on Kafka," *Classics and Commercials* (New York: Farrar, Straus & Cudahy, 1950).

II.
Jewish, Hebrew, or Israeli Literature?

One Literature in Two Languages

I

Bees give us honey, and literati give us—literature. Don't look to bees for that specific purpose. They gratify people with their sweet honey involuntarily. They are not aware that their honey brings relief to ailing lungs. And who knows? If bees could talk, perhaps we might hear the deep sighs and oaths with which they curse their bitter luck at being made to give up their sweet honey.

What is the relevance of all this? It is relevant with regard to our literature of these last few years.

A new type of person has developed among us who is a writer not only on Mondays and on Tuesdays, but all year round. This new type has made a firm commitment to produce literature. His eyes see only whatever has the marks of a literary theme. His heart beats only when it is moved by a literary impression upon it, and everything mundane assumes a literary form. Such a person produces, intentionally or not, with great effort and hardship what is termed "literature." They have me to thank for the appearance among us, from time to time, of a hefty volume of slender booklets entitled *Sifrut* (*Literature*) today, *Literarishe Monatshriften* (*Literary Monthlies*) tomorrow, and the day after tomorrow *Kunst und Leben* (*Art and Life*); a *M'orer* in London, a *Revivim* in Lemberg, a *Reshifim* in Warsaw, and a *Ha'atid* in Berlin-Cracow.

My friends, don't look for some sort of unified direction in all these essay collections. Dr. Joseph Klausner, S.Y. Horowitz, and his regular adversary, Haradetsky, are all seated around one table at *Ha'atid*; Hillel Zeitlin and Reuven Breinin are united with David Frishman in the *Sifrut* camp. Chaim Brenner in his *M'orer* and *Revivim* mixes together Moshe Kleinman with M.Y. Berdyczewski. In the *Literarishe Monatshriften* three singers from three different Yiddish factions—A. Veiter, S. Gorelick, and S. Niger—have united into a single choir. And in the *Birnboim Wochenblatt*, I.L. Peretz has met up with one A. Kleinman and with Birnboim himself. *Hashiloah* was the only journal that for a time remained pure as gold and did not, Heaven forbid, mingle with anyone else. And since Nahum Sokolov appeared in what was formerly Ahad Ha'am's house organ he too has lost his innocence and his distinctiveness in such collections.

II

Many people complain that our literary undertakings are nipped in the bud. There is grief for the young *M'orer*, which departed this world too soon, and for the *Literarishe Monatshriften*, which did not survive beyond its infancy. But as a loyal reader, I don't share these views. I am convinced that we have lost nothing. Only the names and the languages of our publications have changed, and our writers have not disappeared at all. If the writers' bad luck brought about the demise of one of the publications, these writers promptly regathered in another, which distinguished itself from the first only by its name and language. If the bright halls of the "literary monthlies" are closed to these writers, they come together in yet another collection, a Hebrew one—and they write in Hebrew. If one publisher closes down his Yiddish shop, another opens up immediately with the same material in Hebrew. If a Zeitlin offers his fiery moralizing articles in Yiddish in the *Heint* today, he will submit the identical piece in the language of the prophets in *Reshifim* tomorrow. Chaim Brenner's articles in *Revivim* can be found in *Heint* under the new heading of "Quiet Words." Namberg does not find it necessary even to change his name when he writes in Hebrew what he had formerly written in Yiddish. What appeared in *Der Yud* under the title of "Oyf Ein Kvartir" ("In One Lodging") now appears in *Sifrut* as "B'maon akhad."

Jewish literature is not going under—Heaven forbid. It is *one* and its name is *one*. It simply comes before the reader in two forms which, like the pans on a scale, swing in opposite directions. Just as nothing is absolutely balanced in nature, so the scales move up and down: sometimes one is at the top, sometimes the other. Today Brenner comes to us in a Yiddish garment. Tomorrow Sholem Aleichem comes in a Hebrew one. Last year Namberg was a Hebraist in *Ha Zman*. Today he is a Yiddishist in *Unzer Leben* and in *Romantseitung*. Does the name, typography, or publisher of a journal really matter? In recent years it has come to be required that a Jewish writer, just like a correspondent in an office, must know at least *two* languages in order to create freely. To commemorate the jubilee of I.L. Peretz, two editions of his *Collected Works* were published, one in Hebrew and one in Yiddish. And when the celebrant himself was asked in which of these volumes one could find the real Peretz, he answered modestly that the sparks of his spirit were scattered in both *Collected Works,* and that in order to comprehend the greatness and unity of his vision you would have to immerse yourself in both collections. At present, plans call for the publication of a Yiddish collected works of David Frishman. And I am sure that when Reb Mendele reaches his seventy-fifth birthday, some will want to proclaim him a Hebraist and publish his collected works in Hebrew. Sholem Aleichem himself has said recently that as long as all of his works have not been translated into Hebrew, the Angel of Death will not be able to overpower him! Nahum Sokolov is not certain whether he, too, will take on a Yiddish guise. His articles in the *Telegraph* could fill a volume no thinner than a *Gemara.* Our literature contains in its inner chambers a Yiddish Bialik, a Yiddish Berdyczewski, and even a Yiddish . . . Klausner. Ahad Ha'am is the lone exception. Yet Ahad Ha'am has said about himself that he is not a writer (see his *Al Parashat Drakhim*) and therefore his *Truth from the Land of Israel* does not have a Yiddish title, although in Yiddish it would appear in almost exactly the same words.

III

Some impassioned readers among us will not admit that our one and only literature has a double language. After the Czernowitz conference,[1] one of our Hebrew writers (now living in America) swore that from that day on he would not stain his pen with a single Yiddish word! And for him such an oath was not a small matter. For with that oath he severed the bond between himself and his mother, who lives in Russia and to whom he is a truly devoted son. And I have also learned that after Sholem Asch's address to the conference, an impassioned Yiddishist began to teach his little boy the Modeh ani[2] in pure Yiddish. This response was no less difficult for the father than the Hebrew writer's oath was for him, for the Modeh ani is without taste in Yiddish, lacking both salt and pepper. Furthermore, their fanaticism did not last long. The Hebrew writer rapidly became the editor of a Zionist paper, and the fanatic Yiddishist has joined a Hebrew teachers' organization, where, everyone knows, only the purest Hebrew is taught.

The Czernowitz resolution faded away like smoke. At the Czernowitz conference, 90 percent of whose participants were writers, it was forgotten temporarily that there actually are writers among Jews. These writers themselves suddenly forgot that it is their fate to gather straw for two kinds of goats, to acquire two languages. It is an old story that participants in conferences are intense idealists and have a tendency to be somewhat sentimental. That is no small matter! After all, they represent all Jews, and they are fighting for national progress! Doctors determined a long time ago that the pulse of a conference participant beats ten times harder than it would under normal circumstances, and that the participant's imagination works five percent harder than usual. American doctors are of the opinion that cold massages, a trip in a hot air balloon, and participation in conferences are the best remedies for tired nerves and anemia.

The average person cannot imagine what a pleasure it is to discard one's own problems for a few days a year and for a change worry about someone else's. For example, if Sholem Asch had not been in such a hurry to write his *Shabtai Zvi* before the conference, when he was so wrapped up in himself and his translators, who needed seventy translations of his newest work, and if he had written his work on the day of the conference, at a time when his soul was full of ideals, his work might well have turned out much better, or, more likely, it might never have seen the light of day. I return to my earlier point. The average person simply has no idea how delightful it is to forget one's own literary problems for a while and to agonize over someone else's woes! If the Czernowitz writers had thought more about themselves than about other people's business, they would, first of all, have taken a strong oath to write in only *one* language; second, they would have boycotted those writers who appear in Hebrew papers; third, they would have pressured Hebrew papers not to publish Yiddish articles in anything but the original. In a word, they should have been faithful to Yiddish and consequently have reduced their own chances for receiving a poor residual honorarium for publishing the same thing twice—in Yiddish and in Hebrew. They should repress the urge to appear in *Sifrut* today and in the *Literarishe Monatshriften* tomorrow.[3] But it is much harder to make such a commitment than it is to pass a resolution stating that Yiddish is our national language. It is easier to be the cause of bloodied scalps among the Czernowitz students, who would sacrifice themselves for a Czernowitz resolution rather than decide not to contribute simultaneously to *Teater Velt*, *Yugent Velt*, and *Sifrut*. Of course, it is much easier for a *writer* to push another writer to the wall with a resolution than to decline an honorarium from a poor Yiddish paper.

I don't mean to stain anyone's honor—Heaven forbid; I just want to demonstrate that the Czernowitz group, acting out of great ideals and equally great love for the people, forgot momentarily that first and foremost they are Jewish writers, and they live and breathe between two languages, even as a bridegroom is escorted to the bridal canopy by two parents.

IV

And does the writer live and breathe between two languages only? Don't our better critics carry within them the spirit of the German language? And in our younger writers, who were educated in the Russian language, can't we discern the spirit of Russian? And don't we hear echoes of French among our colleagues, the Palestinian writers (Ben-Ami, Hermoni)?

True, we have among us language artists—such as Bialik, Sokolov, Abramovitch, Sholem Aleichem—who occasionally write in a language that might cause one to conclude that not one word has crept into Jewish literature that is not thoroughly Jewish in nationality. There are probably likely to be among us talented writers who strive to create the spirit of a Hebrew language that should be the natural convergence of Biblical language, prophetic language, Mishnaic language, Midrash, and the juridical, philosophical, and mystical language of the *Gemara*, medieval philosophy, Kabbalah, and Hasidism. Ahad Ha'am, Berdyczewski, Zeitlin, and And— these are the talented writers who strive to achieve such a blending of the various pure elements in the Hebrew language. However, Hebrew is also a mixture of the spirit of many other languages. And I continue to have great doubts whether the generation of writers in *Eretz* Israel (who are already as far removed from Russian as from a Russian pogrom) can really understand the language of Brenner, Shafman, and And.

The spirit of the German language is the same everywhere. It does not matter who uses it: a German, a German American, or a Swiss. The same is true for the French language even though the Belgians, the French Swiss, and the French themselves originate from different peoples. Not so with the Hebrew language, whose spirit is different in every country. For the spirit of a strange language peeks out from under the mask of words. As for Yiddish, it is even worse. Its purity is a thousand times more suspect than that of the Hebrew language. For besides the present, Hebrew has a history and a literature of thousands of years, and thanks to which one can still hope some day to create a language with a pure national spirit. But Yiddish has only a *present*. It would never occur to anyone to make a synthesis of Ze'ena u'R'ena,[4] Isaac Meyer Dik, Aksenfeld, Ettinger, Shomer, Yiddish folk songs, Alikum Zunser, the Zionists, Bundist brochures, and American literature. If we were to compare the Hebrew language to an island in a sea of foreign languages that would engulf it, to what can we compare Yiddish? Perhaps to an inn along a dirt road, where people stop over as if they were at home, but where no one stays longer than a short while? Only the present can make Yiddish a literary language, only from the present does it derive its existence. But our present is such that it cannot and will not create anything genuine. The creation of a language, or of any new enterprise, can take place only in an atmosphere of calm and quiet, into which the cries of the marketplace and the sighs of want do not penetrate. But a wandering people cannot construct such a quiet environment. Not only can it contribute nothing to its language but it also impoverishes and weakens that language by its eternal wandering.

* * *

And what, in a nutshell, is the point? It is that we have two languages and a dozen echoes from other foreign languages, but that we have only *one* literature. And therefore the reader who seeks to become acquainted with the currents of Jewish life, to comprehend the spirit of the Jewish individual and multitude and how they find expression in Jewish literature, that reader dares not separate Hebrew writers from Yiddish ones, Mendele, Bialik, Sholem Aleichem, Berdyczewski, Feierberg, and others—all are representatives of our literature, all embody a piece of Jewish life in their writing; all of them are Jewish artists, even though they do not all use both languages to express their artistic motifs.

V

On the wide streets of a southern Russian city the crowd festively carried the picture of Shevchenko, crowned with laurels and encircled with Ukrainian flags. From a distance it appeared to be a religious procession bearing the holy icons of the church or of the Virgin Mary. In this fashion the newly liberated nations in Russia pay homage to their spiritual representatives, the originators of a national literature.

For the significance of literature at this very moment cannot be sufficiently appreciated. On the surface it signals differentiation, but at the core lies the sign of collective bonding. Everything that separates—binds, and whatever binds naturally, organically, has the right to demand that it be viewed as something that *should* and *must* develop freely.

As long as a people has no literature, it can be considered mute. The individual may speak, but the people are silent. A genuine literature is the magic box that contains the spirit of the people with all its sorrows, hopes, and ideals, future and present. Literature is the oral scripture that becomes the written one, and that far surpasses that first Bible. Those who keep exclusively to their oral scripture soon turn to stone and are erased from the book of nations. The Karaites provide the best example: they seem to have the same origin as we; one of them might nowadays well be able to trace his lineage back to King David. Yet no one considers the Karaites to be a nation. At the constituent assembly, in the choir of nations, their voice will not join in song.[5]

The literature of oppressed peoples has always been their own territory, where they feel entirely at home. At the very least it has proved a kind of ex-territoriality, something like Franz Josef's palace or an English embassy in a foreign land. On the threshold of the building the foreign country's authority ends. Behind the walls of such a building, be it in Turkey or Persia, a man could live as if he were entirely at home, with no one having any power over him except his own national community.

We Jews have been able to survive history because of this ex-territoriality. Heine once likened the Bible to a fatherland for the Jew, one that he carries along in his baggage. And the term "People of the Book," with which history has crowned us, clearly contains the notion that our earth, our very home, has always been literature. Obviously, we must take the term *literature* in its broadest sense. Everything that expresses the spiritual movements of a people, be it science, philosophy, journalism, or poetry, and that *is accepted by the people*, makes up what can be proudly called *national literature*.

VI

From its inception our literature has nearly always been a *bilingual* one, and those among us who cannot separate literature from language—that is, the cultural values that have been accepted by the masses from the languages spoken by the intellectuals and the people—can in no way come to terms with this fact. They do not want to acknowledge that, for us, bilingualism is such an old ailment that it has long ceased to pose a threat to the Jewish organism. They close their eyes to something that has been recognized by every Jew who is familiar with the history of our two-thousand-year-old literature.

For this bilingualism is already present in the Bible. When, in the course of his studies, the heder boy reaches the books of Daniel and Nehemiah, he suddenly falls into the Chaldean of the Persian Jewish historian trying to tell his story. And when he studies the sections in *The Ethics of the Fathers*, one of the finest chapters in Jewish literature, he must also come to a stop before words in Aramaic. And when this youngster begins to study the *Gemara*, he comes to experience what has always been characteristic for Jews—speaking in two languages as a matter of course. And out of the modest little Mishnah grows the voluminous Talmud, all in Aramaic.

This same bilingualism infiltrates all corners of Jewish cultural and religious life. The Onkelos translation of the Bible into Aramaic makes up one-third of the sacred ceremony of the Torah reading,[6] as every Jew is obliged to read the weekly Torah portion twice in the language of Moses and once in the Aramaic translation. And we also find Aramaic in the songs and liturgy of the prayer book.

Later, when the Jews were thrust into the Arab world, a whole Jewish philosophical literature came into being in Arabic. Even Maimonides's renowned *Guide for the Perplexed*, which until recently played such an important role in Jewish spiritual life, though almost as old as Methuselah, was written in Arabic.

From the fifteenth century on, an inspirational literature developed in the second language—Yiddish. Just as the Jews once adapted Arabic at first for their daily business and later for their intellectual interests, so they later adapted the old German tongue, for their wanderings caused them to become strongly bound to the Germans.

Also from the fifteenth century on, the finest Jewish intellectuals sought to give the people books in Yiddish. Writers from Eliahu Bachur to Abramovitch strove to provide for the Jewish masses even a small portion of what has always delighted the Jewish mind. And with time the *Ze'ena u'R'ena* became for the people what the Onkelos Bible had been for the Jews before the Second Destruction of the Temple, when the masses of people could no longer understand Hebrew and therefore had to be given translations in their synagogues.

From these little-noticed facts we can conclude that bilingualism accompanied the Jews even in ancient times, even when they had their own land, and they were not as yet the wanderers they are now. Therefore, language never took on the character of a holy shrine (as is now the case for the Poles). Shortly before the Second Destruction, as well as later, the *form* had already ceased to play first fiddle. The wish to implant deeply certain spiritual treasures was stronger than the desire to confine the people within the framework of a single language. And because that spiritual wish always carried the stamp of what we can boldly call a *modern democracy*, our intellectual leaders made no great fuss about language. Better a bilingual nation than one that has only one language meant for the intellectuals and not for the people.

As a moral-religio-philosophical system, Judaism is not something held in the hands of the few. Its strength comes from its being shared by *all* classes. As early as the Pentateuch we find passages such as the one in which Moses, the lawgiver—arriving as Eldad and Medad are prophesying before the Jewish encampment—says: "If only all Jews were prophets."

Consequently, the intellectual representatives of the people never dealt with the language problem, and, instead, always adapted themselves to the language spoken by the great masses.

Translated by Hana Wirth-Nesher

Editor's Notes

1. This gathering, held in Bukovina in August, 1908, was the first international conference to deal with the role of Yiddish in Jewish life. The conference passed a resolution proclaiming Yiddish as a national language, after heated debates between ardent Hebraists who recognized Hebrew as the only national language of the Jewish people and committed Yiddishists who saw Yiddish as the only living language of the Jews in contrast with Hebrew, the language of prayer. This resolution marked a turning point for Yiddish in terms of its cultural prestige. Baal Makhshoves attended this conference along with other well-known literary figures, among them Abraham Reisen, I.L. Peretz, and Sholem Asch. Mendele and Sholem Aleichem endorsed the conference's resolution, although they were unable to attend due to illness.

2. The initial words of a prayer (literally, "I give thanks") said immediately upon waking in the morning.

3. *Sifrut* is a Hebrew publication and *Literarishe Monatshriften* is a Yiddish one.

4. One of the most widely read books in Yiddish up to the end of the nineteenth century, *Ze'ena u'Re'ena* is a paraphrase of the Pentateuch, an adaptation aimed at women readers.

5. The Karaites are a Jewish sect that came into being in the eighth century and are characterized primarily by their denial of the talmudic-rabbinical tradition. Baal Makhshoves argues here that their lack of a written tradition excludes them from nationhood.

6. The Onkelos is a translation of the Bible into Aramaic from the second century C.E.

BARUCH KURZWEIL

Notes on Hebrew Literature

THE VALUE and significance of a spiritual creation, such as literature, can never be measured solely in terms of the status and socio-political circumstances of the human group out of which it originates. There is no consistent, direct ratio between political power or prestige and the wealth and variety of spiritual creativity; indeed, at times one can definitely establish an inverse ratio between periods of cultural efflorescence and periods of growth and consolidation of political power. There can be little doubt, for example, that nineteenth century Russian literature stands head and shoulders above the Russian literature of the present century, a century in which Russia has achieved a heretofore unknown political eminence. Similarly, there can be no question that the Germany of the end of the eighteenth and beginning of the nineteenth centuries constituted a ranking spiritual, cultural force despite the fact that from a political viewpoint, it was relatively weak. Yet, the Germany of the end of the nineteenth century up to World War I had clearly lost its former cultural preeminence, despite its tremendous political power.

These are timely reflections with which to launch a survey of Hebrew literature during the first decade of the Jewish state. For the literary historian is constrained to disentangle himself of emotional involvements as well as from any politico-national bias that can only serve to distort his judgment. He must distinguish carefully between the "is" and the "ought" even as he must properly assess spiritual-cultural data and know what may be anticipated under existing conditions. Yet, there are those who, from the very inception of the State of Israel, have not tired of turning to its writers, and especially to the younger generation, with such pathetic demands as "Give us *the* Israeli novel," or "We look forward to *the* heroic epic of the new Israel." Such demands and anticipations lack all meaning. It is possible to plan agricultural production; industrial output can be speeded up. The forces of spiritual creativity cannot be evoked by command.

A sober account, free of sentimental national hyperbole, of the achievements of Hebrew literature during the first decade of statehood must reckon with three fundamental factors. First, such account must carefully distinguish between the three different groups that have determined and still determine the course of Hebrew literature. These groups differ in age and in the spiritual climate they inhabit. We shall return to them in detail in the course of our discussion. Second, we must focus our attention on the heterogeneity of the various cultural communities of Israel. As yet, no dominant cultural center powerful enough to evoke universal mimesis has been established. Presently, we have a mosaic of contradictory elements, some of which may be revealed ultimately as the foundation stones of a great national culture. Third, the enormous exigencies involved in security and absorption of immigration make inordinate demands upon Israel's strength, spiritual as well as physical.

This essay is not concerned with an analysis of the last two factors. Essentially, they are the proper domain of sociologists, demographers, economists, and statesmen. The literary critic's essential concern is the clarification of the first factor—that is, the nature of the three groups that have put their impress on Hebrew literature during the past decade. However, no literary study, such as ours, can ever for a moment lose sight of the conscious link between the first factor—the very essence of our study—and the two that follow. Only thus can the picture drawn hope to reflect the truth.

II

After *the enemy had destroyed my home*, I took my little daughter into my arms and *I fled* with her to the city. Panic-stricken, I ran day and night, seized by terror until I arrived, an hour before dark, *on the eve of the Day of Atonement* at the courtyard of the *Great Synagogue*. The mountains and the hills that had accompanied us disappeared . . . This Synagogue and these houses of Torah had not left my vision all these past days, and if I forgot them by day, *they would move into view in my dreams at night and while awake* . . . I turned my thoughts away from all that the enemy had done to us, and I began to reflect on the approaching Day of Atonement . . . Would that they might appoint a worthy *Baal Tefillah* to stand before the Ark. *In these latter generations*, the number of leaders in prayer who really know how to pray has dwindled. *The cantors who proudly* display their voice with their songs and yet dull the heart, only they have grown in number. *And I am in need of strengthening, certainly my little daughter, an infant who has been uprooted from her place.* (Emphasis added)

—S.Y. Agnon, "Et Knisat Hayom"

The above quotation is from a story that, from several viewpoints, is symbolic and characteristic not alone for S.Y. Agnon's great epic writings.[1]

The inner horizons the story reveals to the reader are shared by Agnon and by the generations of writers whose spiritual physiognomy was decisively formed by European *Galut* Jewry. Beyond all individual differences, whether of talent or poetic form, the prose of Agnon, the great poems of Uri Zvi Greenberg, the profound incisive stories of Hazaz, the revelations of personal mysticism and the probings of the self of S. Shalom—all possess common elements. Even the poets closest to Bialik, the great epigones of his poetry, such as Yaakov Cahan, Yaakov Fichman, and Zalman Shneour continue, in this first decade of Israel's independence, the literary tradition that is characteristic of the "Old School" of Hebrew literature. *Galut Jewry* and *European culture* have put their ineffaceable stamps on this generation of writers. Even a writer like Abraham Shlonsky, a revolutionary from the point of view of both literary form and social ideology, belongs to this group. The individual differences among the members of this coterie are negligible when contrasted with the chasm that separates all of them from the members of the "Third Group," S. Yizhar, Moshe Shamir, Aharon Meged, Benjamin Tammuz, A. Amir, S. Tanai, A. Gilboa, and Abraham Huss, most of whom are native-born.

Between these two aforementioned groups, there is an intermediate group, writers who are presently in their forties. In part, they too are European-born and, for some, this fact has been decisive for their spiritual horizons. While they have spent most of their lives in Israel, they have nevertheless not adapted themselves to the paths in literature chosen by the "Israeli Group." The late Yitzhak Shenhar, whose writing drew from the sources of the European tradition, is a typical member of this intermediate grouping. The literary development of some members of this group reveals an almost tragic picture that will claim our especial attention. In some instances, this particular development does not work itself out until the writer has approached fifty. On the other hand, a strong, independent personality from among this group occasionally succeeds in dictating to the new literature the terms of his talent and personal expression and thus overcomes the crisis of his generation. This solution was indicated by two poets who are worlds apart in both ideology and literary approach: Natan Alterman and Yonatan Ratosh. The first has become a kind of semi-official poet laureate of the ruling class responsible for the direction of the new Israel. The second is the aesthetic and ideological firebrand of the opposition movement, and the symptomatic importance of the latter is not to be minimized. Ratosh is the father of the "Canaanite" school, and the mentor of the "Young Hebrews." Actually, their movement is the final, logical consequence to be drawn from secular Zionism. Those who prepared and created the ideological foundations on which the

Young Hebrews have reared their structure now stand aghast and repelled by the work of their own hands.[2]

Having briefly touched on the variety of the trends and groups that make up Israel's literary activity in this past decade, we turn again to the quotation from Agnon that stands at the head of this section. A close analysis of the quotation in the context of the story as a whole proves rewarding. It discloses that the essential thematic material of Agnon's latter stories is identical with that found in all the poets of the "Old Guard." The theme of the disintegration and the destruction of *galut* Jewry, certainly an integral part of modern Hebrew literature, receives enormous meaning and weight *with the physical destruction of the European Galut.* The most serious literary works of the past decade seek to grapple with an interpretation of the unprecedented national calamity and with the mysterious riddle of the tragic, fateful conjunction of the two major events of Jewish existence: the fearful slaughter of European Jewry and the rise of the State of Israel. For decades now, modern Hebrew literature as expressed in the works of its leading representatives has moved between the poles of destruction and renewal. Now, in the light of the stormy, terrifying situation of a paradoxical present, it is constrained to a new effort to plot the full meaning of the dialectical polarity in the life of the nation.

"The enemy destroyed our house." As in all stories of Agnon, so here, too, *house* carries a wide, inclusive connotation. We ran "in haste and in flight." "Day and night, the flight of terror and panic." "One hour before dark on the eve of the Day of Atonement," a late hour before the great repentance—return of the remnants of the people. There we stood near "the courtyard of the Great Synagogue" of the nation. "Fire had taken hold of the children's coats." Of all the lovely garments with which we sought to cover our nakedness in *galut,* "only a coat remained." It too had caught fire. The fire raged both from within and without. Spiritual and physical destruction. "We fled in panic, it was the flight from destruction. We took nothing with us." Thus we stood naked, "an hour before dark," an hour before the darkness of destruction on that bitter Day of Atonement that was the tragic day of return and repentance. We stood near the courtyard of the Great Synagogue in the land of our fathers. Bereft and empty, we stood together with the remnants of a young generation that had been reared without Torah because of a planned, willful evasion of the values of religion and the tradition. With what shall we now cover ourselves since cruel fire has consumed both our true and our imaginary possessions? With what shall we cover the nakedness of the young generation? "And now that her coat had caught on fire, I had no garment with which to cover my daughter. I turned here and there and looked for something with which my daughter might cover herself. I looked but found nothing. Whatever place I searched was empty."

The situation on the eve of the Day of Atonement differs radically from the hour of return and repentance of the lonely wayfarer in *Oreach Natah Lalun*. Now, the fire and the destruction are almost total in nature. The penitent wayfarer does not travel slowly in the "old-fashioned train that goes to my city." This is no nostalgic return to the Garden of Eden of childhood that has vanished. For all its tragic quality, such return at least affords the joy of painful lingering in the midst of the vanished world of childhood. "From Jerusalem, the wheels of the coaches rolled between mountains and hills, valleys and ravines. At each station the train stopped and waited. . . ."[3]

Here, in the collection of short stories *Ad Heynah*, the way to the Great Synagogue is marked only by "a flight of panic and terror, day and night." The vistas that once accompanied us, they too left us. "The mountains and hills that accompanied us departed and went their way."[4]

The Jew, the remnant of the survivors, has been deprived even of the vistas of his childhood that betrayed him. Just before dark, he discovers that he stands naked. The fire has consumed everything. He has neither clothes nor books. Even the corner in the Synagogue into which worn-out books are thrust can provide nothing to save him from the shame of emptiness. "I thought that I would go to the corner where torn books are stored away . . . I found nothing there to cover my little girl." Not even torn books are to be found in the *geniza*. The young generation *lacks clothes because it thought it could be a generation without books*. It was trained to disregard the holy books it did not read. Now, like the little daughter of the poet, it has nothing wherewith to cover itself. "When books were read, they would be torn. But now that books are not read, they are not torn. Where shall we flee and where shall we hide? Our house has been destroyed and the enemy covers the roads. If by some miracle we escaped, shall we then count on miracles?" This short story of Agnon's penetrates to the depths of the problems of Jewish existence as they are depicted by the writers of the first group.[5] The motif of departure and return receives here an extraordinarily rich symbolic meaning.

Another significant epic work, executed on a large canvas, Hayim Hazaz's tetralogy, *Yaish*—one of the truly outstanding literary works of this decade—opens with the motif of departure.[6] To be sure, in this rich, many-hued epic, the motif of renunciation takes on a special color, one essentially different from those in Agnon's stories. But with Hazaz too the problem of renunciation of *Galut* is treated in its full acuteness. It is no accident that Hazaz deliberately sought to lay bare the *Galut* life of a community whose forms of life recall the situation of the Middle Ages.

Hazaz is the only Hebrew European epic-writer who has discovered for our literature the inner life of Yemenite Jewry. In his book *Hayoshevet Baganim*,[7] Hazaz astounded the Hebrew reader by his perceptive revelation of ways of thinking and feeling that were heretofore unknown to us. This work was but his first step in what became his sustained effort to present to us the life and vital forces of a community still steeped in a primitive mode of life. Hazaz is attracted by the play of elemental forces. He is possessed by a passion for crystallizing into literary form the powerful dynamic instincts that have as yet been untouched in any effective way by an abstract spirituality. Hazaz's purpose is to trace with all the precision of a worker in a laboratory what seems to him the *sickness of galut Jewry.*

In *Yaish*, the novelist-researcher dispenses with the elements likely to "disturb" his research. European culture is totally absent. Since there is no enlightenment, one can peer directly into the "sickness of *galut* Jewry" and its conflict with a social organism healthy to the core. This pre-enlightened community of Yemenite Jewry of seventy-five years ago offers the possibility of a new appraisal of the full worth of *galut* Jewry. We may be certain that in its native setting we will discover all the stigmata of "a peculiar psychology, fantastically inverted, what one might call night-like, different from that of any people or human creatures anywhere." Its distinguishing characteristics are "Galut, Kiddush Hashem, the Messiah . . . a three-fold cord. The *Galut* is our pyramid whose base is *Kiddush Hashem* and whose apex is the *Messiah* . . . and the Talmud is our *Book of the Dead.*"[8]

It is clear that Hazaz's attitude to *galut* is utterly negative. His great novel *Yaish* serves him as a persuasive literary illustration of the need for *renunciation* for the sake of *return* to *normal* life. Hence, the motif of return bears no religious-metaphysical meaning in Hazaz's writing. The return completes the act of renunciation of spiritual existence. In the atmosphere of this night psychology, the purpose of the return is an absolute secularization. Obviously, Hazaz's concept of renunciation-return is diametrically opposed to the same pair of concepts as treated by Agnon. In Hazaz's writings, these concepts bear a distinct anti-religious character. In this regard, Hazaz continues the anti-traditional line of modern Hebrew literature. Hazaz thus gives to the motif of return a meaning directly opposite to that found in the poems of Bialik, Greenberg, or Lamdan, or in the prose of Feierberg and Agnon. It is well known that Tchernichowsky confesses to his *return* to the world of Apollo-Dionysus, to the goddess Tamuz, to the false prophets, and to the gods of fertility. Clearly, this *inverted return* is tantamount to a *renunciation of Judaism.* This interesting thematic material of modern Hebrew literature carries important implications in its links, both hidden and overt, for the realities of the new State of Israel. The renunciation and return of the heroes of Agnon, for all the variety of their situation, always lead to the threshold of the Synagogue and the actualization of the Day of Atonement—that is, to an increase of metaphysical and religious tension. In Hazaz, the theme marks a conclusive abandonment of transcendentalism. Hence, the ecstatic mystic Yaish, once having left Yemen and come to Jerusalem, becomes convinced that here, in the ancestral homeland, the link between earth and heaven has been irreparably broken. There, in Yemen, he was vouchsafed mystical visions when the heavens were opened and he held converse with angels. With his first step toward an earthly, normalized life in the land of Israel, everything has come to an end:

> Two weeks had gone by from the time they had entered Jerusalem and Yaish had not succeeded in ascending on high as he was wont. What was this? . . . He felt depressed. A baffling mystery. "Instead of the merit of the sacredness of the Holy Land aiding me to soar aloft, height above height, to eminences of God not yet attained, that I might gaze at the cover of the celestial chariot or that I might enter into the palace of the Messiah . . . From heaven, I have been informed: 'Be good enough and stay at home.' What is this?. . . . Have I sinned against God? Have they erred in heaven or has this been caused by the land of Israel?"9

For Yaish, there are only two possible resolutions of the enigma. Both of them are bound to work an inevitable revolution in his way of seeing the world, Judaism, and its values. The fact that in the land of the patriarchs, in Jerusalem, the link with Heaven has been broken, can be explained by one of two assumptions—first, that "Heaven has erred." But if "Heaven has erred," then all the divine revelations have not only lost their validity as absolute truth but, being rooted in error, they must inevitably be misleading. Second, if the "land of Israel is the source" of the breach with the heavenly sphere, then there can be no question that *all that the Jewish tradition has taught about the religious, transcendental character of the land of Israel is an exploded legend.* Either assumption leads to the identical conclusion: The religious mythos, and with it the basis of Judaism, has been destroyed. Yaish, however, still waits expectantly. But his final disillusionment is not long in coming: "However, he received no answer, neither in word, deed, vision, nor dream. All his efforts yielded nothing. *The heavens were closed to him and were not opened for him again for the rest of his days.*"10 Here, Hazaz seems to say that the renunciation of the *galut* for the sake of the return is the ultimate liquidation of the position of traditional Judaism. This return is the end of the dominion of the transcendental and the crowning achievement of the process of "here and now," of the absolute secularization of Judaism. The theme is common to both Agnon and

Hazaz but in the latter it receives a development diametrically opposed to that of Agnon. All the heroes of Agnon in their panicky flight, whether from external enemies or from the "enemy" within (the loss of inner certainty), possess one common characteristic.

In each of them there abides the consciousness that "this Synagogue and these houses of Torah-study did not depart from before my eyes for a moment. And if I forgot them by day, they would manage to come to me at night in a dream or while awake." This is the destiny of those who leave and return, whether their return succeeds, as did that of Yudel in *Hachnasat Kalah*, or whether it ends in tragedy as it did for Menassah Hayim in *The Crooked Shall be Straight*, or whether it be the ill-starred return of Yizhuk Kummer in *T'mol Shilshom*. The narrator in *Oreach Natah Lalun* reveals the same rhythm of flight and return that culminates in renunciation—flight return. The demonic events in the stories of *Sefer Hamaasim* are cast in the same pattern of the ineffaceable inner presence of houses of prayer and Torah within the souls of the strange heroes. The various poetic actualizations of the confusion of the modern Jew in situations that lack unequivocal resolution, all the strange metamorphoses of renunciation and return, every attempt at desertion and panicky flight— all of them still leave open the possibility of finding a refuge place, albeit a dubious one, in the shadow of the Synagogue and house of Torah in anticipation of a cleansing, purifying Day of Atonement. Not so in Hazaz. In his stories, the movement of renunciation/return drives toward the exclusive spiritual horizons of the younger writers—an absolute secularism that has ceased to concern itself seriously with the Jewish tradition of the *galut*. Though the stock of ideas in the work of Hazaz, like those in the poetry of Tchernichowsky and Shneour, include almost all of the characteristic spiritual elements to be found in the writings of the "Third Group" (the "Canaanites"), there is a vast difference here. Hazaz, a product of Russian Jewry, knows intimately the *thesis* against which he launches his *anti-thesis* in *Yaish*. He knows from first-hand experience the life of the Jews of Europe, formed as it was in the likeness of the Jewish religious tradition. This Judaism obtrudes only at the very limits of the conscious horizon of the young Israeli writers. For them, it is a matter of remote, tedious history, hardly more than a spiritual fossil; at best, it is an archeological exhibit.

III

In 1951 a book of poetry appeared that may be described unqualifiedly as the mightiest lyrical expression of the tragic destiny of our people. No other literary work proclaims with such moving power the awesome polarity of *destruction and rebirth* as does Uri Zvi Greenberg's *Rechovot hana-har*.[11] By the searing quality of his visions, by the prophetic pathos of his castigation, and the noble, lyric tenderness of his words of encouragement and consolation, Greenberg has become the most important poetic inter-preter of our people's fate during these past two decades. The poems of *Rechovot hanahar* served a liberating function. They aroused and bestirred the people out of the state of dazed shock that followed the destruction of European Jewry. Moreover, the work is the supreme poetic expression of the Jewish historic consciousness of Jewish destiny. The past and the present, the remote and the near-at-hand, the life of the founders of the people, the periods of the First and Second Commonwealth, the wander-ings of the exile, the exaltation and degradation of the people—all is fused into the single, meaningful, synoptic vision of the poet. For all its lacerat-ing quality or rather, precisely because of the depths of sorrow out of which it speaks, it opens vistas to a bright proud future for the Jewish people. Greenberg proclaims a vision of Israel's preeminence, of its reli-gious mission among the nations that demands the renewal and establish-ment of the *Kingdom of Israel*. The present can be understood only out of an absorption in the past, and its presence in the recesses of our soul is the sole guarantee of our future.

> What will come again has ever been;
> What has not, never will.
> I trust in the morrow
> For I face the image of the past:
> This is my vision and song.
> *Selah*, Hallelujah, Amen.[12]

From the point of view of form and structure, *Rechovot hanahar* carries forward the possibilities inherent in expressionism and surrealism. Green-berg's use of figurative expressions abandons all the accepted poetic de-vices of the type of poetry known as "realistic." The visionary character of his poetry, from its very beginnings, calls for means of expression quite different from those ordinarily employed by modern Hebrew poetry be-fore his appearance. Something of the long, infinite breath of a mighty storm at sea vibrates in the powerful rhythm of these poems. From the melodies of Jewish fate, the abysmal woe of the elegies, the exultant hope and outburst of joy at the great future of the people whom God has raised to the heights of eternity, an intoxicating music arises. Greenberg is about the only poet of our time whose poetry remains unvitiated when it be-comes the trumpet of actuality. For the great poet can live the life of gray actuality from a perspective of poetic transformation.

Notes

1. S.Y. Agnon, "Im Knisat Hayom," in *Ad Heynah* (Jerusalem: Schocken, 1952).
2. See Baruch Kurzweil, "The New 'Canaanites' in Israel," *Judaism*, 2 (January 1953): 3–15.
3. *Oreach Natal Lalun*, 7.
4. Agnon, "Im Knisat Hayom," 171.
5. Ibid., 171–77.
6. Hayim Hazaz, *Yaish*, 4 vols. (Am Oved: Tel Aviv 1947–52).
7. Translated into English by Ben Halpern under the title *Mori Sa'id* (New York: Abelard-Schuman, 1956).
8. Hayim Hazaz, *Avanim Rotchot* (Am Oved, 1950), 233, 235.
9. Hazaz, *Yaish*, 4:244.
10. Ibid.
11. U.Z. Greenberg, *Rechovot Hanahar* (Jerusalem/Tel-Aviv: Schocken, 1951).
12. Ibid., 37.

YONATAN RATOSH

Israeli or Jewish Literature?

ISRAELI OR JEWISH LITERATURE? was the topic of a recent series of radio debates, with a framework reminiscent of many similar radio discussions, beginning even before the establishment of the State of Israel and dealing with literary, educational, or other matters. Within this framework, we heard statements about the motherland and the nation, rootedness and spiritual confidence, simplicity and loyalty, established and progressively evolving values—while, juxtaposed against these topics, we heard about the continuity of a generations-old tradition, of synthesis with the values and heritage of centuries, of broad horizons joined with profundity.

It should be noted that non-Israeli Hebrew literature—at any rate, that of the later generations in Eastern Europe, up to Agnon and Hazaz—was primarily the literature of the collapse of a lifestyle and its values, the literature of destruction, as it was so well analyzed by none other than Dr. Kurzweil, that great devotee of a universal Jewish literature.

Be that as it may, the practical side of the issue perplexing authors, educators, thinkers, and public figures is—as one of the lecturers in this series, Ms. Amir (Pinkerfeld), put it—whether the new will develop alongside the old, in opposition to it, or within its framework.

The exact formulation of a question often leads halfway to its solution, and so it is appropriate to ask whether the problem that concerns us—Israeli or universally Jewish literature—is stated accurately enough.

After thinking it through carefully, we find ourselves asking what is the significance of the "or" that stands between Israeli and universally Jewish literature? Are the two really mutually exclusive? Some have refuted this suggestion, saying at last, correctly and logically, that no Jewish literature is—or ever was—completely isolated from any country, any place. Jewish literature in Germany differs from Jewish literature in Italy. Each of these differs, in turn, from Jewish literature in Russia, and the same applies to all the remaining Jewish literatures in their respective countries. Jewish literature as a whole is, in fact, no more than the sum of Jewish literature, country by country.

If we were to formulate the question in full, we should have to use the terms "Jewish-Israeli literature" and "universally Jewish literature." It would then be immediately self-evident that the very crux of the question has no foundation or meaning. It is impossible for Jewish literature in the State of Israel not to be *Israeli*, and this does not apparently contradict its being part of a universal Jewish literature. Why, indeed, should Jewish-Israeli literature be singled out from among the remaining local Jewish literatures for adverse discrimination? Why that "or" after all?

This seemingly unnecessary "or" that divides the two is, however, emotionally basic. This is the essential force of the problem. The fact that the discussions surrounding this question have continually been renewed and perpetuated for so many years is clear evidence that it exists and remains unchanged.

Thus, it seems that the question is simply not formulated accurately enough, which is likely to blur rather than clarify the contrast between the two phenomena.

We could perhaps differentiate more clearly between these two categories if we were to remember that Jewish literature does not now exist—and has not ever existed—in the Hebrew language alone. Sholem Aleichem, for instance, did not write in Hebrew—he wrote in Yiddish and, incidentally, in Russian, too. Similarly, H.N. Bialik, Yehudah Halevi, and the Rambam did not write in Hebrew alone. Jewish literature exists in America today in Hebrew, Yiddish, and English. It also exists in German and in Russian, and existed, at one time, in Arabic, as well. Hebrew was undoubtedly the holy tongue, the language of the culture, thought, and science of the Jews for generation upon generation, just as Latin was that of the peoples of Europe throughout the Middle Ages. But Jewish literature does not exhaust itself in Hebrew, is not bounded by Hebrew, is not identical to Hebrew literature.

It may help to expand our perspective a little if we recall that Hebrew was once a very noble, international language, and that in the Middle Ages Hebrew was at times one of the general languages of science—rather than a Jewish language alone. This was true in medicine, for example, and every doctor worthy of the name might have been presumed to know Hebrew, as with Latin in our day. We might also remember that in the sixteenth century in Hungary, not only Jews but learned nobility and other Gentiles were supposed to know Hebrew no less than Latin and Greek. They even wrote poems in Hebrew as part of the learning process. Therefore, not only is Jewish literature not limited by Hebrew, but, to be accurate, literature in Hebrew is not exclusively Jewish.

Similarly, it might help to remember that, as far as people are concerned, nothing in Israel is exceptional in the Jewish world. For instance, some Jews were farmers in Argentina and in Russia as some are in Israel; and, it goes without saying, Jews serve in the military all over the world. Nor are Jewish prime ministers and ministers a phenomenon unique to Israel; we need only to recall France, for example. What is special about our existence here is not, therefore, to be found in any particular detail: not in agriculture, not in the army, not in the navy, not in government. What is special is solely the totality of these things—the fact that we are the people of the *land*, the fact that we see ourselves as the people of the land, as native-born, as a nation.

And if we view Judaism as a unique form of existence, singular among the world's nations, whose laws are inapplicable to it—in short, in the same light as Judaism sees itself—it will be difficult for us not to conclude that the very uniqueness of Israeli literature lies in the fact that it is not *Jewish*. The literary critic Dr. Kurzweil, whose name we have already mentioned, has insisted time and again that Israeli literature is not Jewish. In his reflections on our self-definition, our coming into being, Dr. Simon of the Hebrew University has also posed the question as to whether we are still Jewish.

Public figures try to ignore this question, to blur it. Politicians seek to minimize the opposition, to portray it almost as a mere official formality for the purposes of identity cards alone. Sociologists, thinkers, and critics all take note of this development, and even if they perceive it to be a negative trend, they fight to counteract it. Dr. Kurzweil and Dr. Simon, like many of their peers, have their say in a spirit of criticism and condemnation. Yet they both point out the very essence of the phenomenon.

And perhaps this is the real question: not *Israeli* or universally Jewish literature, an illusory opposition that a little reflection reveals to be without foundation, but *Jewish* or *non-Jewish* literature, *Jewish* literature or *national* literature.

*   *   *

It may be difficult even to determine where Jewish literature ends and this new, national literature begins. But this difficulty does not alter the essence of the fact—just as it is perhaps difficult to determine precisely when someone from England who immigrated to Australia ceased to be English and became Australian, or in which generation the descendant of immigrants became American. Nevertheless, it is generally a clear *collective* fact that many English people immigrated to Australia, and today, only the Australian nation exists there; that the Australians are not English; and that in America, the American nation exists in its own right.

Much respect is due to Jewish literature in its various languages; we do not seek to detract from its worth. It undoubtedly attained many fine achievements. We have all learned from Jewish literature in Hebrew—but this learning may be likened to the biological inheritance of each individual. A certain American might, for example, bear the greatest resemblance in looks and personality to some grandfather or distant cousin overseas of an older and different nationality. But from a national perspective, there is no resemblance at all, the two are entirely different. A nation is not a biological fact, but a social, territorial formation with its own values. This formation holds true for individuals and for works of literature that draw upon other literatures, but that fundamentally exist in a separate system of evolution with its own rules and values. Jewish literature, as we have already stated, may be of great importance, but it is not our literature. Every teacher of literature in every school in Israel knows this fact to be true and has felt it daily for years. Its very content, framework, problems, and solutions are remote from us—so much so that in practice, notwithstanding its great importance, it remains extremely foreign, despite all of the efforts of teachers and spiritual leaders. A new and different literature is evolving here.

And maybe here, in the schools, is to be found the root, partial but essential, of many of the faults that teachers and educators list in their pupils, the native Israeli writers: narrowness of vision, superficiality, Levantinism. Ultimately, Levantinism is nothing more than the result of an incompatibility between the values of the acquired culture and the actual way of life and spiritual values of the student. France has a great culture, but in the Levant she produced Levantines. It is impossible to see how Levantines could fail to grow up here, even in the lap of Jewish culture, which may be great and valuable intrinsically, but which is foreign to native Israelis in all respects, whether they find it praiseworthy or disgraceful.

Perhaps the main problem facing criticism in our generation is the very definition of our culture itself. One cannot fail to see that only on the basis of a correct definition of our independence will we be able to learn and benefit from the literatures of our neighbors without imitation or self-effacement. Obviously, we might learn more than a little from universal Jewish literature, from Jewish literature in the Hebrew language.

* * *

Jewish literature, universally Jewish literature, argues in the name of continuity. We need to be precise: Universal Jewish literature does not develop naturally or directly. It is made up of many separate literatures, as we have already stated. Each literature is the fruit of a different country, with a frame of reference specific to it alone. Each one has an existence in its own right. The links of continuity are not particularly strong nor particularly uninterrupted. Such continuity as there appears to be is the effect of external influence; less actual than the result of abstraction, deliberation. Above all, it is a continuity in time alone, hovering in the temporal world. From the point of view of place, for example, we are left with extreme detachment, that quintessential detachment that has become familiar to us.

Jewish literature argues in the name of broad horizons: in the name of that Judaism that embraced the four corners of the globe. And here, too, we need to be precise. Judaism has known many countries and peoples, settled among them, was received by them, and explored the depths of all the problems arising as a consequence of this movement. But from a certain perspective, the perspective of its neighbors, might this situation not also reflect a certain narrowness, hand in hand with breadth of vision? For all that Jewish literature treated, it saw from the point of view of the problems and the need of Jewish existence, and from this perspective alone.

At any rate, with respect to the national literature being created in Israel, it is possible that the continuity and breadth of horizons characteristic of Jewish literature might have a negative influence. For us, Judaism's wide horizon means, in practice, restricting one's immediate, real, geographical horizon to the dimensions of the present State of Israel, to the areas of Jewish settlement alone before the establishment of the State. It means, in practice, restricting one's focus of interest solely to the Jewish community, in the past, present, and even the future; it means, in practice, a sectarian approach, slightly narrow and shortsighted—a type of detachment from the country as a country, from its inhabitants insofar as they are the inhabitants of the country, from its events insofar as they are the events of the country.

The continuity of Jewish literature is by no means a continuity of place. In this place and in this country, for a literature of land and nation, this very continuity assumes a vast and heavy void spanning generations upon generations, of cities and countries beyond our boundaries of knowledge, interest, and spirituality. For the purpose of an indigenous, national literature, neither achievements of a way of life elsewhere nor pipe dreams and yearnings for the banks of the Rhine and the Vistula will be able to fill this void. The only literature that could spring from the lap of universal Jewish literature, within the framework of time and place in the Jewish world, would be a meager and detached literature—not the literature of the motherland, but at best the literature of the provinces.

The choice is between such a literature and a native, rooted literature, a literature of nationhood—one that will break out of that closely guarded wall and expand historical and territorial horizons; one that will open hearts and minds to the continuity of time in this place; one that might ultimately be able to embrace people as people, rather than as Jews, members of a certain community, and the world as world, rather than as a stage for the generations of the wandering Jew. On the broad, deep, firm foundation of the motherland, it is possible to open minds and hearts in all directions.

But for the sake of this future, for the sake of the reception and development of national values and problems, freedom is necessary, liberation from the framework of Jewish literature and values, from the contents and problems of Judaism.

To put it bluntly: take the case of an old building. It is impossible to build a newer and better—or, at any rate, more suitable—building in its stead without first clearing away the old. Or, to put it more simply, take the case of a chick in its shell. It has to pierce its shell, to crack it open, to shake it off in order to emerge into the daylight. Failing this, it will be destined to suffocate within.

* * *

Like so many great fundamental questions, this one too can be summarized with the utmost simplicity. We have here two systems of values.

The one: the Jewish people, the Zionist movement of rebirth, the Hebrew language, the land of Israel. The Jewish people—scattered, in its formation if not in its very inception, in exile (in Babylon). The Zionist movement—which arose far from the land of Israel and was given the poetic name for Jerusalem, the Holy City. The Hebrew language—which the majority of the Jewish people do not speak. A language that served only as the language of holiness and culture (for the educated, of course), not as a living language. The land of Israel—a term that, during the period of its realization in the classical Hebrew era, applied only to the area of the Samarian kingdom, and did not include the Negev, the Coastal Plain, Judea, or Jerusalem: a very late euphemism, which to this day has no defined meaning (and perhaps precisely because of this vagueness, it is so widespread and acceptable).

The second value system is very much more simple: a Hebrew nation—in its own land; a Hebrew movement of rebirth—in its own land; the

Hebrew language—the language of the nation; the land of the Hebrews—together with all its periods, its events, and its problems. Hence, the fundamental problems of our culture and our policies alike.

The choice facing our literature is actually the choice between these two systems of values: between the values of the Jewish Diaspora and those of the Hebrew *nation*.

The name of our country—Israel—was chosen at the time precisely because of its lack of clarity, as a kind of compromise that evaded the need to decide between these two sets of values, between the definition of the state as the Jewish state and its definition as a Hebrew state. Let's leave politics to politicians. But when it comes to matters of the spirit and to literature, let's call a spade a spade, and state matters with precision.

It seems that much of the blurring of the problem and the opinions surrounding it stems from the very term *Israeli literature*. For, no matter how we define it for the purpose of our debates, the actual choice facing us will remain unaltered. The problem is, then, Hebrew literature as opposed to Jewish literature. We shall have to resolve this problem in the framework of our lives; we shall have to arbitrate between these two choices: Jewish or Hebrew.

Does the fact that the majority of inhabitants of the State today are recent arrivals, or at any rate of foreign birth, have a bearing on this choice? Surprising as it may seem, an open mind leads us to conclude that we cannot assume this to be true. The reasons are many. But first and foremost, already today the relative majority in our midst is undoubtedly the native population born and raised here. And this is the only population that is growing, that will keep on growing year after year, ceaselessly, regardless of regime or political stance. In contrast to any other populace that comprises emigrants from any of the lands of the Jewish Diaspora, this public is already the mainstream of the educated class in Israel, in every profession, in every field. Its share is destined to grow progressively from year to year. This public, which is destined to determine the face of the country in every respect, is also the very public that is producing, and that will continue to produce, our writers.

It is this same public that is being called on to decide between the two alternatives. Can there really be any doubt as to how it will decide? The question is only with what degree of self-consciousness this decision will be made, and with what measure of wholeheartedness, honesty, and integrity. In other words, the sole question is: What will be the standard of our Hebrew literature?

And for the common good, we can but hope that this standard will rise and flower rapidly.

Translated by Louise Shabat Bethlehem and Hana Wirth-Nesher

DAN MIRON

Modern Hebrew Literature: Zionist Perspectives and Israeli Realities

GATHERINGS OF PEOPLE interested in the Jewish literature situation tend to pressure our thinking in the direction of streamlining, of eliciting from the chaotic reality of that situation some unifying pattern. Both as literary people and as historians we are conditioned in this direction. Indeed, the more chaotic the surface of the object or situation we investigate, the stronger our urge to expose the hidden order beneath. My point, to put it succinctly, is that in investigating the contemporary Jewish literature scene, we should refrain from applying our habitual reductive procedures. We should rather accept it for what it is, a fragmented array of diverse, independent literary developments, which, nevertheless, come into contact in a common artistic commitment to the imaginative probing of the possible significance or significances of the Jewish experience under contemporary circumstances.

There is no such thing as a unified Jewish literature, and there has not been one since the fragmentation of our national culture at the end of the eighteenth and beginning of the nineteenth centuries. Indeed, one of the inherent and most significant characteristics of Jewish history in modern times is that it produced no one Jewish culture but many variants of possible Jewish cultures or sub-cultures. To the same extent it could not produce one Jewish literature. Rather, it produced two or three or four independent Jewish literatures as well as many Jewish-oriented literary developments, which evolved within the contexts of non-Jewish literatures.

Of course, the so-called new or secular Hebrew literature of the last two hundred years always regarded itself as the true and legitimate custodian of national literary creativity. It appointed itself a *tsofeh leveyt yisra'el*, "a watchman unto the House of Israel," an institution responsible for the moral and cultural well-being of the nation. But its claims were always challenged by its great rival, the literature of the Hasidic movement, which regarded it as illegitimate, profane, and non-Jewish. Neither were these claims acceded to by Yiddish writers, secularized though they were. And Yiddish literature itself, once it had attained some cultural status by the beginning of the twentieth century, was quite ready to declare itself the only legitimate and truly contemporary Jewish literature.

The fragmentation of the Jewish literary expression in modern times indicates the basic difference between each of the "new" Jewish literatures and the "normal" national literatures, a difference that often makes comparisons difficult and analogies misleading. A decision on the part of a German, a Frenchman or a Spaniard to become a writer and contribute to his national literature need not involve any a priori ideological commitment, beyond a commitment to literature itself. During the last two hundred years, however, a Jew's commitment to literature was inextricably bound up in an ideology: a secular Hebrew literature, a secular Yiddish literature, Hasidic Hebrew-Yiddish literature, a Jewish literary expression in a non-Jewish language, and so on. Even the total assimilationist made a similar commitment in a negative fashion. By his very choice of language and context, every Jewish writer expressed loyalty to a certain conception of the national culture and indicated his faith in its further development toward a specific national-cultural goal.

Many writers worked within the framework of more than one Jewish literature. Indeed, bilingualism and even trilingualism were not only common but also "natural" under the specific cultural conditions. Abramovitch said that for him writing in both Hebrew and Yiddish was like breathing through both his nostrils. For some time, only those with the keenest ideological motivation refrained from such dualities. This bilingualism, however, does not indicate the existence of a single, unified bilingual or multilingual literature, as some theorists (Sh. Niger and Dov Sadan) have claimed. It indicates, instead, a unique cultural situation, which made functioning within more than one literary context possible and, for many writers, even necessary. No matter how consistent they were, multilingual writers actually adapted their work to different, often contradictory, ideological contexts, which directly influenced the aesthetic and ideational structure of their work. They did that even when writing the *same* work in more than one language, as many of them did. Actually, it is through a comparison of the two versions of such works that we can best detect the characteristics of the different, even contradictory contexts to which the work in question has been adapted.

A Jewish writer, therefore, choosing to become a writer, had also to opt for a certain national ideology, which directed him toward participation in one Jewish literature or another. This does not mean, of course, that ideological struggle was impossible *within* any one of the above-mentioned Jewish literatures. It was, and it often unleashed stormy polemics. These struggles, however, were caused by the friction among rival versions of one overall ideology. Such were the struggles of Labor-Zionist writers against Revisionist-Zionist writers in *Eretz* Israel during the 1930s, or those of the Communist Yiddish writers in the Soviet Union against the Socialist-Bundist ones in Poland between the two World Wars. Such struggles often surpass in ferocity the campaigns against "external" adversaries.

This friction led to yet another difference between modern Jewish literatures and "normal" national ones—namely, most "normal" national literatures have but one overall goal: to give literary expression to the national entity as such. Each of our Jewish literatures had a "goal" in a different sense. Evolving within its specific ideological frame of reference, it was meant to be not only an expression of the nation but also its guide. It had to direct it, to point to it the correct cultural path (according to its specific ideological bias) and criticize it for not following it. The ideological element also tended to promote the programmatic and didactic functions of literature over the purely expressive ones.

Since the establishment of the State of Israel, this entire cultural complex has been largely eliminated. Israeli literature, for better or worse, has approximated "normalcy"; that is to say, it is being created without any a priori ideological commitment except the commitment to literature as such. Non-Zionist and even anti-Zionist writers contribute to it, as do Arab writers, provided that they live in Israel and write in Hebrew. This, I submit, constitutes the one decisive difference between Israeli literature and all other Jewish literatures in the past and the present. Yet, far from creating a unified Jewish literature, the advent of an Israeli literature has even further complicated the cultural situation. For now, in addition to many contesting Jewish literatures, there is a differentiation to be made between "abnormal" and "normal" ones.

Theories which predicate the existence of a single, all-encompassing Jewish literature are bound to remain ingenious tours de force which fail to carry conviction. The arguments they develop are always more interesting than persuasive, and even where they are substantiated by solid historical evidence, ideological wishful thinking takes precedence over empirical observation. These theories offer us much brilliance, but also a particular kind of obfuscation. The proportions of the past are blurred, subtly but persuasively. Literary figures of peripheral significance are endowed with absorbing interest, while major writers, unaccounted for by the theoretical scheme, are brushed aside. As for future perspectives, literary reality proves

repeatedly how inaccurate predictions made within such theoretical contexts can be, and since the literary future is always cited as the final proof
of any given theory, it is the future which most fully exposes the theorist's
myopia.

Zionist expectations for the development of modern Hebrew literature
offer a telling instance of the inadequacy of theory. I will offer two sets of
historical examples, the first drawn from the formative years of Zionism as
well as of modern Hebrew literature in the 1890s, and the second from the
late 1940s and early 1950s, when the founding of Israel led to the search
for a new Hebrew *Eretz* Israeli literature. In both cases, literary thinkers of
the first order presented highly interesting theories predicting the future of
our literature. Examining the shortcomings of these theories and predictions, we can perhaps chasten our own urge to offer encompassing explanations of the contemporary literary situation.

II

To invoke old Ahad Ha'am as the first illustration may raise a few eye-
brows. Ahad Ha'am's severe limitations as a philosopher of Judaism, ideologue of spiritual Zionism, and literary mentor of his age have long since
become painfully obvious, and today only his direct style and graceful
essayistic exposition are still valued. Indeed, even as he reached the zenith
of his career, with the foundation of the literary monthly *Hashiloah*
(1896), a group of young writers, led by M.Y. Berdyczewski, vigorously
challenged his conception of Hebrew literature as a vehicle for Judaic self-
knowledge. Subsequently, Ahad Ha'am was often charged with insensitivity to the aesthetic-emotive impact of belles lettres. Dov Sadan went so
far as to identify him as one of the three culprits responsible for Bialik's
failure to realize his full poetic potential.[1]

Yet, Ahad Ha'am did contribute the first carefully thought-out Zionist
"theory" of Jewish literature. Among the founders of Zionist thought, he
alone seriously pondered the problematic situation of Jewish literature in
his own day as well as in the foreseeable future. His starting point was a
devastating critique of Jewish literature in modern times. Since the emergence of the Jewish Enlightenment toward the end of the eighteenth century, he maintained, all first-rate Jewish literary talents found their way to
non-Jewish literatures. Writing in foreign languages for foreign audiences,
they strove to incorporate their work into traditions and values unrelated
to their national heritage. What Jewish traces or characteristics survived
only added spice to a dish meant for non-Jewish consumption. Those
writers who wrote for Jewish audiences in foreign languages maneuvered
themselves into a spiritual ghetto. Since they knew they would be read

only during the two or three decades their readers needed to integrate their interests with those of the surrounding culture,[2] such writers accepted in advance an extremely short literary life expectancy. The task of establishing a national literature was left to other writers, usually the least talented or poorest equipped intellectually, who dedicated themselves to writing in their national language, Hebrew, for readers who have already developed some rudiments of a secular, humanistic *Weltanschauung*. Determined further to humanize these readers by revitalizing their atrophied aesthetic sensibility, these writers too were doomed to failure. Their outpouring of lyrical poems, didactic epics, allegorical dramas, and eventually also sentimental novels failed to develop a genuinely poetic idiom in Hebrew. Their supposedly elevated, highly ornamental imitation of biblical Hebrew was devoid of aesthetic or intellectual impact. This failure stemmed not from lack of talent and literary culture or from their adherence to a misguided poetics, but from the linguistic situation per se.[3]

Ahad Ha'am's analysis of this situation was thoroughly up-to-date and, in the context of contemporary Hebrew criticism, he was certainly an innovator. As early as 1893, he formulated his idea of poetic language:

> To the extent that there exists an inherent difference [as far as literary usage is concerned, D.M.] between a language which lives in speech and one which lives in books—it bears only upon emotion (that is, upon emotive expression), because emotions are activated not only by the plain concepts indicated by the literal meanings of the words of the language, but also by the abundant subtle images which are associated with every spoken word through its constant use, and which coexist with it in the depths of the soul, where the speaker cannot sufficiently analyze and clarify them even to himself. This subtlety of feeling cannot, therefore, be sustained in a language which is not spoken. However, when it comes to clarity of thought it is the written word rather than the spoken one which counts. Every civilized nation actually possesses a special written language for the purposes of spelling out its thoughts and cogitations, and this is often very different from the language used in speech.[4]

Here, to use somewhat anachronistic terminology, Ahad Ha'am postulates a truly connotative language as the only soil out of which an emotive literary idiom could grow. Words influence us poetically only when they activate secondary and associative shades of meaning derived from personal and immediate usage—that is, from speech. This assumption eliminated the very possibility of a contemporary poetic expression in Hebrew. Under the existing linguistic circumstances, Ahad Ha'am believed, Hebrew could sustain only a literature rooted in denotative language, a literature of concepts rather than emotions, aiming at clarity of thought rather than the aesthetic activation of the reader's feelings. Rather than devaluing belles lettres, as the critics of his editorial policy charged, Ahad Ha'am's

theory shows that he was motivated by despair rather than by disdain.
Even the sentence which so infuriated Berdyczewski and his followers (in
Ahad Ha'am's programmatic introduction to the first issue of *Hashiloah*),
that "as for sheer poesy, the outpouring of the emotions over the beauty of
nature, the sweetness of love, etc.—whoever cares for it will find it in
languages of other nations to his heart's content"—although unhappily
phrased, conveyed a feeling of "sour grapes" rather than lighthearted dismissal.[5] Ahad Ha'am kept reminding his opponents that he, too, craved
"sheer poesy" in Hebrew, but that he could not disregard the difference
between the desirable and the possible.[6] The nation had realized its full
poetic potential only in the Bible, which was composed in *Eretz* Israel by
native Hebrew speakers, who enjoyed political and cultural independence.[7] To regain the emotive-aesthetic dimension, Hebrew would have to
be written once more under the same conditions, and therefore the emergence of a truly poetic Hebrew literature depended on the slow evolution-
ary realization of the Zionist ideal. For the time being, he argued, the
nation would have to do without such a literature.

For those who proposed Yiddish as a national language, Ahad Ha'am
had nothing but contempt. Yiddish, like all other ancillary Jewish "jar-
gons," was to him a passing peripheral phenomenon. With chilling accu-
racy and total lack of empathy, he prophesied its eventual decline. Although the language seemed at the time to seethe with the connotative
richness necessary for nourishing genuine poetic expression, it still lacked
for him the real intimacy, which only a direct connection with the national childhood could produce. A national literature, he argued, like a single
poet's work, could not be written in a language acquired late in life and
severed from the earliest communal memories. As Yiddish had no "real"
past, it could look forward to no real future. If they were not to be lost to
the nation, all works of value written in Yiddish would have to be translated into Hebrew.[8]

III

Deducing the chances of a national Jewish literature from basic Zionist
social and political principles, Ahad Ha'am produced the only logically
sustained Zionist literary ideology. But, of course, he was wrong: Literary
reality refuted his theory even as it was being propagated and debated. For
a time, in the late 1880s and early 1890s, his analysis could seem correct at
least to those readers who, in their violent ideological and aesthetic disap-
proval of the literature of the *Haskalah*, grossly underestimated its intellectual, artistic, and linguistic achievements. A whole century of vain literary
efforts seemed to lie before them. Contemporary Zionist literature, with its

vague, sentimental, and hyperbolical avowals of love for old mother Zion and her miserable children, the Jewish people, seemed even worse than the critical-satirical literature of the *maskilim*. For a Europeanized reader with a taste for neatness and order, like Ahad Ha'am himself, Hebrew literature had little to offer and its prospects seemed dim.

Within less than a decade, however, and not without Ahad Ha'am's active help, Hebrew literature and particularly its belles lettres flourished in a way no one could have predicted. The appearance within a few years of Bialik, Ahad Ha'am's spiritual disciple, changed the poetic structure and aesthetic level of Hebrew verse. Prose fiction, under the influence of such figures as Abramovitch and Berdyczewski, suddenly matured to the extent that it could join the most advanced European literatures in experimenting with the modernist techniques of Impressionism, Symbolism, and Stream-of-consciousness. Sometimes, such experiments even preceded their equivalents in Russian, French, and English. The Hebrew essay, in no small part through Ahad Ha'am's efforts, acquired a grace, sophistication, and sense of innate culture that put it on a level with its European models. Just how these sweeping changes were possible is not our present concern. What matters is that they did occur, and in so doing, refuted Ahad Ha'am's predictions.

Zionism equated cultural freedom with political independence, and therefore prescribed linguistic "normalcy" as the only base for a full-fledged artistic literature. The great Hebrew masters of the first quarter of the twentieth century, some of whom were ardent Zionists, demonstrated that such "normalcy" was not an artistic *sine qua non*. Abramovitch, Bialik, Tchernichowsky, Berdyczewski, Gnessin, Agnon, Yaakov Shteynberg, and many others, wrote poems and stories, in which aesthetic-emotive impact was achieved without reference to a connotative spoken language. Instead, they developed a connotative idiom by returning to the ancient literary sources, with which all contemporary Hebrew readers were, to some extent, familiar: Bible, Mishnah, Talmud, Midrash, and so forth. While most of their predecessors in the *Haskala* attempted to *reproduce* a pseudobiblical language by amassing quotation and allusion, these new writers drew upon the whole continuum of postbiblical sources as well, and constructed their own intricate system of allusion and counter-allusion, quotation and misquotation, imitation and parody. Thus, their language could resonate with a near infinity of associations and nuances. Connotative language and multilevel text structures had never before been so prevalent in Hebrew literature. Indeed, this language appears to have been too rich and dense for such sensitive writers as the short-story master G. Shofman, the poet David Fogel, or even J.H. Brenner. However, they too, in a way, refuted Ahad Ha'am's notions: when they relied, in part, on a semblance of spoken Hebrew, they strove not for additional connotative richness, but for a leaner, more direct and stark style.

With Yiddish as well, Ahad Ha'am's predictions proved totally misguided. No matter what the future held, at the time, Yiddish literature swarmed with talent and energy. Abramovitch, Sholem Aleichem, and Peretz, as well as their younger followers, produced great prose fiction, while Yiddish poetry groomed itself for the leap into modernist brilliance. Without the direct linguistic continuity Ahad Ha'am judged indispensable for a national literature, Yiddish writers managed to evoke, stylistically and thematically, the sense of historical depth.

During the first decade of the twentieth century, Berdyczewski, Ahad Ha'am's old opponent, formulated his own explanation for these developments. In schematic form, his argument runs as follows:

1. Emotive expression in literature can be achieved in an unspoken language provided that the existing literary lexicon is constantly put to use in new ways, emerging from an ongoing, ever-growing emotional awareness. Emotive states engender fresh and effective expression, and not vice versa: "A cistern from which you draw water, be it as pure and good as it may, will not become a well before you further sink and dig it."[9]

2. Modern Hebrew developed naturally (that is, out of authentic emotional needs) in writing and artificially in speech (à la Ben-Yehuda), and, therefore, authentic literary expression in Hebrew can be achieved only within the framework of the unspoken, literary idiom: "As long as we are the people of the book, and only the people of the book, it is enough—and that, too, is a miracle—that we possess the language of the book."[10]

3. In contemporary Hebrew literature, the painful sense of national deficiency and deprivation produces the strongest and richest works. Hebrew literature functions best as "a negative poetry" that does not depend in any way upon a "normal" full-life experience. Only the poets of the *Kera' shabalev*, "rent in the heart," who deeply feel and express the abnormality of the Jewish situation, including the abnormalities and deficiencies of its linguistic circumstances, can create our national literature.[11]

4. A literature which expresses a deficient life experience need not be inferior to one which emerges from a sense of full possession of oneself and one's environment, as long as the deficiencies are experienced and recognized. Such recognition actually gives the "poetry of distress" an edge over the "poetry of comfort."[12]

5. Jewish national literature can and must be written in more than one language, but the differences between the various languages must not be blurred. Poetic work can exist in only one, unique linguistic matrix. Therefore, the writing of the same work in more than one language (a

widespread phenomenon in Jewish literature at the time) is anti-aesthetic and educationally harmful.[13]

Berdyczewski's assertions contradict Ahad Ha'am's literary rationale at every point. Where Ahad Ha'am regarded a national literature as a future possibility, Berdyczewski saw it as a reality. The former believed that only the Zionist solution could resolve the Jewish cultural quandary, while the latter believed that the direct and deeply felt expression of the same quandary formed the basis for Jewish literary creativity. The spiritual Zionist envisaged a national literature flourishing within the framework of the Hebrew-speaking *merkaz ruhani*, "spiritual center," in *Eretz* Israel, while Berdyczewski, whose Zionism was terrestrial and political, actually created it, while living in Germany, far away from Hebrew readers (let alone speakers) and dividing his cultural interests between the Jewish literary tradition and German philosophy and poetry.

Berdyczewski's literary thinking differs fundamentally from that of Ahad Ha'am not only in his cultural realism, his acceptance of the actual, but also in his understanding of authentic literature as an expression of an emotional need. Consequently, he refused to accept Ahad Ha'am's seemingly logical differentiation between the desirable and the possible with regard to literary achievement. The need to express a sense of the beauty of nature or the sweetness of love would produce the linguistic tools necessary for the task. Knowing only his *need* for nature and love, the poet might not say much about them per se. His would be a "negative poetry," a "poetry of distress," the only authentic poetry possible under the circumstances.

IV

We shall turn now to our second example, Hebrew Israeli literature of the late 1940s and 1950s. Founded at the beginning of the century, the literary center in *Eretz* Israel came into its own in the 1920s and 1930s. By that time, the modernized and growing Jewish community there included a substantial contingent of native Hebrew speakers, and early in the next decade a generation of native Hebrew-speaking writers began to appear. By that time, the repression of Hebrew and Zionism in the Soviet Union and the invasion of Poland by the Nazis had put a tragic end to the long history of Hebrew literature in Eastern Europe. After a short period of growth and expansion in the 1920s and 1930s, the small American center of Hebraists was already on the wane and soon most of its active members would either immigrate to Israel or disappear as writers. Thus, Hebrew literature was being written almost solely in *Eretz* Israel, and soon, in the independent State of Israel, by a young generation of *Eretz*-Israeli-born, native Hebrew speakers who had fought and won the war. At last, Hebrew literature seemed to enjoy the conditions of normalcy and independence that Ahad Ha'am had identified as the prerequisites for true creativity.

And yet, literary thinkers were not comfortable with the situation. The destruction of European Jewry and the founding of the State of Israel prodded them into hectic literary theorizing. Such great turn-of-the-century writers as Abramovitch, Frishman, Tchernichowsky, and Brenner were banished for their acerbic and supposedly unempathic criticism of traditional Jewish mores.[14] Others, particularly Agnon, were elevated as positive models. Most readers and critics, particularly of the older generation, found the present generation disappointing. The literature produced by the young sabras struck these readers as flat and provincial, lacking in the resonance provided by European and Jewish cultural resources. Their writing was assumed to be limited to their immediate experience, which did not reach even to the various aspects of the *Yishuv*. In short, this *dor rishon lige'ulah*, the first generation to be fully delivered from the crippling circumstances of the exilic situation, left much too much to be desired. Even favorably inclined critics urged the young writers to equip themselves intellectually, lest they squander their only asset—the vivid, first-hand experience of the war—and be left to face their barrenness or resort to stop-gap mannerisms.[15]

Thrown into turmoil, literary thinkers asked the basic questions once again: What was the guiding principle of Hebrew literature? What were its future prospects? What if any would be the links between ongoing Israeli literature and the literary tradition? Would this literature remain in any sense a *tsofeh leveyt yisra'el*—that is, would it concern itself in any significant way with the large, worldwide Jewish ambience and with the lessons of Jewish history? Beneath this ferment, the foreboding remained—in Dov Sadan's words, a "gnawing dread, which our heart did not reveal to our mouth"—lest the entire Zionist literary experiment arrive at a cultural dead end.[16]

Of the welter of theoretical schemes that emerged, I will outline three. The poet Yonatan Ratosh, the founder and ideologue of the Movement of Young Hebrews, dubbed the Canaanites by its adversaries, formulated his thoughts over a long period of time, starting in the late 1930s. During the War of Independence, his theory of a new Hebrew literature severed from its past, or from what he called "Jewish literature in the Hebrew language," reached its final crystalline form.[17] In the early 1940s, the critic Baruch Kurzweil shifted focus from German and other European literatures to the works of Agnon and the ongoing denunciation of the early works of the sabra writers. By the 1950s he, too, was ready with an encompassing theoretical formula.[18] Through two decades of literary criticism and scholarship, Dov Sadan slowly evolved the grandest theory of all. Emerging in 1950 in the form of a compact little book entitled *'Al sifrutenu—masat mavo (On Our Literature—An Introductory Essay)*, his theory subsumed everything written by Jews for Jewish reading publics during the preceding two hundred years.[19]

Ratosh believed that Jewish literature had always been multilingual and therefore could never be differentiated linguistically. Hebrew, as the language of prayer and inter-Jewish communication, functioned for many generations as its linguistic core, but Jewish literature was written as well, not only in other Jewish languages (such as Yiddish or Judezmo), but also in Arabic, German, Russian, English, and so on. A concern for the fate of Jewish coreligionists and for the religious Jewish tradition provided the common thread. Since the three determining characteristics of nationalism —a national territory, a shared political national history, and a national language—were lacking, a true national literature was impossible. Rather, modern secular Jewish literature continued the old religious literature, decoding in various languages the experiences of those Jews who, although they had lost their faith, had not yet lost their sense of separateness. In recent generations, it had become—in America, in *Eretz* Israel, and in other places—what Ratosh calls "an immigrants' literature," focused on the alienation and pain of acculturation of the Jew outside his habitual historical context. Place was entirely secondary: The immigrant mentality vitiated its significance even for Jewish writers working in Hebrew in *Eretz* Israel. Thus, for instance, Natan Alterman's cycle of poems purporting to describe the Israeli summer revealed only his immigrant experience of unbearable heat and dryness. Alterman had not the slightest inkling of the "real" Israeli summer.[20]

Hebrew literature must be differentiated from Jewish literature, even from those parts written in the Hebrew language. Thus, Bialik, Agnon, Uri Zvi Greenberg, and Alterman could not be regarded as Hebrew writers. Hebrew literature constituted the literary expression of the Hebrew nation and therefore must be written by Hebrews rather than by Jews. Although the new Hebrew nation was in the early stages of formation, the characteristics of nationalism and therefore of a national literature were already present: common territory—the land of Canaan, one national language, and a shared political history. This literature exhibited a natural flair for the landscape and cultures of the so-called Semitic space, the fertile crescent of the Middle East, and for this area's ancient cultures. The formation of the new nation and its struggle for survival provided its central core.

Although its historic thinness was not necessarily harmful, the young Hebrew writer could strive for linguistic and cultural depth by exploring the rites and myths of cultures of the land. Ideological servitude to the Jewish-Zionist past was the chief threat to this literature. Ratosh detected a residue of such a servitude even in the works of S. Yizhar, the most talented and essentially "Hebrew" among the young Israeli-born writers.[21] In a public lecture delivered before the 1948 war had subsided, Ratosh identified the dangers posed by contact with the values and literature of an "obsolete" Jewish culture:

> Culturally, the problem is whether at the center of the new Hebrew culture looms the Jew, the immigrant, and the *oleh* with his problems of acculturation, while the native-born Israelis, as far as this culture is concerned, are merely sons of immigrants, already acculturated *olim*, or whether at the center there are the natives, the Hebrews, the children of the land of the Hebrews. If the second is the case, then those who arrive in the country are merely immigrants, whose problem is not one of acculturation but rather one of assimilation, and who, generally speaking, will not succeed in fully assimilating. Only their sons, themselves children of the land of the Hebrews, will be Hebrews. This perspective stands, of course, in total opposition to that of the immigrant literature—and the major cultural task it postulates is that of the liberation of the Hebrews, the children of the homeland, from the value system of the Jewish generation of immigrants. This war, the Hebrew war of independence, is as much a struggle over the past as it is a struggle over the formation of the present and the vision of the future.[22]

Ratosh, however, was confident that the birth of the new Hebrew nation was decreed by history and that full delivery from the old Jewish matrix was a mere question of time, and of a short time at that. Jewish literature in the Hebrew language was at an end, while Hebrew literature was writing its opening paragraphs. There was no need for Hebrew readers and writers to treat the great Jewish-Hebrew masterpieces of the past with disrespect. Ratosh, himself, admired the poetry of Bialik and contributed much to the understanding of the poet's most complex work, "Megilat ha'esh" ("The Scroll of Fire").[23] But these masterpieces must not be read as part of the new national literature. For better or worse, this literature would deal with national experiences totally unassociated with any past Jewish experience.

Baruch Kurzweil interpreted the history of Jewish culture and literature in terms of a myth of a lost paradise. Paradise was the continuum of the traditional-religious Jewish way of life. This metahistorical continuum had consisted of two complementary factors: the regulatory system of the religious law based on the revelation at Sinai and the basic preliminary *Erleb-nis* of the individual Jew whenever and wherever he was, that is, "the primal certainty that life with all its phenomena loomed against a hovering backdrop of sanctity, by which it was measured and evaluated."[24] While demanding a strict control over natural instincts and human passions, this experience had also been tremendously comforting. It had integrated a personal, omniscient and omnipotent God into daily life.

Kurzweil valiantly defended this harmonious vision of tradition against any intrusion by jarring historical fact. Thus, for Kurzweil, Scholem's analysis of the tradition as a dialectic system full of contradictions and antinomies was anathema, a mere demonization of Judaism.[25] Similarly, he brushed aside as peripheral all symptoms of secularism in premodern Jewish history and rejected the notion (accepted by Bialik, Lachower, Scholem, Schapira, and others) that modern, secularized Jewish culture and literature might have evolved not only under foreign influences but also out of sources indigenous to the tradition itself. The breach with the *Judische Einheitskultur*, an expression Kurzweil quoted from Max Wiener, was a totally novel and revolutionary phenomenon.[26] Changing economic and social conditions in eighteenth-century Europe had opened the garden gates and let in the snake of Enlightenment. Since then, Jewish culture as such—for there was only one legitimate Jewish tradition, however it adapted to changing circumstances, as, for example, by Samson Raphael Hirsch, the founder of the so-called Frankfurt Orthodoxy—was engaged in a losing battle. The history of modern, secular Jewish culture is the story of the battle, and ironically, the closer the new, secular culture drew to victory, the closer it approached its own demise. As long as Jewish culture concerned itself with the authentic religious tradition, even by rejecting and fighting its influence, it could still possess some of its energies or be illuminated by its lingering afterglow. As soon as it managed to banish the haunting presence of the tradition, Jewish culture itself fell apart, for nothing except the presence of the Jewish faith could hold together that spiritual or cultural system.

Nowhere was this better illustrated than in the so-called "new" Hebrew literature. From its inception in the second half of the eighteenth century, this literature was, according to Kurzweil, nothing more than the continuous expression of "a spiritual world, which was stripped of primal certainty" of the divine presence. While its early phases were marked either by a naive belief in the feasibility of some reconciliation between tradition and secular culture or by a gleeful, all-out war waged against tradition, mature artists such as Bialik, Feierberg, Berdyczewski and Brenner recognized the hideous sight of the absurd which emerged from beneath their facile Zionist hopes and aspirations.[27] Agnon was the last and perhaps the greatest of these tragic masters and, therefore, Kurzweil systematically read his works as expressions of doubt, despair, and impending chaos rather than as complex aesthetic reactions to the modern Jewish condition, in which faith and doubt, hope and despair, balanced one another.[28] Over the more recent literary scene loomed the figure of Uri Zvi Greenberg, who rejected the absurd and commited himself to a vision of a renewed Jewish-religious continuity. But Greenberg was an isolated phenomenon, and, moreover, the political implications of his vision of a renewed Sinai illustrated the grave moral and intellectual dangers of any attempt to recover the tradition.[29]

The cultural impasse resulting from the development of modern Hebrew literature was manifest in the new Israeli writers. Their Zionism and socialism provided no criteria for evaluating reality, so they were reduced to "a literalization of life," a reportage-like flatness. Their raw, nonselective naturalism was, however, preferable to intellectual pretensions which would inevitably expose them as overblown nullities, "zeros as big as a wagon's wheel." Kurzweil also preferred their work to the faddish symbolic games played by second-generation Israeli writers such as A.B. Yehoshua, Amos Oz, and Aharon Appelfeld. Those few Israeli writers —Mordecai Tabib, David Shahar, and one or two others—who produced worthwhile work owed their success to their uncharacteristic biographies, which had exposed them, as children, to some authentic religious experience.[30] Without a major infusion of spiritual energy, Jewish culture and literature could not survive. As no source for such energies was imaginable, Kurzweil foresaw only further degeneration of the Jewish literary situation.

Dov Sadan, too, regarded modern, secular Jewish culture as a historical experiment which had already or would soon use up its resources. With its greatest creation—the State of Israel—complete, this secular culture should give way to a new Jewish culture capable of putting to spiritual-cultural use this mighty political vehicle. Adopting the best achievements accumulated through the two-century-long secular detour, this new culture would realign Jewish life with the old religious tradition.

To Sadan, the crisis of secularism was not as tragically final as it was to Kurzweil. The confrontation between Jewish tradition and the European secular Enlightenment gave birth not only to Zionism and Jewish Socialism, but also to two massive Jewish cultural movements that offered religious answers to the dilemmas of modern times: the Hasidim and their rabbinical adversaries, the Mitnagdim. Out of this crisis emerged, then, not one but three, and perhaps more, Jewish literatures: the literature of the Enlightenment, which eventually split into the so-called modern or "new" Hebrew and Yiddish secular literatures; the literature of the Hasidim, written both in Hebrew and in Yiddish; and the halakhic literature of the Mitnagdim. In addition, Jews created literary works for half-secularized Jewish reading publics in various European languages. All these constituted parts of one modern Jewish literature and, though bewilderingly various, this fragmentation need not be permanent. The vital parts of this literature—those written in Jewish languages (for the foreign ones were bound to peter out)—could reunite as soon as a synthesizing principle was found.[31]

Versed in psychoanalysis, Sadan understood the fragmentation of Jewish literature as a reflection of a schizoid personality. While the secular literary movements occupied the upper, rationally regulated layers of the national consciousness, the spiritual movements took root in deeper layers, closer to the nation's emotional loyalties as well as to its subconscious. For the national personality to redeem itself, the various sequestered parts must be reunified. Such a cure was possible because that personality was not as sick as it seemed. Many of the divided selves were vital and each, at its best, included some parts of the others. To prove this point, Sadan brilliantly analyzed the works of the great Hebrew and Yiddish masters of the last two hundred years, discovering in all of them, even in the poetry of the "pagan" Tchernichowsky, the deep roots of the Jewish religious experience. The works of Bialik and Agnon seemed to him to approximate most illuminatingly a Jewish *kuliyut,* "wholeness," and so investigating them became the center of his life's work. Unlike Kurzweil, Sadan emphasized both the modern and traditional aspects of these writers' works.[32]

An ardent Zionist, Sadan regarded the present as a time of both crowning achievement and grave crisis. Without the fragmentation of national consciousness, Jewish spiritual tradition would not have allowed the creation of the political tools necessary for the survival of the Jewish people. But now that the State had been created, there was a danger that it would not be informed by the Jewish spiritual tenor—hence, his "gnawing dread, which our heart had not revealed to our mouth." However, there was no reason to lose heart. Ongoing dialectical development would lead from thesis to antithesis and eventually to synthesis.

For years, Sadan refrained from commenting on the literary activity of the sabra writers. Only in 1954, with the publication of Moshe Shamir's historical novel, *Melekh basar vadam (King of Flesh and Blood),* did he break his silence. This novel, he argued, was the long-awaited breakthrough, the opening of *Derekh merhav* (a path leading to a wide and open place, and the title of his article on Shamir's novel).[33] In his novel, Shamir deals with the confrontation pitting the mundane *raison d'état* of the Hasmonean king, Alexander Yanai, against the values of the Torah as represented by the Pharisees. The author, then in his Marxist-Stalinist phase, interpreted the collision as expressing class-struggle and as foreshadowing impending social revolution [which he dramatized in his sequel to the novel, the play *Milhemet beney or (The War of the Enlightened)*]. To Sadan, this political interpretation was rationalization, reflecting the author's need for ideological consistency. What counted was Shamir's ability to reach into the depths of Jewish history and his readiness to interpret this history from the vantage point of the official religious tradition of the early rabbis. From J.L. Gordon on, almost all modern Jewish writers identified their cause with the biblical kings rather than the prophets, or with the freedom fighters of the last days of the Second Temple rather than their opponents, the custodians of the Law. Reenacting on a grand scale the confrontation between the mundane and the spiritual contenders in Jewish history, Shamir chose to identify with the latter. This choice could and should be a new beginning, opening the way for other Israeli writers to realign themselves with tradition.

V

These three theories point in utterly different directions. Ratosh envisaged a flourishing literature, sustained by a strong neo-Hebrew identity and by its closeness to the ancient soil of Canaan. Kurzweil maintained that literature would become progressively hollowed of the last remnants of authentic cultural significance, shallow, levantine, aping undigested foreign fashions. Sadan foresaw a neo-Judaic renaissance, produced by writers who miraculously bridged the chasm separating present from past, Israel from the Diaspora, the mundane from the sacrosanct, Hebrew from other Jewish languages, the active conscious self from its subconscious underpinnings. And yet, these mutually exclusive theories emerged from one crisis, which all three critics interpreted as the crisis of a new culture negotiating the terms of its existence vis-à-vis its traditions. That Ratosh included among these traditions the so-called "new" Hebrew literature, while Kurzweil identified the emergence of this culture in the second half of the eighteenth century, and Sadan identified a continuous existence of the past alongside and within the new literature, should not blind us to the similarity, indeed, the parallelism of their theoretical constructs.

This parallelism reveals the common seriousness and integrity of these three brilliant intellectuals as they fathomed the depth of a major cultural crisis and courageously carried their convictions through to their logical conclusions. Where popular propaganda culture predicted the glorious continuation of triumphant Zionism, they saw grave dangers and the need for sweeping cultural change. However, the parallelism also indicates their common rigidity and the limits of their powers of observation. From our vantage point thirty years later, these three responses can be likened to the faces of Oedipus in Sophocles' play. One, drawing the most primitive conclusions from his quandary, sets out to kill his father and live ever after with the motherland, the old-new Canaan. He is the Oedipus who solves the riddle of the Sphinx, the young king at the opening of the play. The second is the king who has already advanced to the point where the death of the father has to be avenged by the castration of the son. The third and wisest of them all—an Oedipus in Colonnus—has visions of reconciliation with his father, who, he says, will come back from the dead. And all three shared the characteristic Oedipal insensitivity to reality.

The streak of unreality in Ratosh's rigid intellectualism is easily detected. Buttressed within the citadel of his logic, Ratosh seems never to have bothered to observe what was really going on outside. His theory was posed on an extremely narrow base of empirical observation. Ratosh did see through the official Zionist vision. In fact, he pinpointed a significant unrecognized component in the psychological and cultural makeup of the *Eretz*-Israeli-born generation who reached maturity around the outbreak of World War II: torn away from the world by the war, tired of the Zionist jargon of their parents, disgusted with European Jewry, who supposedly let itself be slaughtered in cowardly passivity, and totally absorbed in the difficult task which history meted out to them, they withdrew into themselves. Ratosh identified this withdrawal, with its inherent self-pity camouflaged as macho toughness, this pathetic camaraderie of boys and girls who knew that many of them would have to die very young, as the formative experience of a new "nation" of heroic "Hebrews." He could not have been more wrong. He misinterpreted his own discovery by isolating it from its historical and psychological contexts. Thus, when the generation on which he pinned his hopes made its great sacrifice and won the 1948 war, the results immediately and utterly destroyed the poet's vision. The State of Israel, once created, asserted its historical significance by opening its gates to Jews from all over the world. Within a few years, the immigrant population outnumbered the old, established population. Problems of acculturation became an integral part of Israeli life. The traumatic experiences of Nazi concentration camps or of the ghettos of Arab towns seeped into the national consciousness, formed it, prescribing the national behavior in war and peace.

Accordingly, almost nothing vital and authentic in Israeli literature of the last twenty-five years resembles, even in a superficial way, the new "Hebrew" literature Ratosh envisaged in the early 1950s. S. Yizhar's *Yemey Tsiklag (Days of Zilag, 1958)*, the last great monument to the mood of *Eretz*-Israeli isolationism Ratosh had defined as the essence of the new Hebraism, was already imbued with the author's sense of an ending. The ordeal of the ending of a shared adolescent experience, which proved to be the only experience Yizhar knew well and could convey effectively, was presented for the last time with all its details fully analyzed and anatomized—for posterity. But even before the publication of *Yemey Tsiklag*, significant, innovative works were published which marked a literary watershed. The great poetic shift which occurred in the late 1950s, and which, I think, is still the most prominent Israeli development in the history of Hebrew literature, was initiated mainly by poets without even the slightest residual "Canaanism." Some of the most prominent among them, such as Yehuda Amichai, Natan Zach, and Dan Pagis, were immigrants, who, although they had arrived in the country as boys, could not and would not suppress their non-sabra mentality. Indeed, they unabashedly put it to poetic use. Preferring cogitation to description, they underplayed the local landscape important to their predecessors. Instead, they strove for wide significance and in some cases (most prominently that of Amichai) examined human experiences and interactions against a backdrop of Jewish models and Jewish history. The Israeli novel, not only as written by the immigrant Aharon Appelfeld, but also by such sabras as A.B. Yehoshua, Amos Oz, Amalia Kahana-Carmon, and Yaakov Shabtai, likewise developed a broad frame of reference, in which there was no place for the notion of Hebrew nationalism in Ratosh's sense. Yehoshua's anti-Diaspora Zionism and insistence on national "normalcy" brings him closer than others to neo-Canaanism. Nevertheless, his version is quite remote from Ratosh's original conception. His sharp, intuitive understanding of the Israeli condition does not allow for any conceptual formulation that does not account for the problematic wider Jewish ambience. In his recent novel, *Gerushim me'uharim (Belated Divorce,* 1982), Yehoshua as much as tells us that the specific Israeli "psychosis" can be understood only against this wider backdrop.

Kurzweil's theoretical scheme strengthened his grasp of a particular set of phenomena in Hebrew literature: the doubt or despair about the continuity of Jewish experience manifested in the turn-of-the-century masters and their followers. He contributed much to our understanding of the darker side of Bialik, Agnon, Brenner and many others. However, the same scheme severely limited his understanding of the direction and values of Israeli literature. This limitation was not due, as has often been suggested, to his negativism and his pugilistic manner; his "cannibalistic" articles and reviews dealing with Israeli writers were often among his best. Equipped with innate detectors of *kitsch*, pretentiousness and sham depth, he accurately identified moot, suspicious spots, of which Israeli fiction had more than its fair share. His critical writing during the late 1940s and throughout the 1950s actually helped the generally better Israeli fiction of the 1960s find an appreciative audience (although he, himself, had no use for it). At the same time, some of his infrequent, positive recommendations and sudden laudatory outbursts, particularly in reference to poetry, embarrassed his readers as all too obvious indications of gross misjudgment, disorientation, and sheer bad taste. Although his theoretical formulations could not numb his sensitivity to what was really bad and worthless, they left him with no criteria for sifting value and achievement out of the chaff of contemporary literature. His worldview, which left no room for a significant Jewish culture after the tradition, was like a strainer, which let out all pure liquids but kept the dregs. Thus he had almost nothing to say about the dramatic developments in Hebrew poetry of the late 1950s. He failed to sense the quality of the early fiction of Appelfeld and detected mostly the weak spots in the works of Oz and Yehoshua. More generally, he could not see that Israeli literature, despite its limitations and all too frequent slips, was maturing and gathering strength, both in its artistic quality and its subtlety as an expression and critique of the Israeli condition.

Sadan has been by far the most creative Hebrew critic in our time. His contributions to the understanding of our literary heritage were as numerous as they were valuable. Nevertheless, his historical scheme resulted in an even deeper insensitivity to the real values and the real difficulties of Israeli literature. Quite simply, no *derekh merhav*, in his sense, was found or sought by the best Israeli writers. Because the reconciliation of tradition and modernity, as Sadan defined it, was not their problem, they find him irrelevant even as they pay respect to his achievement and unique personality. His extravagant praise for Shamir's historical novel is a case in point. The novel, a considerable achievement in its day, was by no means a new beginning in Hebrew literature and by now has become an episode of secondary importance in the development of Israeli literature. Shamir broke no new paths as far as the art or the ideological commitment of Israeli literature were concerned, and his attempt at a realistic recreation of Jewish history in the days of the Mishnah found no followers of any significance. Indeed, Shamir said nothing in his novel about the Israeli political and cultural situation that he had not already said in a more direct and less contrived way in his earlier novels, *Hu halakh basadot (He Walked in the Fields), Tahat hashemesh (Under the Sun),* and *Bemo yadav (With His Own Hands),* which Sadan had not regarded as of particular importance.

When a work such as Pinchas Sadeh's *Hahayim kemashal (Life as a Parable),* which appeared two years after *King of Flesh and Blood,* actually effected a new start in Israeli fiction, Sadan did not seem to have noticed. With the first collection of poems by Amichai, Zach, Avidan, and their colleagues, which appeared during the second half of the 1950s, the Israeli literary scene was fundamentally changed. Whereas Shamir produced a heavy stylistic replica of the Hebrew of the Mishnah for purposes of historical verisimilitude, these poets discovered new rhythms and inflections in spoken Hebrew in the effort to express the Israeli condition. Yet Sadan preferred Shamir's glorified plaster statue to these living literary forms simply because Shamir pointed in the direction Sadan thought Israeli literature should develop. Conversely, Sadan ignored most of the innovations in the Israeli fiction of the 1960s and 1970s because they did not advance Israeli literature in the recommended direction. Current Israeli literature exposes his vision of reconciliation with the tradition as so much wishful thinking. Never before have its vital and creative parts been so far from the synthesis Sadan preached. Facing the neo-Judaic upsurge, which inevitably nowadays goes hand in hand with extreme right-wing politics, most Israeli writers see not a resurrected father, but a frightening hybrid—an enemy whose cultural victory would be the downfall of everything for which they stand.

Against the backdrop of theoretical failures identified in this essay, it would be folly to predict possible future directions of Israeli literature. At the present moment, however, this literature, at its best, is evolving as an anguished expression of Israeli dilemmas and a sharp critique of Israeli mentality. It is written with the understanding that the Israeli condition is not only one variant of the human condition, but also expresses one nuance, albeit a special and, perhaps, central one, of the Jewish experience under present-day circumstances. Developing according to its own inner logic and under the impact of specific Israeli conditions, Israeli literature still tells us something significant about Jewish existence today. So do non-Israeli writers from their various vantage points and within the contexts of five or six non-Jewish literatures: American, French, English, Russian, and Latin American Spanish. There is no indication that this fragmented literary conglomerate will ever amount to a unified Jewish national literature. There are, however, good reasons for the various independent entities which form this conglomerate to establish better contacts with each other, to learn from each other's experience, to recognize the difference within the similarity and the similarity beyond the difference.

Notes

1. Dov Sadan, "In the Light of Synthesis" [Hebrew], in *Beyn din leheshbon* [*Between Account and Reckoning*] (Tel Aviv: Dvir, 1963), 9.

2. Ahad Ha'am, "Resurrection of the Spirit" [Hebrew], in *Kol ketavav*, 5th ed. (Tel Aviv and Jerusalem, 1956), 173–86.

3. See Ahad Ha'am's early article, "Language and its Literature" (1893) in *Kol ketavav*, 93–97.

4. Ibid., 94.

5. Id., "The Purpose of *Hashiloah*," in *Kol ketavav*, 128.

6. See his answer to Berdyczewski et al., "Need and Capability," in *Kol ketavav*, 128–32.

7. Ahad Ha'am, "Language and its Literature."

8. Ahad Ha'am, "Resurrection of the Spirit."

9. M.Y. Bin-Gorion [Berdyczewski], "On the Matter of Language" [Hebrew], in *Kol ma'amarav [Complete Essays]* (Tel Aviv: Am Oved, 1952), 179.

10. Ibid.

11. Berdyczewski, "In Our Poetry," in *Kol ma'amarav*, 174–75.

12. Berdyczewski, "The Aesthetic in Poetry," in *Kol ma'amarav*, 173.

13. Berdyczewski, "Language and Booklore," "Duality," and "A Blurring of Borderlines," all in *Kol ma'amarav*, 181–92.

14. See Avraham Kariv's series of reassessments in his *'Atarah leyoshnah [The Crown Restituted]* (Tel Aviv: Dvir, 1956) and *Mishilshom 'ad hena [From Yesteryear Till Now]* (Tel Aviv: M. Newman House, 1973).

15. See, for instance, David Kena'ani's early survey (1949) of Israeli prose fiction, "Learn Well" [Hebrew], in *Beynam leveyn zemanam [Authors vis-à-vis Their Time]* (Merhavia: Sifriat Poalim, 1956), 137–49. See also Simon Halkin's pioneering overview of 1952 of Israeli poetry, "Recent Poetry Collections by the Young" [Hebrew], in his *Derakhim vetsidey derakhim basifrut [Paths and Byways in Literature]*, vol. 1 (Jerusalem: Akademon, 1969), 101–37.

16. Sadan, "A Path Leading to an Open Space" [Hebrew], in *Beyn din leheshbon*, 283.

17. See his public lectures, "Jewish Literature in the Hebrew Language" and "Israeli vs. All-Jewish Literature" [Hebrew], in Yonatan Ratosh, *Sifrut yehudit balashon ha'ivrit [Jewish Literature in the Hebrew Language]* (Tel Aviv: Hadar, 1982), 37–50.

18. Baruch Kurzweil, "The Fundamental Problematics of Our New Literature" [Hebrew], in *Sifrutenu hahadashah: hemshekh o mahapekhah? [Our New Literature: Continuity or Revolution?]* (Jerusalem and Tel Aviv: Schocken, 1960), 11–146.

19. The essay was republished in Sadan's *Avney bedek* (Tel Aviv, 1962), 9–66.

20. See Ratosh's article, "The Land from Afar," in *Sifrut yehudit balashon ha'ivrit*, 73–82.

21. Ratosh, "Flight to Reality," in *Sifrut yehudit balashon ha'ivrit*, 53–58.

22. Id., "Jewish Literature in the Hebrew Language," in *Sifrut yehudit balashon ha'ivrit*, 41.

23. See Ratosh's articles on Bialik in *Sifrut yehudit balashon ha'ivrit*, 111–70.

24. Kurzweil, *Sifrutenu hahadashah*, 16.

25. See his articles attacking Scholem in *Bema'avak al'erkhey hayahadut [In the Struggle for the Values of Judaism]* (Jerusalem and Tel Aviv: Schocken, 1969), 99–240.

26. Kurzweil, *Sifrutenu hahadashah*, 17.

27. Kurzweil, "The Fundamental Problematics of Our New Literature."

28. See Kurzweil's essays on Agnon in *Masot 'al sipurey Shay Agnon* (Jerusalem and Tel Aviv: Schocken, 1963).

29. See Kurzweil's essays on Greenberg's poetry in *Beyn hazon leveyn ha'absurdi [Between Vision and the Absurd]* (Jerusalem and Tel Aviv: Schocken, 1966), 3–99.

30. Kurzweil's articles and reviews dealing with Israeli writers were collected posthumously in *Hipus hasifrut hayisra'elit [In Search of Israeli Literature]* (Ramat Gan: Bar-Ilan University, 1982).

31. See Sadan's "Introductory Essay" (n. 19) and his "Concluding Essay" in *Orhot ushvilim [Paths and Ways]*, vol. 1 (Tel Aviv, 1978), 173–84.

32. See Sadan's essays on Agnon in *'Al Shay Agnon*, 2nd rev. ed. (Tel Aviv, 1978).

33. Sadan, *Beyn din leheshbon*, 283–300.

III.
Yiddish Language, Jewish Culture?

DAVID G. ROSKIES

The Story's the Thing

STORIES, IT WAS ONCE BELIEVED, offer a temporary reprieve from death. So
Scheherazade stayed her execution at the hands of the sultan with fantasy,
suspense, and eroticism enough to last a thousand and one years. So too
the seven noble women and three amorous men who fled the plague-
ridden city of Florence in 1348. While they did nothing to alleviate the
collective horror, they managed to stave off their own fear of death in a
ten-day-long contest of bawdy and irreverent tales. But six centuries after
Boccaccio, when poet Itzik Manger assembled a minyan of Holocaust survivors in an imaginary bunker, each Jew hailing from another part of
Europe, he could finish no more than two stories of this modern Decameron.[1] The muse simply failed in the face of such catastrophe.

How much redemptive weight can stories bear? For Walter Benjamin,
one of this century's most outstanding literary critics, storytelling was the
answer to modern angst. Storytelling conjured up a world of communal
listening, of young and old alike sharing and shaping the collective memory of the folk—a world where each individual storyteller, according to
Benjamin, was a master of local traditions, rooted in the soil, or a mercu-
rial type just returned from his travels. Whether a master of local or exotic
tales, Benjamin's storyteller inhabited a moral universe of "experience"
rather than an alienated world of "facts." The storyteller used "transparent
layers" of personal and collective experience, of wisdom and practical
knowledge gained over centuries in much the same way as a craftsman
used the tools and techniques passed down from master to apprentice. By
choosing Russian storyteller Nikolai Leskov (1831–95) to occupy the center of this idyllic, preindustrial landscape, Benjamin implicitly repudiated
the Nazi image of the past, complete with Teutonic knights and pagan
blood lust, and the Nazi vision of a racially purged Europe.[2]

Stories, however ephemeral and insubstantial, can stay the executioner's hand, or offer a humane counter vision in a world gone mad. In

119

quieter times, when the stakes are not so high, stories may bestow a blessing that is neither physical nor moral but rather ecological. Contemporary
writers, critics, preachers, and politicians revive the art of storytelling so as
to recycle some part of the past before it is leveled or polluted forever.
What is rescued is then dignified with the name Tradition.

In the Jewish world, the temple of storytelling is the 92nd Street "Y" in
New York City. This is where Elie Wiesel—with disheveled hair, piercing
eyes, and an exotic French accent—mesmerized audiences by retelling
midrashic and hasidic tales. In Benjamin's scheme, Wiesel was both an
authentic source of local lore, having been born and raised in the Hasidic
heartland of the Carpathian Mountains, and a teller of exotic tales, having
passed scathed and scarred through the valley of death. Few could command the same authority. But since then a native-born generation of
storytellers has come of age. Each season they share the stage at the "Y"
in a series titled "The Oral Tradition: Jewish Stories for Adults."

The title says it all, for the "Oral Tradition" translates into the rabbinic
concept of *torah shebe'al peh*, the "Oral Torah." In an extraordinarily bold
move, the rabbis described Moses as receiving two Torahs at Sinai—one
divinely inscribed and inspired, and the other already incorporating what
all future generations of sages would discover.[3] Until, that is, these orally
transmitted teachings were in turn codified into the Mishnah and still
later the Talmuds, thus bringing the oral learned tradition to an end. How
clever, then, to take the translation at its word so as to open the process up
again; to underline the spontaneity of a live speech-act; to turn story into
Scripture and bestow an aura of sanctity on a modern form of entertainment. What better way to bolster the shaky stock of Tradition in a secular
world than with the rising capital of oral storytelling.

Those who perform at these storytelling sessions are neither scholars
nor rabbis. They are American-born Jews who are part of a nationwide
movement for the "preservation and perpetuation of storytelling" and
they hone their craft at regional conferences and workshops. The largest
such gathering is the Annual Storytelling Festival held in Jonesborough,
Tennessee. Peninnah Schram, a popular figure at the 92nd Street Y, was the
first to perform an explicitly Jewish repertoire at the Festival (which up
until then coincided with the High Holy Days). Here, in the heart of rural
America, where "there were no airplanes overhead but, yes, there was a
train that could be heard occasionally from the Sister's Row Tent," she told
the story of "The Nigun" (the hasidic melody) that inspired an outpouring
of joy and brotherly love.[4] In postindustrial America, where storytelling is
an endangered species, one has to travel far afield in order to create a
temporary habitat where the folk traditions can breed and interpollinate.

The effort seems to have paid off, however, for no sooner are the stories told than they are issued in book form, stimulating ever new anthologies of Jewish tales and inspiring a new genealogy with Peninnah Schram and friends as its latest heirs.[5] The "Jews we all know are the masters of Storytelling," pronounced Bea Stadtler to her audience in Cleveland one day, when introducing them to Peninnah Schram. "Everywhere they go, Jews are always telling stories. So, from Abraham, to Isaac, to Jacob, to Joseph, to Moses, to the Baal Shem Tov, to his grandson Rabbi Nahman of Bratslav, to Isaac Bashevis Singer, Peretz and S. Y. Agnon, stories have been passed down from generation to generation."[6] No matter that three millennia or so and several dispersions separated Moses from the Baal Shem Tov. No matter that modern Yiddish and Hebrew literature could be born only once Hasidism was presumed dead. If the Rabbis could invent a *shalshelet hakabbalah*, a chain of transmission from Moses to the Men of the Great Assembly, then why not claim equal status for the storytellers?[7]

Because medium is nine-tenths of the message in the art of storytelling. At the 92nd Street Y, storytelling has to fit the mold of adult Jewish education: just enough parochial content to make it educational; just enough entertainment value to make it profitable. The same stories retold in Tennessee to an audience of fellow practitioners will mean something else again. This audience watches out for the storyteller's technique and picks up echoes of similar tales from other ethnic traditions. Neither live audience has much in common with the practice of Jewish men studying sacred texts out loud. Not only are the latter heir to a learned tradition that devalued stories and storytelling, but they are also working within a closed circle, in which even the meaning of the tales is governed by strict rules of interpretation. The reason one needs to learn the art of storytelling nowadays at conferences and workshops and the reason Bea Stadtler's chain of transmission is missing so many links is that stories were preserved within the warp and woof of Tradition itself, or not at all.

Until, that is, the Enlightenment gave the Jews of Central and Eastern Europe a secular culture of their own in which the measure of modernity was the distance traveled from the house of study—from folklore, fantasy, and storytelling. How a grand storytelling "Tradition" was born precisely out of these discarded relics of the past is the story that I shall outline here, with special reference to Yiddish language and literature. For of all Jewish subcultures, Yiddish is the closest to the living, singing, praying, and talking folk; and the historical ground covered by modern Yiddish writing is coterminous with that of the Enlightenment in its various guises; and of all modern Jewish movements, secular Yiddishism had the most to lose in its love affair with modernity.

Looking back to the beginning of the nineteenth century one clearly sees that the traditional culture received a new lease on life on the very threshold of modernity. Hasidism was the moving force in this revival, primarily on account of its appeal to myth. The repertoire of medieval miracle tales, exempla, and even romances (which circulated in the form of Yiddish chapbooks) was easily updated and adapted to dramatize the powers of the *zaddik*, giving rise to the largest body of hagiographic literature ever produced by Jews.[8] Kabbalah, in addition, provided Hasidism with an esoteric scheme for subjecting almost any text to an allegorical reading. The simplest folktale could yield profound clues to the cosmic struggle for *tikkun* if properly interpreted or reordered in the light of Lurianic kabbalah. This, as is well known, was Nahman of Bratslav's method of retelling the "stories that the world tells."[9]

Tsarist tyranny also played a hand in preserving traditional norms. For twenty-six years, from 1836–62, all but two Jewish printing presses were closed down in the Jewish Pale of Settlement. This effectively blocked the publication of anything that even hinted at heresy and it meant that any reformer had to learn the art of camouflage if he (there being no women involved at the time) wished to see his work in print. The first generation of Eastern European *maskilim* learned very quickly that Hasidism could best be beaten at its own game, by providing a starved reading public with a good story, by adopting the speech pattern of a *maggid*, replete with scriptural references and personal anecdotes—in short, by subverting the very traditions that were seemingly being revived. Once the printing monopoly was rescinded, the *maskilim* launched a frontal attack on Jewish "medievalism" through parody and satire, but the lessons learned in the art of camouflage stood them in good stead when, at the end of the century, it suddenly became clear that modernity had exacted too high a price. As they saw the entire medieval structure collapse economically, socially, and morally, the intellectuals began to seek some new form of cultural expression that would transcend the present squalor and project a sense of collective and individual pride. This is when they rediscovered the great repository of the national genius—folklore.

Thus, storytelling came to play a pivotal role in the course of Jewish self-discovery. Along with a modernist trend that absorbed the techniques and sensibilities of European culture, from satire to surrealism, there was a countermovement to return to the sources of Jewish literary tradition. Yet this latter trend also did not come from within. It took the example of German neoromanticism, Russian populism, and Polish positivism to convince the generation of Peretz, Berdyczewski, and Sholem Aleichem that there was anything worth preserving in Jewish folk culture. And since in those days the study of Jewish folklore was still in its infancy and there were as yet no journals of Jewish literary history, writers had to do their own field work. Looking back on his first field trip to "the provinces" in

1890, Peretz had one of the characters turn to him (that is, to Peretz as the implied narrator) and say: "Kugel is his Judaism. Maybe your Judaism is stories."[10] What Peretz reveals in this brief episode and more fully in "Stories," an almost sordid account of the life of a modern Jewish writer,[11] is the extent of his own estrangement from the values of "the folk." Having fallen from grace, the modern Jewish writer who chose the path of return would have to carry a double burden; he could appropriate the folk tradition only in the name of values completely foreign to the folk. His was a creative betrayal of storytelling.

Peretz, to be sure, was not the first Jewish writer to use traditional forms for subversive ends. As Peretz himself recognized, all roads led back to Nahman of Bratslav, whom he hailed as the harbinger of modern Yiddish culture and whom he enlisted as the narrator of a series of visionary parables.[12] Unlike Peretz, who read Nahman as an allegorist, the approach to Nahman's *Tales* that most directly answers our own needs is the autobiographical. If we follow the lead of contemporary scholars,[13] we discover a composite portrait of the *tsadik-hador* (the preeminent *zaddik*—that is, Nahman himself) as a Marrano (The King Who Decreed Conversion), as both the father grieving for his dead son and the much-maligned *zaddik* whom the son so longed to see (The Rabbi and His Son), as both the lonely genius plagued by doubts and the simpleton living by absolute faith (The *Hakham* and the *Tam*). Such contradictions bespeak a modern sensibility that we would view as being far more subversive than the radical messianism hidden away in the structure and symbolism of Nahman's *Tales*.

In this sense Nahman emerges as the first real modern and his *Tales* do indeed anticipate the future. This tug-of-war between the formal requirements of the folktale—a cast of God-fearing Jews, a mythic plot, and stylized language—and the subversive tendencies born of the author's despair: this irreparable rift between the real and the ideal becomes the substance of modern Jewish storytelling from Nahman's time on. The modern stylized folktale becomes at once an emblem of loss and an exemplum of the wholeness that might someday be restored.

Nahman, for all his angst, was still firmly rooted in the traditional world. For him to tell stories to his chosen disciples was no more strange than to teach them through homilies on the *Zohar*, though the relative status he gave to storytelling was surely a departure from past cultural norms. For Peretz, in contrast, and all the writers who followed, storytelling was the path of most resistance. To be a professional writer meant to master European forms, to cultivate a "literary" style, to cater to a differentiated audience. For moderns to choose storytelling was an ideological statement in and of itself.

Given the questionable loyalty of the writers who now chose to employ

the tools and themes of traditional storytelling, how was one to know
their intention? Was every neoromantic tale a call to traditional faith?
Were vehicle and tenor always supposed to agree? Did the use of symbols
from other than Jewish culture already signal a subversive twist? Was there
anything that all modern folktales had in common, a shared concern or
perspective on life? Peretz, the pathbreaker and tireless experimenter in all
forms of stylized folk narrative, can supply us with some of the answers.

Since this essay is not the place to present all the evidence, the following must be taken on faith: (1) that Peretz's neo-Hasidic tales are
among his most humanistic works and as such are totally at odds with
Hasidic teaching; (2) that for Peretz the supernatural is knowable and
essentially benign; and (3) that miracles underscore human freedom rather than divine providence. Sometimes the betrayal of the traditional story
is obvious, as when Peretz shifts his attention away from the *zaddik* and
onto the simple Jew, frequently a woman.[14] At other times he reserves the
twist for the end, as when the Litvak says "If not higher" when asked about
the miraculous ascents of the Rabbi of Nemirov.[15] The Rabbi's acts of
kindness are greater than any miracle—a humanist position if there ever
was one. Still, these are all positive tales, attempts to rescue a secular faith
from a sacred plot. Peretz, however, never fully abandoned the parodic
techniques he had perfected in such early stories as "Kabbalists" (1891)
and "Bontshe the Silent" (1894).[16] One of Peretz's most celebrated works
in *Folkstimlekhe geshikhtn* (*Stories in the Folk Vein*) is, in fact, a brilliant
parody. It is the story of "Three Gifts."[17] What the casual reader neglects to
see is that the tale of the gifts is embedded within a frame tale about a
thoroughly mediocre soul who did not know the difference between good
and evil when alive and is therefore consigned to permanent limbo after
death. Bribery being its only recourse, this soul finally wins a place in
Heaven by presenting the ministering angels with three stigmata of Jewish
martyrology. The head angel ends with a typical *pointe*: "Ah, what beautiful gifts! Of course, totally useless—but to look at, why, they're perfection
itself!" Which is to say: there is no denying the beauty of such deeds, only
their total effect is to redeem an unworthy soul. Jewish self-sacrifice, Peretz
seems to be arguing, makes no difference on the global scale of human
mediocrity. This radical thrust can be better understood against the backdrop of the Kishinev pogrom and of the angry response it provoked
among Peretz's generation of intellectuals. And so the pious tale about
three exemplary martyrs becomes a bitter exposé of the Jewish and human
predicament.

Here, the vehicle of the story and the ideological tenor clash openly, yet
many readers, even in Peretz's own day, were so taken in by the folksy
facade as to miss the subversion altogether. Perhaps this was a measure of

how estranged the readers themselves had become from the religious ethos of the folk, of how desperately they now clung to stories as a surrogate for faith.

Through his use of folklore and fantasy, Peretz mainly argued the case for humanism, that we are like angels, capable of self-transcendence (if not higher), of achieving a state of ethical perfection through the powers of love, music, art, and individual striving. If the modern, stylized folktale stood for anything in particular, it was the search for transcendence in a world that had broken with tradition. Unlike the modern Jewish novelists who may have shared the same concern, the storytellers exploited traditional narrative forms in order to highlight the possible continuities or the impossible contradictions between a dimly remembered past and a fragmented present.

The dualism of Der Nister, a writer of the next generation, was informed by the darker side of Peretz's vision. Der Nister's point of departure in the hypnotic symbolist tales that he, alone among Yiddish writers, mastered, was the divided soul of humankind, fated to live with irreconcilable forces that tear one apart. While his stories invite, nay, demand, a psychological reading, Der Nister articulated the language of the soul in terms borrowed from Christianity, Bratslav Hasidism, E.T.A Hoffmann, and the Russian symbolists.[18]

Yet to write of the divided soul in perfect story form already intimated a redemptive possibility. Der Nister's recurrent plot, the tale of a quest (or a quest-within-a-quest-within-a-quest), belied any Freudian determinism, even if the quest ended in suspended animation. For through the abyss, the mud, the black enameled cellars, the demonic love, and the debauchery that characterized life on earth, Der Nister could see the way clear to personal redemption, especially when the artist himself appeared in the guise of redeemer ("Bove-mayse, or A Tale of Kings").[19]

Which brings us, in the inexorable logic of modernism, to the use of storytelling as a self-reflexive genre. Paradoxically, it is to Sholem Aleichem, the least "modern" of modern Jewish writers, that we must turn for the fullest exploration of storytelling as a verbal medium. While Der Nister calls attention to the archaic, repetitive, and circular features of his narrative style, which distances the reader from the story told, Sholem Aleichem uses the syntax, cadence, intonation, code switching, diglossia, and wordplay of spoken Yiddish to eliminate the boundary between text and reader. Even when read silently, his stories "speak." But Sholem Aleichem's stories-in-monologue are also *about* language, in more than one respect. Benjamin Harshav has recently described the use of "metalanguage" by Sholem Aleichem's monologuists, Tevye in particular, by which he means their ability to jump from the immediate reality to metaphysical ques-

tions.[20] And while Tevye may be considered Sholem Aleichem's most perfect storyteller, the speaker of the perfect language,[21] he is by no means
Sholem Aleichem's only fictional stand-in. In the traveling salesman
aboard the third-class train compartment, Sholem Aleichem discovered a
new kind of narrator for tales of dissolution in the industrial world, and
one of them, at least—the storyteller who jumps off at "Baranovich
Station"—is as much a spokesman for the powers of art as for the terrors
suffered by a powerless people.[22]

With Isaac Bashevis Singer, both the repertoire and ideology of modern
Jewish storytelling come full circle. Miracles that occur in his stories are
hieroglyphics of the holy, much as they function in the Bratslav tales. For
Singer, as for Nahman, evil is a metaphysical problem, a question not of
man's free will, but of God's. A familiar tale, when retold by the devil—or
by any one of his henchmen—is Singer's most effective way of dramatiz-
ing this potential for evil in the universe. And once the devil takes over,
anything can happen. In "Mayse Tishevits" ("The Last Demon"), for instance, the familiar plot (borrowed directly from Peretz) is deliberately
truncated.[23] After the virtuous rabbi twice succeeds in thwarting the se-
ductions of the very likable demon-narrator, we are programmed to expect
that the third test will make or break him. Yet, in this version there *is* no
third trial. The Germans come and murder the Jews of Europe, leaving no
one worthy of being tested. The demon's work pales in comparison with
the work of human demons. The full indictment against mankind is left
for the demon to deliver, a repudiation of the secular humanism championed by Peretz and his school. As Nahman improved upon the universal
folklore repertoire, Singer improved upon the modern secularized folktale.
In Singer's hands storytelling is used to subvert the modern subversion.

As the last of the demons, who draws his sustenance from the letters of
the Jewish alphabet, Singer's narrator is also a stand-in for the writer. Here
the story as a self-conscious genre reaches its culmination, for never before
has a story been told to an absent audience and never before has a storyteller been reduced to communing with a disembodied language.

Yet the story of modern Yiddish storytelling does not end here. It is a
recurrent tale of loss-and-retrieval, with each generation of moderns discovering anew the power of stories to close the ever-widening gap between
the world of shared experience and the consciousness of the individual
storyteller, and as such, it cries out for a satisfying ending. Since I have set
my version of the story squarely within the Yiddish-speaking world, I dare
not, at story's end, use sleight of hand to conjure up other worlds of Israeli,
Franco-Jewish, or Anglo-Jewish fiction in order to argue for hidden
continuities—that a dybbuk, say, of Peretz, Sholem Aleichem, Der Nister,
or I. B. Singer somehow entered the writings of Nissim Aloni or Steve

Stern.[24] Perhaps I should reveal, however, if only to tie the end of this essay up with its beginning, that Stern's fanciful tale, "Shimmele Fly-by-Night," takes its inspiration from Itzik Manger's "The Adventures of Hershel Summerwind," of the unfinished Decameron.[25]

Fortunately, I have found within Yiddish culture itself, in its newest and, in some ways, least hospitable home—the State of Israel—a born-again storyteller in the person of Yosl Birshteyn. How Birshteyn discovered his natural storytelling talents on the airwaves of the Israel Defense Forces is a modern Jewish story if there ever was one, and I promise to tell it some other time. Meanwhile, I draw the tentative conclusion that as much as Yiddish culture kept storytelling alive, to create a seemingly unbroken chain of transmission, it was the rediscovery of stories by successive generations of Jewish rebels, revolutionaries, and immigrants that gave Yiddish a new lease on life. And that is surely redemption enough for the People of the Lost Book.

Notes

1. See Manger's "Afterword" to *Noente geshtaltn un andere shriftn* [*Intimate Figures and Other Writings*] (New York: Itzik Manger Jubilee Committee, 1961), 516.

2. Walter Benjamin, "The Storyteller: Reflections on the Works of Nikolai Leskov" (1936), in *Illuminations*, trans. Harry Zohn, ed. Susan Sontag (New York: Schocken, 1968), 83–109.

3. See Jacob Neusner, "Oral Tradition and Oral Torah: Defining the Problematic," *Studies in Jewish Folklore*, ed. Frank Talmage (Cambridge, Mass.: Association for Jewish Studies, 1980), 251–71. Neusner argues that, historically, "Oral Torah" was synonymous only with the Mishnah and that the full-blown concept of a dual Torah is of late amoraic provenance.

4. Peninnah Schram, "Telling Stories at NAPPS," *The Jewish Storytelling Newsletter* 1 (Winter 1986): 7.

5. For a convenient, though uncritical review of the field, see Peninnah Schram, "Current Collections of Jewish Folktales," *Jewish Book Annual* 49 (1991): 73–84.

6. "The Storyteller's Introduction," *The Jewish Storytelling Newsletter* 1 (Winter 1986): 4–5.

7. *The Fathers According to Rabbi Nathan*, trans. from the Hebrew by Judah Goldin (New York: Schocken Books, 1974), chap. 1.

8. Joseph Dan, *Hasippur hahasidi* [*The Hasidic Story: Its History and Development*] (Jerusalem: Keter 1975); Gedalia Nigal, *Hasipporet hahasidit* [*The Hasidic Tale: Its History and Topics*] (Jerusalem: Y. Marcus, 1981).

9. Nahman of Bratslav, *The Tales*, ed. Arnold J. Band (New York: Paulist Press, 1978); Dan, *Hasippur hahasidi*, chap. 3.

10. I.L. Peretz, "Dos vaserl" ["The Brook"], retroactively appended to his *Bilder fun a provints-rayze* (1891), but first published in 1904. In *Ale verk fun Y.L. Perets*, 11 vols. (New York, 1947–48), 2:197.

11. Peretz, "Mayses" (1903), in *Ale verk*, 3:462–77. For an English translation, see Maurice Samuel, *Prince of the Ghetto* (Philadelphia: Knopf, 1948), 133–50.

12. Peretz, "Reb Nakhmenkes mayses" (1904), in *Ale verk*, 4:187–208.

13. Joseph G. Weiss, *Mehkarim behasidut Braslav* [*Studies in Bratslav Hasidism*] (Jerusalem: Bialik Institute, 1974); Arthur Green, *Tormented Master: A Life of Rabbi Nahman of Bratslav* (Tuscaloosa: University of Alabama Press, 1979), esp. 223–26.

14. Dan, *Hasippur hahasidi,* 39. For examples of heroines, see Peretz's "A Passion for Clothes" and Ber Horowitz's "The Dybbuk," both translated from the Yiddish in *Yenne Velt: The Great Works of Jewish Fantasy and Occult,* ed. Joachim Neugroschel (New York: Simon and Schuster, 1978), 353–70.

15. "Oyb nisht nokh hekher" (1900) in *Ale verk,* 4:98–102. For an English translation see *A Treasury of Yiddish Stories,* ed. Irving Howe and Eliezer Greenberg (New York: Viking, 1954), 231–33.

16. "Mekubolim" (Hebrew, 1891; Yiddish, 1894), in *Ale verk,* 4:20–25 and "Bontshe shvayg," in *Ale verk,* 2:412–20. For English translations see *A Treasury of Yiddish Stories,* 219–30.

17. "Dray matones" (ca. 1908), in *Ale verk,* 5:81–92; *Yenne Velt,* 114–22.

18. The only critical study of Der Nister to date is by Khone Shmeruk, "Der Nister's 'Under a Fence': Tribulations of a Soviet Yiddish Symbolist," *The Field of Yiddish, Second Collection* (The Hague, 1965), 263–87. The largest sampling of his stories in English is in *Yenne Velt.*

19. 1920; in *Yenne Velt,* 460–542.

20. Benjamin Hrushovski, "The Deconstruction of Speech: Sholem Aleichem and the Semiotics of Jewish Folklore" [Hebrew], afterword to this translation of Sholem Aleichem, *Tevye hehalban vemonologim* (Tel Aviv, 1983), 195–212.

21. See my *Against the Apocalypse: Responses to Catastrophe in Modern Jewish Culture* (Cambridge, Mass.: Harvard University Press, 1984), 163–83.

22. "Station Baranovich" (1909), in *The Best of Sholem Aleichem,* ed. Irving Howe and Ruth R. Wisse (Washington, D.C.: Simon and Schuster, 1979), 61–70. See also Wisse's comments on the story on pp. x–xi.

23. I.B. Singer, "Mayse Tishevits" (1959), in *Der shpigl un andere dertseylungen,* ed. Khone Shmeruk (Jerusalem, 1975), 12–22. For a loose English translation, see *The Collected Stories* (New York: Farrar, Straus & Giroux, 1983), 179–87.

24. On Franco-Jewish writers, see Judith Roumani, "The Portable Homeland of North African Jewish Fiction: Ryvel and Koskas," *Prooftexts* 4 (1984): 253–67. On Steve Stern, whose turn to Jewish storytelling uncannily recapitulates the careers of modern Yiddish writers, see Janet Hadda, "Ashkenaz on the Mississippi," *YIVO Annual* 19 (1990): 93–103, and Steve Stern's own autobiographical statement, "A Brief Account of a Long Way Home," *YIVO Annual* 19 (1990): 81–91.

25. In Steve Stern, *Lazar Malkin Enters Heaven* (New York: Penguin Books, 1986), 87–112. Manger's story is most readily available in *A Treasury of Yiddish Stories,* 438–46.

RUTH R. WISSE

Two Jews Talking:
A View of Modern Yiddish Literature

ONE MODE OF CONFRONTATION, or encounter, recurs so often in Yiddish
poetry and prose, and with such obvious success, that we might consider it
the natural form of the literature. From the moment that Mendele the
Book Peddler gets entangled with his counterpart, Alter Yaknehoz, on the
road to Glupsk, two Jewish males have been meeting on the Yiddish page
in discussion and debate.[1] The two Jews form a tiny island in the midst of a
threatening or simply alien sea, and whether they are friends or opponents, strangers or relatives, contemporaries or separated by a generation,
they provide for as long as they remain locked in conversation the moral
context within which everything else must be weighed and understood.

In what is perhaps the single most famous such work of Yiddish fiction,
Tevye tells Sholem Aleichem how he became a dairyman, how he almost
made a fortune but didn't, and how he lost his five daughters and his
homestead during the successive social and political upheavals of his time.
The stories trace the disintegration of traditional East European Jewish
civilization, but each time Tevye concludes a section of his biography—
"You know, Panie Sholem Aleichem, let's talk about something more
cheerful. What do you hear about the cholera epidemic in Odessa?"—he
affirms the coherence of that civilization. Readers have always recognized
Tevye's adaptability and moral strength as an assurance of the culture's
resiliency, but the presence of Sholem Aleichem as a listener is an important part of that confirmation. As long as the simple villager is able to
amuse the Russified city gentleman, and as long as this gentleman still
responds appreciatively to his every quip and allusion, the basis of a common culture is demonstratively secure.[2]

The same frame device of a distraught parent speaking to Sholem Aleichem serves the same purpose of pacification even in so late and bleak a

work as "A Thousand and One Nights," written during World War I.[3] On
board ship, an unstable and very temporary haven, the bereaved father
describes the final destruction of his town, the tag line showing how heavy
the humor has grown: "Let's talk of happier things. Wasn't there a pogrom
in your town? Didn't they hang Jews there? And by the way, where are *you*
running from, Mister Sholem Aleichem?" Here, no less than in the Tevye
episodes, and in many of Sholem Aleichem's train and travel stories, the
effects of disjunction and uprootedness are greatly tempered by the evidence of intimacy and identification between two Jewish strangers.

Since modern Jewish literature developed as a consequence of the Enlightenment, it was naturally preoccupied with the relations between Jews
and non-Jews, and with the secularization of Judaism that was one of its
wholehearted aims. Whereas this process of secularization took place in
Western European countries gradually, over a period of centuries, and
within several distinct national frameworks, the East European Jews discovered a ready-made body of secular thought which they scrambled to
assimilate and to adapt to their own situation. Yiddish literature was the
most important medium in the dissemination of these new ideas. The
conversation between Jews proved an ideal vehicle for exploring and assessing the process of Jewish modernization, since it established an authentic internal ground, a linguistic and cultural island, from which the
"flood"—a term that reappears in Yiddish fiction—could be withstood.

Not surprisingly, the conversation between Jews was a form much used
by the great Jewish intellectual, I.L. Peretz, both in his fiction and in his
essays, like the biting one, "On History," that opens with a Jew of the
author's acquaintance sitting down beside him on a Warsaw park bench to
inquire why he is looking so sad.[4]

> "Graetz is dead," I answered.
> "God's will!" said my acquaintance. "Was he a local?"

Peretz uses a Socratic dialogue with this traditional, simple Jew to pro-
pound his own ideas about the importance of history as a force of national
cohesion in a secular age. He phrases his argument in homey midrashic
analogies and familiar terminology—a skill that Peretz must have mastered in his long years as an educator of adults—so that the Jewish "student" can recognize himself comfortably in the argument that is being
made, and more readily accept its conclusions.

From within the shelter of the home culture, the intimacy of the Yiddish conversation allows for the free expression of new ideas, and of new
attitudes about the world. In such dialogues the author's point of view is

normally entrusted to one of the characters, but since the good author can seldom control his characters as thoroughly as he intends, even some of the most didactic works assume a human complexity.

Among Peretz's "hasidic" stories, to bring but one example, is a slight thing called "A shmues," which consists entirely of a conversation between two former antagonists, Reb Shakhne, a follower of the Kotzker Rebbe, and Reb Zerakh, a Hasid of Belz.[5] Once upon a time, in the heyday of Hasidic rivalry, these men had fought bitterly. Now they merely engage in a light quarrel over the relative importance of the Haggadah and the *kneydlakh*, that is, of the spirit and the body. The story has many of the familiar qualities of Peretz's fiction, including an atmosphere of decline, a sharp, legalistic dualism of points of view, the use of traditional garb for the exposition of contemporary issues.

Reb Shakhne, defender of the *kneydlakh*, takes for his text, "You shall not return to his master a slave who has fled from him." The body, normally the thrall of the soul, should be allowed to enjoy its freedom on Passover, the holiday of freedom, without having to return to its taskmaster. "Here, body, grab a *kneydl*," and without spiritualization feel in your own free right the enjoyment of a mitzvah.

Reb Zerakh, the antagonist of the story, has no patience for such self-indulgence. For him the mandatory joy of Passover lies in the reading of the text, especially in the recitation of the plagues and the *Shfoykh khamoskho*. This invitation to God to pour out His wrath upon the nations, and the account of the plagues that God once visited on the enemies of Israel, should be repeated seven times instead of once! After the torment and persecutions suffered by the Jews, this ceremony of verbal aggression does his heart good.

We know from other sources that Peretz detested this passage of the Haggadah, and the exclusivist tendencies of some of his contemporaries. This dialogue between Hasidim is a platform for the generous humanism of the "materialist" as opposed to the mean national instincts of the Jewish "spiritualist." It suggests that whereas the materialist is kindly, responsive to the basic physical needs that unite all mankind, the spiritualist is divisive, fostering categories of uniqueness and hatreds of which the Jews have been the chief victims. Reb Shakhne, the author's spokesman, is granted the decisive final word. He attacks Zerakh in a long and complicated argument that concludes as follows: "Israel shall not rejoice as do the nations! You are not a peasant! Vengeance is not Jewish!" Jews are supposed to recite the plagues with a sad mien, with compassion for those who were once sacrificed to their bid for freedom; Jews do not hate.

Of several fascinating aspects of this story, here baldly summarized, I will pause on only one—the unintentional paradox that underlies Peretz's

argument. When Reb Shakhne, the humanist, attacks his opponent's nationalistic pleasure in the Haggadah, his primitive vengeance against the
goyim, he expresses a national arrogance far more profound than Zerakh's.
Reb Zerakh's expression of rage is merely an attempt at getting even: *If I
cannot do you any harm in return for the harm you have been doing me all these
many centuries, let me at least express through God my belief in His Vengeance.*
Shakhne's humanism, on the other hand, gives voice to an essential national superiority. "You are not a peasant! Vengeance is not Jewish!" Jews
are thus credited by Peretz through Shakhne with an innate moral distinctiveness that has succeeded their religious idea of election.

As long as it remains within the religious framework of Halakha and
prayer, the Jewish idea of election depends upon God, on manifestations
of His grace, His power. In his contempt for this idea of exclusiveness, the
Jewish humanist actually went much farther. He placed on the Jews an
onus of morality that depended for its realization upon *them*. They were to
be the conscience of the world, holding themselves to a perpetually higher
standard of judgment—and holding "peasants," or non-Jews, to an explicitly lower standard of judgment. Reb Shakhne's position in this argument,
ostensibly the open, generous, and liberal view of the world, thus implies a
degree of national hubris far greater than anything that Reb Zerakh, with
his *Shfoykh khamoskho*, could voice.

The internal dialogue between Jews transformed action into speech, the
events out there, of which the Jews were so frequently the victim, into a
controlled reinterpretation of those events. The action was now in the
argument. In the hands of a master like Peretz, the traditional talmudic
duo, Reuben and Simon, became exponents of sharp contemporary debates, a compressed verbal drama. The occurrences that triggered the
arguments—pogroms, expulsions, new political and ideological pressures
—remain the background while the Jews assault one another on how
these challenges had best be met.

With the rise of modern Jewish ideologies the Yiddish dialogue was put
to partisan use even more sharply than Peretz had done. Eliezer Shteynbarg was the genius of this form in the period between the world wars.
Equally devoted to the enrichment of Yiddish and the promotion of democratic socialist ideals, Shteynbarg revived the fable as a contemporary
instrument that could combine entertainment with instruction, delight in
verbal play with pointed moral teaching. In his poetic fables the pragmatic
needle stands up to the bayonet, the industrious brush raps the elegant
shoe, and the nightingale sings unappreciated by the belching pig. Almost
impossible to reproduce effectively in another language, the fables owe
much of their wit and charm to the interplay of male voices that begins in

casual banter and then rises to staccato final thrust. So, after complaining at length to the whip on his back, the horse receives his answer:[6]

"Shut up!"

(*The whip cracks now, like a sharp tongue*)
"I know very well that dragging
A cart like this with your stomach nagging
Means nearly emptying each lung.
Let me give you a tip —
You keep getting the whip
Not for not pulling; but you're due for
Being converted into glue for
Not getting the point, for letting yourself, you ass,
Be harnessed up and brought to such a pass!"

In Shteynbarg the Jewish voices are often interpreters of a "Marxist dialectic" and, in fact, the sparring of these two outlooks, the Jewish and the Marxist, can be the very point of the fable. The traditional Jewish speaker is *balebatish*; he is the comfortable bourgeois—or, in the case of the cited fable, the compliant Jewish victim. The cutting voice of the whip belongs to the political realist who uses the familiar language of intimacy—the Yiddish dialogue—to get across his tough new message.

Of course the internal dialogue could not suit *all* the purposes of Yiddish literature, and during the period of geographic dispersion and modernization those Yiddish writers who set their faces to the world preferred to interpret themselves and their constituency as part of the general, universal fabric. Sholem Asch's novels of St. Petersburg, Warsaw, Moscow, and New York placed the Jews within the mainstream of current events and had them speak the undifferentiated languages of their new surroundings. There were novels of steel and iron, epics of ancient Prague and developing Kentucky, stories of the cross and the sickle that proved the interpenetration of Jew and world. Then too, the emphasis of many Yiddish writers, particularly after World War I, fell on the effects of disjunction and discontinuity, on the breakdown of Yiddish communication rather than on its cozy familiarity. In the stories of David Bergelson, when a disaffected intellectual is quoted as saying, "The world is dirt, as I am a Jew," we hear the dead fall of a phrase that was once a weighty oath, now reduced to an ironic tic.

Yet during the very period that Yiddish literature grows most universal in its inclinations, the years between the wars, the Yiddish writers themselves seem to take over the dialogue that once belonged to the characters. The internalization of historical processes, and the translation of the argument with external powers into an argument with one another becomes an instinct among Yiddish writers and intellectuals, perhaps for much the same reasons that it was originally enshrined in fiction. An outgrowth of the Enlightenment, and a manifestation of its progressive will, modern Yiddish writing mocked above all the internal, self-referring quality of Jewish life. The first literary generation exposed the casuistry of the rabbinate, the stagnation of the Jewish economy, the political impotence of the Jews who conducted European affairs from the benches of the local bathhouse, the cultivated ignorance of the Hasidic courts. They promoted reform based on the self-adaptation of the Jews to surrounding cultures and languages. As a result of these reforms, Jews soon began to function in Russian and Polish, and with emigration, in English and Spanish, consigning Yiddish to the sidelines, and relegating Yiddish writers of the later generation to marginality in the very pursuit of modernization that their forebears had championed.

Mendele Mokher Seforim's satire of the *shtetl* showed the comic helplessness of Jewish men who sublimate their frustration in aggressive debate. One does not have to be a satirist to note the same thing happening among Yiddish writers when the sphere of their influence contracts, especially in America where it happens most rapidly. Immigration after 1924 was reduced to a trickle. The Anglicization of East European Jews becomes manifest in their children, who pretend not to understand, let alone speak, their mother tongue. In Palestine the linguistic battle between Yiddish and Hebrew had tipped decisively in favor of Hebrew. The single bright spot on the horizon appeared to be the Soviet Union where Yiddish culture was subsidized by the State, and enjoyed a distinct influence. As their own sphere of influence contracts, and the personal difficulties of making a living add to their isolation, the Yiddish writers draw in among themselves, with the intensity of internal conflict compensating to some degree for the palpable decline of audience.

One moment in the history of Yiddish literature seemed to bring this process of internalization to a head, and may serve in place of a text as an exemplification of the problem. A crisis among the Yiddish intelligentsia — and not, of course, among them alone—occurred in late August, 1929, following the Arab massacres of Orthodox Jews in Hebron and Safed. In itself, this violence would have triggered a familiar reaction among Jews all over the world, across all ideological lines. But as we now know, the Kremlin leadership, in a shift of policy, declared the Mufti's campaign of terror against the Jews to be the beginnings of the Arab revolution, and insisted that its Yiddish voice in America, the *Morgn frayhayt*, adopt its position. The *Frayhayt*, which had been since 1926 under the control of the Soviet Central Committee, reversed its first spontaneous reaction to the pogroms as an act of excessive violence, and condemned the "Zionists-Fascists" who had provoked the Arab riots, hailing the Mufti as the liberator of his people.

At this point, an entire roster of *Frayhayt* writers publicly severed their connection with the newspaper and launched an independent weekly. The founders of *Vokh*, the breakaway paper, included some of the most prominent Yiddish voices in America: Moyshe-Leib Halpern, Isaac Raboy, Joseph Opatoshu, Aaron Glanz-Leyeles, Ephraim Auerbach, Lamed Shapiro, Menahem Boreisho, and Halpern Leivick, the last three of whom became the editors.

Because these writers of *Vokh* broke with the Communist *Frayhayt* on the issue of Palestine, it is often mistakenly assumed that in the struggle between socialist and nationalist affiliation, they chose the nationalist, anti-Communist side. But the process was hardly that simple. Actually, the break with the Communist newspaper over a question of national sensitivity was painful to these writers, because it appeared to show them up as rank chauvinists whose narrow self-interest made them turn their backs on the ideals of universal advancement. It was therefore necessary to stress, more than ever before, their essential loyalty to the underlying principles of the Societ Union, which remained undiminished by their defection from the *Frayhayt*.

Thus, the main energy of the writers of *Vokh*, in its short duration, was invested in transforming the global struggle over Palestine into a purely internal Jewish conflict. It is not the Soviet Union that is held under suspicion, but the local Jewish Communists of New York: "We have not separated ourselves from the revolutionary movement or from the Soviet Union, but from the *Frayhayt* editorial staff."[7] Within the first few issues of what was announced as a cultural weekly, there were attacks by Leivick, Shapiro, and Opatoshu on the writers who had remained with the *Frayhayt* and on the "assimilationism" of the Left. Even stronger is the attack on the "reactionary chauvinist forces" of the Right: by Ephraim Auerbach on Melekh Ravitch of the Warsaw Bundist *Folkstsaytung*; by Lamed Shapiro on Hayim Nahman Bialik as the figurehead of Palestinian Zionism; by Menahem Boreisho on Ludwig Lewisohn as the representative of American Zionism, and so forth. As the other Yiddish papers respond in kind, charges and countercharges are hurled with what seems clearly to be displaced aggression. When a staff writer of the Zionist daily, the *Tog*, denounces the *Yevsektsia*, the Jewish branch of the Russian Communist party, for insisting that Yom Kippur be declared the national work day of the Ukraine, an editor of *Vokh* leaps into battle:

> If with a knife at our throat we would have to choose: you [Zionists] or the *Yevsektn*, we will choose the *Yevsektn*. Not because they please us, they don't. But they are young, and behind them stands a great and fruitful

idea. If they are blind in certain things, they may in time begin to
see . . . they have the potential; YOUR camp is the generation of the
desert—in every respect. It is perhaps brutal to say so, but your time has
passed . . . forever.

The image of the knife at the throat, while instinctively correct, elicits a
characteristically oblique response. Rather than inveigh against the Arab
hordes, the British mandatory powers, the Kremlin leaders, the forces *holding* the knife at his throat, the Yiddish polemicist turns his rage against
those within his own situation who are responding differently to the knife
at their throats.

There seems to be a revealing parallel between Reb Shakhne's position
in the story, "A shmues," and the consequence of *Vokh*'s editorial attempt
to demonstrate its universality. In the very act of denying a parochial
loyalty and repudiating an outdated Jewish allegiance, the writers of *Vokh*,
like Reb Shakhne, are more profoundly insular and parochial than those
whom they accuse of it. While those who speak bluntly in their own self-
interest are at least able to recognize and identify the forces ranged po-
tently against them, the voices that try to avoid the narrowness of a national identification end by denying the reality of the rest of the world. The
greater the outside pressure, first from Communist anti-Jewishness, later
from Fascism and the competing interests of the British and the Arabs, the
more passionately we find these anti-nationalist Yiddish writers quarreling
among themselves.

The poet, Joseph Rolnik, with customary sweetness and delicacy, gives
us the flavor of the thirties in miniature:[8]

I and the poet Isaac Raboy
are next-door neighbors.
Maybe I drop in at his place
or he comes over to me.

Between us—me and him—
only plaster over some lath.
Each one hears the other walking
—I on the right, Isaac the left.

We go back twenty-five years
together—to Henry Street.
Like one family then. And now
they call us the "old timers."

I work in a word-stable,
and he at marten and mink.
I lean a little to the right
and he is thoroughly left.

We talk like good old friends,
we talk plainly and honestly,
though he's left through and through
and I—just a bit on the right.

And when we remember Levine's Café,
those five steps up,
a soft warm dew starts
to melt through our limbs.

And when we remember home,
Mir is mine, his Rishkan,
I'm no longer a little bit right
and he's not left anymore.

My father owned a flour mill,
his father—wagons and horses.
Our wheel turned in the water
and his ran over the earth.

We talk of Sabbath and weekdays,
about all kinds of foods,
what we prepared for the holidays,
what they were cooking in Rishkan.

We talk like old, good friends,
we speak from the heart and honestly
—though he is left through and through
and I just a bit on the right.

In this poem, called "Neighbors," Rolnik moves gently from the political tensions that separate the two writers to the common memories of childhood and their young manhood on the Lower East Side that continue to bind them. He seems bemused by the inevitability of the refrain, left and right, that has become a new component of their intimacy. In order to keep talking, however, these two Jews must return to the past, avoiding the present ideological barriers between them. For all its air of wry innocence, the poem makes us aware of the stupefying hold that political categories had over the two writers and of their shrinking little world.

The war erased most of the socialist-universalist rhetoric of the 1930s. The scope of the catastrophe overwhelmed the Yiddish writers, who tried, like most of the Jews left in the world, to find comfort in the emergence of the Jewish state. When the Yiddish dialogue resumed in the war's aftermath, there was little remaining trace of the animus against the Zionist Right. Invoking the traditional past that once united them, the speakers regroup on an autonomous island of discourse where their attitudes about themselves and the outside can be freely aired. Of all the Jewish writers, those who wrote in Yiddish were collectively affected by the war far more critically than their colleagues in other languages, since it was their partic- ular linguistic base that had been obliterated.

Aaron Zeitlin's *Monolog in pleynem yidish*, written in 1945, reestablishes a circle of intimacy after the mass destruction of European Jewry and the mass assimilation of American Jewry.[9] The American *landsman* who stops Mister Zeitlin on the New York Street has come to America years before, and this accidental meeting with the poet affords him the chance to remi- nisce and to reflect. He is certainly less appealing than Tevye as a represen- tative figure of the ordinary Jew, but he is capable of a terrible pathos when he says:

> *Ay kent understend, ay kent!*
> *Take pleyin farbrent?*

The Anglicized Yiddish of the speaker, even more than the saga of his disaffected children, shows how much has been forfeited in the process of Americanization, while their shared memory of Warsaw—"Just burned to the ground? Just like that?"—sharpens the pain of all they have lost. The two Jews briefly recreate a ground for mourning.

Postwar Yiddish literature has a true existentialist quality: the sign of "No Exit" appears in the childlessness of so many of its characters, and in their obsessive engagement of one another, as if everything now depended on its outcome alone. Chaim Grade's famous story, "My Quarrel With Hersh Rasseyner,"[10] is really about the resumption of Jewish argument within the very heart of the existentialist city of Paris, yet its Jewish sur- vivors struggle for meaning under the wings of a God they still share, however differently they interpret His Presence. Since it takes as its subject the proper relation of their conversation to their surroundings, this story may be the most self-conscious example we have in Yiddish fiction of two Jews talking.

The story is avowedly autobiographical, though it goes without saying that Grade invests himself in each of the two characters. The "author," Chaim Vilner (which was Grade's name in his yeshiva student days), tells of three meetings he had between 1937 and 1948 with Hersh Rasseyner, once his fellow student at the Mussarist Yeshiva in Bialystok where they were taught to purge themselves of the evil impulse. The first encounter occurs many years after Vilner had left the yeshiva to become a secular Yiddish poet. The second takes place in 1939, under Soviet occupation. Rasseyner accuses his former classmate of responsibility for "them," for the Soviet occupiers who joined the Germans in carving up Poland between them. Vilner tries to shrug off the charge: "I am no more responsible for them than you are for me." But in this section it is Rasseyner who has the last word, since he does indeed consider himself responsible for his lapsed fellow Jew and thereby holds Vilner responsible for the political ideals that he had championed through much of the thirties.

In contrast to these brief opening sections, the third encounter, describing their reunion in Paris in 1948, covers forty pages of running dialogue of exceptional intellectual and emotional range. Rasseyner's incarceration in a death camp during the war has softened him, deepening his religious fervor and intensifying his opposition to worldliness. Having shepherded many young boys through the war, Rasseyner now runs a shuttle of orphans from Europe and Morocco to Israel, saving their lives and shoring up their spirits. He is more than ever convinced of the need for religious self-discipline. The war presented him with such irrefutable proof of the need for Jewish Law in the face of barbarism that he is astounded by Vilner's unrepentant humanism.

Vilner, for his part, will not turn his back on the world. The statues of Paris remind him of the glorious contributions that Gentile poets and thinkers and scientists have made to civilization. The deeds of the few righteous Gentiles whom he met in his own wartime odyssey confirm his trust in human kindness. For Chaim Vilner, the murder of innocents in the death camps raises the question of God's mercy, not Man's, and he is astounded no less than Rasseyner by his colleague's tenacity in the face of such contrary evidence. Thus, we have two Jews locked in debate who refuse with equal stubbornness to yield to despair, the one of God, the other of Man.

That two Jews continue their argument throughout and beyond the years of Soviet treachery and German genocide is the surest confirmation of Jewish continuity. Their physical survival, however symbolic, is here only an opportunity to reveal their great resources of mind and faith. The story ends with Vilner's embrace of Rasseyner, and his affirmation that they will continue their quarrel. Grade has used this running argument between two former yeshiva *bokherim* not to promote one point of view over the other, but to dramatize the vitality of the internal Jewish dialogue, which no external powers have been able to dull.

Two distinct voices of the kind that we have in Grade create the artistic equivalent of human choice. Isaac Bashevis Singer, a less affirmative writer, is generally inclined to the use of monologue: His self-impelled narrators are sucked to their inevitable doom, or else, if they are demons, they entice their victims into a similarly unavoidable net. Even when he writes about the process of modernization, which held out the prospect of choice, Singer often reverses the direction of the characters' movement. His Jews are not seen to be leaving their origins. Instead, the centripetal force of the

Jewish world pulls all of modern civilization into its vortex. Singer's fiction recreates the present as the past, or as a Jewish Sheol.

For Isaac Bashevis Singer, the inner circle of two Jews talking, when he resorts to it, is very tightly circumscribed. In a novel called *Der bal-tshuve*, the author-narrator meets at the Western Wall in Jerusalem the penitent of the title, who tells "Mr. Singer" the story of his life, much as Tevye had once poured out his woes to Mr. Sholem Aleichem.[11] A survivor of the Holocaust, the penitent celebrated his liberation by embarking on a life of self-indulgence in greed and pride and lechery. But by the time he tells his tale he has become a resident of Meah Shearim, the ultra-orthodox section of Jerusalem whose hundred gates are kept shut against the encroachments of modern temptation. Singling out humanism as the most dangerous of all modern self-deceptions, the penitent extols the traditional Jewish civilizing structures of law and prayer, ritual and study, which alone can guarantee the Jew his happiness.

Since the returning Jew expresses his satisfaction with Judaism, readers may wonder why his confession is such a gloomy and disturbing document. Perhaps because the circle of intimacy has been drawn so tight as to shut out not only the world, but most of its Jews. "Mr. Singer" in this novel is the *only* Jew to whom the penitent is prepared to tell his story, as if acknowledging how narrow the culture has grown. While Sholem Aleichem, listening to Tevye's enthusiastic encounter with all the many new challenges of his time, was so charmed that he determined to make all the world aware of this marvelous man, "Mr. Singer's" hero forces upon him a story of progressive withdrawal from temptation into self-imposed protective custody. It feels in this book, as in much of I.B. Singer's fiction, as if we are standing at the very end of time, within a universe so unbalanced and amid human impulses so wicked that our only safety lies in the constriction of binding laws, even if we no longer believe in their divine source, and even if there is no longer any joy in their observance.

Modern Yiddish literature, which arose to the promise of emancipation, turned in the postwar period away from its own failed hopes. Yiddish poets grew liturgical. Sometimes they appeared to be setting up the familiar scheme of two Jews talking, but with God as one of the parties. In the absence of answering voices of other Jews, God became the target of argument. Jacob Glatstein writes:[12]

God, wherever You may be
there all of us are also not.

Kadia Molodowsky writes:[13]

God of Mercy
Choose another people
for the time being.

H. Leivick's last book of poems was entitled *Poems to The Eternal One*.

Two Jews talking initially provided Yiddish authors with an indepen-dent platform from which they could scout out their surroundings. The pitched argument was an indigenous Jewish form, evoking generations of student-scholars, the Jewish equivalent of duelers or knights-errant. The familiarity guaranteed the intimacy within which secrets may be revealed. The two Jews were able to talk about their love affair with the world.

But the progress of the affair was not smooth. The cultural record of Yiddish shows how dazzled the writers were by the higher idealism of the Socialist Bride in particular, whose dowry included the promise of accep-tance into universal society. When the Bride turned skittish, the suitors began quarreling among themselves. They remained locked in furious combat long after her betrayal.

In the normal process of cultural transmission, one generation studies the legacy of its predecessors, and comments on their achievements and failings. The aging generation of Yiddish writers does not have any such prospect and suffers the limits of its abbreviated influence. Many of them, chastened by history more than anyone has a right to be, returned to a traditional framework of discussion, even if only to take up the old poses of internal rebellion. There being, as they felt, no one to listen, they did not find it necessary to offer much of an explanation of their past or interpretation of error.

Those of us who inherit the world of Yiddish, even in part, are invited to bury and to praise. But I resist the impulse to eulogize. I wish, instead, that we could continue the Yiddish tradition of two Jews talking at least long enough to go over the ground of Yiddish literature once again with the engagement of participants: to appreciate its power, but no less, to recog-nize its capacity for debasement.

Notes

1. This particular reference is to the frame story of Mendele Mokher Seforim, *Fishke der krumer [Fishke the Lame]* (1869 and 1888). But examples of this device can also be found in a number of other works by Abramovitch, particularly the ex-tended allegory, *Di kliatshe [The Nag]* (1873), which consists largely of such conver-sation. Among earlier Haskala writings, Yoysef Perl's *Megale tmirin* [The Revealer of Secrets] (1819), is written in the form of correspondence between two hasidic followers of the same Rebbe, and provides one model of this method in prose, while in poetry some of the rhymed fables of Shloyme (Solomon) Ettinger present two animals thinly disguised as two Jews talking. One might also consider, as an exten-

sion of this literary habit, the actual correspondence between such literary pairs as I.L. Peretz and Y. Dinezon or Sholem Aleichem and Mordecai Spector, which often imitates and parodies this convention.

2. These thoughts are more fully developed in my article, "Sholem Aleichem and the Art of Communication," B.G. Rudolph Lecture in Judaic Studies (Syracuse University, 1979), and in the introduction to *The Best of Sholem Aleichem,* ed. Irving Howe and Ruth R. Wisse (Washington, D.C.: Simon and Schuster, 1979).

3. Sholem Aleichem, "Mayses fun toyznt eyn nakht" (1915), in *Ale verk fun Sholem-Aleykhem* [*The Complete Works of Sholem Aleichem*], vol. 28 (New York, 1917), 135–232. Partially trans. Sacvan Bercovitch, "The Krushniker Delegation," in *The Best of Sholem Aleichem,* 232–44.

4. I.L. Peretz, "Vegn geshikhte" (1891), in *Ale verk fun Y.L. Perets* [*The Complete Works of I.L. Peretz*], 11 vols. (New York, 1947–48), 8:40–47. Trans. Sol Liptzin, "On History," in *Peretz,* 296–309.

5. I.L. Peretz, "A shmues" (1900), in *Ale verk,* 4:141–44. Trans. Joseph Leftwich, "A Conversation," in *The Book of Fire* (New York and London, n.d.), 133–36.

6. Eliezer Shteynbarg, "Dos ferd un di baytsh," in *Mesholim* [*Fables*], vol. 1 (Czernowitz, 1932). Trans. John Hollander, "The Horse and the Whip," in *A Treasury of Yiddish Poetry,* ed. Irving Howe and Eliezer Greenberg (New York: Viking, 1969), 233.

7. All following references appear in *Vokh,* which began publication on Friday, October 4, 1929. See definition of aims, Editorial, 4 October, 1929; H. Leivick, "Why We Left the *Frayhayt,*" October 4, 1929, 4–6; "In the Spotlight" (signed Ephraim Auerbach), October 18, 1929, 16–17; Lamed Shapiro, "Under the Pealing Bells," November 8, 1929, 6–8; Editorial of 18 October, 1929. See also A. Leyeles, "The Mufti's Sleeve," 4 October, 1929, 13–14: "We have absolutely not become Zionists because of the Palestinian tragedy. If it were possible, we became even greater enemies of political Zionism than before." Speaking from the standpoint of historical determinism, Leyeles feels that Zionism has been dealt a "deserved blow" by the pogroms, but adds that they cannot be expected to dance for joy at the event.

8. J. Rolnik, "Shkheynim," in *Naye lider* [*New Poems*] (New York, 1935). Trans. Irving Feldman, "Neighbors," in *The Penguin Book of Modern Yiddish Verse,* ed. Irving Howe, Khone Shmeruk, and Ruth R. Wisse (New York: Viking Penguin, 1988).

9. Aaron Zeitlin, "Monolog in pleynem yidish" ["Monologue in Plain Yiddish"], in *Lider fun khurbm un lider fun gloybn* [*Poems of the Holocaust and Poems of Faith*], vol. 1 (New York, 1967), 98–104.

10. Chaim Grade, "Mayn krig mit Hersh Rasseyner," *Der yidisher kemfer* 28 September, 1951, 33–44. Trans. in slightly abbreviated form by Milton Himmelfarb, "My Quarrel with Hersh Rasseyner," in *A Treasury of Yiddish Stories,* ed. Irving Howe and Eliezer Greenberg (New York: Viking, 1953), 579–606.

11. Isaac Bashevis Singer, *Der bal-tshuve* [*The Penitent*] (Tel Aviv, 1974).

12. Jacob Glatstein, "Roykh," in *Shtralndike yidn* [*Radiant Jews*] (New York, 1946), 16. Trans. Chana Faerstein, "Smoke," in *A Treasury of Yiddish Poetry,* 331.

13. Kadia Molodowsky, "El khonun," in *Der meylekh Dovid aleyn iz geblibn* [*Only King David Remains*] (New York, 1946), 3–4. Trans. (different version from the literal given here) Irving Howe, "God of Mercy," in *A Treasury of Yiddish Poetry,* 289–90.

BENJAMIN HARSHAV

The Semiotics of Yiddish Communication

You may have heard charming, appealing, sentimental things about Yiddish,
but Yiddish is a *hard* language, Miss Rose. Yiddish is severe and bears down
without mercy. Yes, it is often delicate, lovely, but it can be explosive as well.
'A face like a slop jar,' 'a face like a bucket of swill.' (Pig connotations give
special force to Yiddish epithets.) If there is a demiurge who inspires me to
speak wildly, he may have been attracted to me by this violent, unsparing
language.

—Saul Bellow, "Him with His Foot in His Mouth"

This and several similar, often quite contradictory, pronouncements by
native speakers of Yiddish seem to attribute to the language a life of its
own, a mentality, a set of values and attitudes, serving as a source of
strength and frustration alike.[1] Clearly, the nature of Yiddish as a vehicle
of communication, as a repository of a whole semiotics of discourse and
"worldviews" of its speakers, is an essential part in the understanding of
the language.

Yiddish speakers have always felt that theirs is quite unlike any other
language and provides them with a highly charged means of expression.
The difference was conspicuous when compared with the rational, well-
ordered, and intellectual but detached or bureaucratic language used in
post-Enlightenment Western societies. Not growing out of high culture
and a refined literary tradition but out of a homogeneous folklore world,
steeped as it was in irrational discourse, quintessential formulas of folk
wisdom, and highly charged intimate family attitudes, the language was
suddenly—in the lifetime of one or two generations—confronted with a
pluralistic and specialized modern world and with elitist culture. Speakers,
making that leap, either despised their "primitive" language or saved from
it precisely the unusual, irrational, folkloristic, or symbolic elements, carrying over their full semantic weight into the new, "European" context:
The very strangeness of Yiddish expressions and gestures when used in
another language served as an emotive, untranslatable "spice" for the initi-

ated as well as a substitute for an authoritative "Bible of quotations" for the new texts.

This leap was acutely felt under the conditions of modern Yiddish litera-ture, written in the big cities of Poland or the Soviet Union or even farther, "on the other side of the ocean"—that is, removed, or having escaped, from its two sources of vitality: the old religious world and a living folk ethos. In some sense, this condition may be typical of much of modern literature in general (we may think of Joyce writing at a distance from Dublin), but in other languages writers could rely on a rich written tradi-tion of literature, philosophy, and other discursive writings. Yiddish writ-ers on the move carried their "world" in their language.

It was even more sharply sensed by those who lived and wrote in other languages, when only vestiges of Yiddish were left—in Bellow's words, "fragments—nonsense syllables, exclamations, twisted proverbs and quo-tations or, in the Yiddish of his long-dead mother, *trepverter*—retorts that came too late, when you were already on your way down the stairs."[2]

Language and Social Psychology

Language as such cannot be "hard" or "delicate" or "explosive," as Bellow's narrator puts it. In the twentieth century, Yiddish has been used for many kinds of discourse, often quite contradictory to whatever might be its "inherent" or accepted nature. This "oral" and popular language has been successfully harnessed to impressionist prose, historiography, lin-guistic and statistical research, political propaganda, or "ivory tower" po-etry. Nevertheless, in social perception, the language did carry a cluster of characteristic features, developed in its unique history and crystallized in its modern literature. The very fact that native speakers may assign such emotive qualities to the language, rather than seeing it as a neutral vehicle for communication, speaks for itself. Let us say at the outset: the bulk of the language and its grammar may be similar to other languages; what marks it as a different medium are special features interspersed by its users, and these are of interest to the popular and scholarly characterizations. Rather than providing a regular grammar of Yiddish or an analysis of representative texts, I shall focus on such "characteristic" features.

By the "semiotics" of Yiddish, I mean a second level of language, built above its vocabulary, morphology, and syntax—that is, the "language" of communication accepted by the speakers of a community: how to behave in human interaction, what to say under what conditions, how to initiate a dialogue, how to go on talking, in what terms to observe the world, and how to express briefly an evaluation or an emotive stance. It comprises a whole network of signals, rules of conversation, encapsulated formulas and labels, allusions to codified and richly connotative life situations.

It seems that, in its popular forms, Yiddish internalized and schematized some essential characteristics of "Talmudic" dialectical argument and questioning, combined with typical communicative patterns evolved in the precarious, marginal, Diaspora existence. These became second nature to many Jews—their typical mental and behavioral attitudes, conversational manners, or even psychological dynamics—and were transmitted to the next generation quite autonomous of the language itself or of the amount of culture acquired by any given individual. When Bellow writes at the beginning of *Herzog*: "Late in spring Herzog had been overcome by the need to explain, to have it out, to put in perspective, to clarify, to make amends," he describes Herzog's psychological state, but he could have described the semiotics of one mode of a typical Yiddish conversation in similar words. In "Him with His Foot in His Mouth" (as quoted in the epigraph to this chapter), Bellow seems to understand this connection: the narrator's "demiurge" inspires him to "speak wildly," attracted to him by "this violent unsparing language" (which, paradoxically, he does not speak at all).

A variety of such undefined attitudes and patterns of thinking and speech have often marked the behavior of Jews—their "Jewish" features—but were also felt to be strange or offensive by the users of another, dominant semiotics and were suppressed by adaptable Jews themselves.

Thematic Components

The semiotics formed in a certain sociolinguistic culture contains a flexible cluster of attitudes and communicative signs and gestures, including typical features as well as options for contradictory possibilities. Though susceptible to recent influences, it often has a conservative core reflecting some kind of "mentality" and set of "beliefs" of a national or ethnic society, as codified in a formative period. This conservative core may reflect earlier stages of beliefs and attitudes, no longer held by the speakers but turned into a "language" to speak. Thus, in European languages, the sun still "sets," though, since Copernicus, we believe that the opposite is true. Many primitive or pagan beliefs are incorporated in proverbs or nursery rhymes of Christian languages and now fulfill primarily communicative, emotive, or aesthetic, rather than referential, functions. Bellow's narrator, claiming that "pig connotations give special force to Yiddish epithets" (in the passage quoted above), probably has no particular attitude toward pigs as nonkosher animals, but he feels the "special force" of pig connotations that combine the negative pole of the kosher taboo system—the very heart of Jewish identity vis-à-vis a Christian society—with the German negative "swine" language, used against the Jews themselves (in the image of the *Judensau*, "Jewish sow"). In *Tevye the Milkman*,[3] Sholem Aleichem has exposed this discrepancy between the attitudes codified in the language and the speaker's present reality, highlighted by the tacit narrator's ironic point of view. Thus, the inferior status of women assumed in the language is inverted in plot by their superior understanding of reality; the lower status of artisans in the language is both exposed and undercut in Tevye's own words: "A man, says I, is like a carpenter: a carpenter lives and lives and dies, and a man lives and dies."

As we have seen, a whole conceptual world and terminology came to Yiddish from the religious domain and was turned into "language," freed from its specific denotations. Even the word "Torah" itself—the name of the holiest book—came to mean, on the one hand, teaching or theory in general and, on the other hand, any kind of practical knowledge, from cooking to teaching children how to tie their shoelaces. This was a secularization not in the sense that the speakers abandoned religion but rather that they expanded religious terminology to nonreligious domains as well, using the intensity or emotive force of the expression and neutralizing its religious denotation (which, of course, could be revived in a specific context). In the terms of its own speakers, it used the "Sabbath" language to serve the everyday life of the "weekdays." Yiddish had no religious obligations, as the "Holy Tongue" did, and thus it could perform such a secularizing function.

Similarly, customs of religious behavior, texts of holidays, and analytical methods of scholarly inquiry permeated Yiddish as part of its semiotic system. You did not have to know Hebrew to use a Hebrew quotation; you did not have to be a "scholar" to exhibit an analytical or "philosophical" attitude or to be inquisitive or critical. All such absorbed attitudes and "folk wisdom" became decontextualized, much as folklore in general (according to Jakobson and Bogatyrev) neutralizes the individuality of a poem's individual author and the particular circumstances of its creation.[4]

Furthermore, in accordance with the open and multidirectional nature of Yiddish as a fusion language, it adopted pieces of beliefs and expressions from other cultures and melted them all into one system. The Vilna marketplace curse, *Kh'vel makhn fun dayne kishkes a telefon*, "I shall make your guts into a telephone" (that is, I shall twist them like a telephone cord), exhibits the same fusion of cultural domains as the earlier *Di kishke hot nit keyn fentster*, "The guts [*kishke*] have no windows" (that is, guts have no display windows; you cannot see what you have put into your stomach, which means that you can eat any junk so long as you fill your stomach). The coarse, disgusting *kishke*—which combines the coarseness of its Slavic, "peasant" sound (when transferred to Yiddish) and of cheap, poor people's food ("stuffed *kishke*") with Yiddish folklore's obsession with problems of the digestive tract—is conjoined with the elegant innovation, the worldly sounding Internationalism, *telefon*. At the same time, the stylistic effect of the worn-out expression, *kishke*, is made strange and refreshed in the new context, while the modern telephone is degraded to the level of *kishkes*.[5]

The semiotics of Yiddish communication has a stable core captured in the "mythology" of Yiddish folklore and placed in that particular, imaginary world of the *shtetl*, which was projected in fiction by the founders of its modern literature and then reabsorbed into the communal consciousness. (The *shtetl* was a small town, predominantly Jewish or having a Jewish area, surrounded by Christian villages and dominated by a foreign power.) The *shtetl* was not the real background of all Yiddish speakers—some lived in villages and most writers and their readers already lived in larger towns or cities—but it was their proverbial, mythological "space," a collective locus of a network of social and ideological relationships wrought in the phraseology of Yiddish folklore and literature. Most modern trends of Jewish life, literature, and consciousness pushed away from the *shtetl*, abandoned it, despised it, or at least saw it in an ironic or nostalgic light. But Yiddish classical literature used the iconography of the *shtetl*, its mythological behavior and language, as a microcosm of Jewish nature: such are the images of Mendele's Kabtsansk and Sholem Aleichem's Kasrilevke. In a sense, this parallels the use of Orthodox Jewish figures and religious symbols as "Jewish" iconography in paintings and sculptures by Max Weber, El Lissitzky, Chaim Gross, or Marc Chagall, though the artists themselves were not "Jewish" in their external appearance. This collective imaginary space was supported by a peculiar Jewish geography; the Golem of Prague, the merchants and Enlightenment writers of Odessa, the intellectuals of Vilna, the fools of Chelm, the small seats of famous Yeshivas (Volozhin, Ponevezh) and of Hasidic dynasties (Lubavich, Satmar, Uman') became symbolic places, in folklore and in literature alike.

Yiddish poetry has profusely employed motifs of "Jewish" imagery as a *store of situational meanings*, as a *language* for expression, even when the poet was far removed from them ideologically or thematically. Often such motifs may not even carry any overt "Jewish" images. Thus, Halpern's poem, "What Do We Know, Dear Brothers" (written when he was associated with the American Communists) employs key situations from the Bible (the Burning Bush, Moses, Samson, King David) without mentioning them by name, and places them within the context of a cosmopolitan, "existentialist" perception of his character, Rabbi Zarkhi:

What Do We Know, Dear Brothers

Three rubberbands on a thin tip top
And a pair of glasses looking out to sea.
Maybe it's Zarkhi's longing that weeps—
What do we know, dear brothers.

And maybe it is not Zarkhi that weeps
But a tree that burns and isn't consumed,
Weeping with branches as if they were arms—
What do we know, dear brothers.

And maybe it is not a tree that weeps
But the silent lament of an eye and a hand
Of a man dying at the threshold of his land—
What do we know, dear brothers.

And maybe it is not a man that dies
But a blind giant a thousand years ago
Weeping over his shorn hair—
What do we know, dear brothers.

And maybe it is not a giant that weeps
But the simple silly instrument
Weeping under Zarkhi's aging hand—
What do we know, dear brothers.
                    —*American Yiddish Poetry,* 428

With time, however, as "Jewish" concerns became more predominant in Yiddish literature—especially after the Holocaust and the establishment of the State of Israel—what had been a mere "language" could easily be inverted and turned into *theme.* Yiddish poetry was suffused with motifs from Jewish religion and history serving largely as authentic imagery for the expression of universal human experiences. Now the poets and their readers could invert that relation and read the imagery as thematic evocation.

Sociologically, the "world" of Yiddish as we know it today—its thematic networks codified in language—was an unusual phenomenon. In one tangled web, it combined semiotic elements of the most prestigious group in medieval Jewish society, the "scholars," as they were absorbed in daily communication (what folklorists call *gesunkenes Kulturgut,* "sunken cultural treasures"), with elements from the life of the impoverished masses of Eastern Europe in the nineteenth century. The appeal of the latter was reinforced in the romantic idealization of the "people" and their authentic vitality by the post-Herderian, folklore-loving Jewish intellectuals. The

Jews in medieval Europe were inherently and nominally (though not actually) a classless society, since they were a "quasi-class" unto themselves in the feudal class structure. Within Jewish society, there was no formal caste barrier for social, intellectual, or economic mobility, and the poor shared with the rich the same conceptual world. All of them were aristocrats of God, "the Chosen People," and any one of them could, in principle, reach the highest levels of learning and prestige.

Thus, Yiddish folklore exhibits a unique combination of attitudes from a socioeconomic lower class with those of an intellectual elite. The Jews were pure but, at the same time, they were, in their own eyes, a fallen aristocracy of the mind, conscious of their history, of their mission, and of ideological attitudes in general. This is why it was relatively easy for a Jew of lowly origin to rise to the highest levels of general society and culture: mentally, he did not have to overcome vertical class barriers (provided he overcame the horizontal religious fence). And this is also why sincere anti-Semitic revulsion toward Jews involved objections to their behavior rather than to their intellect.

Therefore, we should not be amazed that the best Yiddish poets of the "Young Generation" in New York were simple workers: Mani-Leib was a shoemaker, Landoy a housepainter, Leivick a paperhanger, Halpern a poverty-stricken jack-of-all-trades. These were not traditional proletarians who turned to writing. They read and discussed the poetry of Pushkin, Blok, Rilke, Hofmannsthal, Baudelaire, Verlaine, and Rimbaud and published translations of their poetry as well as those of Chinese, Japanese, and Indian poets. Shoemaking was merely a necessity; after all, a poet had to make a living, and professional jobs were not available. Socialist ideology enhanced the poet's pride in being a real shoemaker, which, along with tailoring, had been the most despised profession in Jewish folklore. In the minds of these poets, as in the folk-consciousness of the East Side Jews in general, being proletarian and poor was a transitory stage, a temporary necessity brought about by the hard course of history, while aristocracy of the mind, ambition to achieve the highest intellectual standards, was inherent in being Jewish or—as they would insist—in being human (whether this goal was actually realized or not is another matter). This is not unlike the theory of the split mind as perceived in Hasidism: while half of one's mind is steeped in the dark of everyday work and worries, the other half should be kept separate, rising high, unifying with God.

Hence the strange combinations we find in the Jewish lower classes (often, in the mothers and fathers of scholars and writers) of semi-illiteracy on the one hand and admiration for learning and for "higher" matters on the other. That is why the same popular Yiddish newspapers that carried

melodramatic stories of love, divorce, hardship, and success also pub-
lished translations from world literature, articles on Spinoza, poems by
Leivick, and novels by Isaac Bashevis Singer. And that is why a starving
Jewish population of London's Whitechapel in the beginning of this
century could support a Yiddish journal with the significant title *Germinal:
Organ of the World Anarchist Organization,* with contributions by Kropotkin
and other ideologues, as well as J.H. Brenner's journal, *Ha-Meorer (The
Waking Bell),* which launched a new, individualistic stage in Hebrew litera-
ture.

At the same time, Yiddish folklore preserved the memories of an earlier
age, when there were fewer Jews, many of whom were occupied in trade, in
changing and lending money, and in traveling. Trade—symbolizing the
mediating function of the Jews as well as their mobility—is almost as
much of an ideal in Yiddish folk-consciousness as is learning. Selling shoelaces or apples or peddling in the countryside was considered a "natural"
Jewish way of life and could—and often did—lead to a better life; keeping
a tiny store was considered more prestigious than any artisan craft. The
popular lullaby goes: *Unter Yankeles vigele/ shteyt a klor-vays tsigele./ Der
Tate is geforn handlen./ Er vet brengen Yankelen/ Rozhinkes mit mandlen,*
"Under Yankele's cradle/ stands a pure white kid./ Papa went traveling,
Papa went trading./ He will bring for Yankele/ Raisins and almonds."
Travel, trade, communication with strangers, observation of differences
between social and religious groups, their habits and languages, and the
irony of such juxtapositions are basic to Yiddish folklore.

And so is the uniqueness of the Jews, their suffering in history and their
difference from others. Though modern Yiddish literature often resists
them, ethnic distinctions are still engraved in the language. A woman is
called a *Jewess,* a man is called either a *Jew* or a *goy,* "Gentile." Since the
image of the *shtetl* implies a Jewish center surrounded by villages, with
their peasants coming to the Jewish market in town, a *goy* often simply
means a peasant. Stereotypically, he may be seen as ignorant, coarse, or
drunk; but he may also be endowed with enviable physical and spiritual
health. A Christian girl is called a *shiksa,* which may carry either the
negative connotation of "a loose woman" or the positive one involving
the attractions of real, sincere, and physical love. Modern Yiddish literature as a whole tried to invert this relationship, which had become fos-
silized in the language, though it still resorted to terminology reflecting
the point of view of an ethnocentric Jewish observer. Such language is
used, for example, in Halpern's famous poem, "Zlochov, My Home," a
scathing attack on the ethnocentric *shtetl* and its ugly Jewish behavior (see
American Yiddish Poetry, 408–11).

Structural Components

Several basic conditions of its history have influenced the nature of Yiddish discourse. One essential fact is that, in a book-oriented society, Yiddish was primarily a language of conversation. Yiddish sentences are replete with gestures of a speech situation. They contain a variety of devices to stress the casual nature of speech, to attract the listener's attention, and to express the speaker's evaluative postures toward the contents of the narrative. Even scholars like Max Weinreich use dialogue markers in their scholarly monographs. Since there was no tradition of Yiddish philosophy or systematic treatises (and very little in Hebrew) and nothing comparable to a Latin syntax to influence Yiddish with written and formal rigor, descriptions in Yiddish tend to be presented not in the form of objective exposition but are imbued with the speaker's attitudes. Positive objects or events are marked with positive evaluative expressions (for example, if a child says something clever, the quote is accompanied by *a gezunt in zayn kepele*, "Health to his little head"); negative ones are fenced with reservations ("Let it be said of our enemies"; "May he have such a black year"); members of contradictory categories (such as Jew and Gentile, man and woman, human and animal) are separated by guarding signals (especially: *lehavdl*, "to be distinguished from").[6] It is a language that conveys strongly the emotive attitudes of the speaker toward the contents of his message (as Bellow and other English-speaking writers have indicated). And it can do so by spicing its discourse with Hebrew, Slavic, or emotively loaded idioms and expressions, or by interposing brief words or interjections with no independent meaning of their own, such as *nu, epes, shoyn, khasvekholile, mishetyns gezogt* (almost untranslatable: "so," "something," "indeed," "already," "God forbid," "in a manner of speaking"), or simply by substituting *shm* for the initial consonants of any noun, to deride it, as in *book, shmook*.

Since Yiddish was primarily a spoken language, the forms of its folklore genres are usually brief. Long forms of discourse were kept for learning, preaching, and argumentation. As we have seen, however, the long forms of most Hebrew texts used in Ashkenaz had no sustained logical or narrative structures of their own and were rather parasitic on primary (or secondary) texts. The major genres of Hebrew writing and formal discourse in Ashkenaz were either commentaries—that is, written or spoken on the margins of some other, established text—or sermons—that is, starting from a quote or the weekly reading of the Bible and shifting, through story, allegory, and parable, to a topical or moral issue and then back to the next quote from the original text.

Typically, such religious and moral discourse—and Yiddish conversation deriving from it—advances not in a straight line, through affirmative statements or the logic of a problem presented in a hierarchical argument, but through many kinds of indirect or "translogical language" (to use Philip Wheelwright's term in *The Burning Fountain*): asking a question; challenging a claim; looking for a counter-argument or an alternative possibility; answering with an example, a simile, or an analogical situation; illustrating a point by telling a story, an anecdote, or a parable; quoting a holy text or a proverb; posing a riddle; telling a joke; leaping to metalanguage and metadiscourse and pondering on the language used and on the purpose of the whole conversation; punning on words; digressing into pseudo-etymology; and shifting, by association of language, from any of those to another topic. These are not the metaphors favored in the Western tradition, but their impact is as powerful as that of any translogical language in poetry or myth. The value of metaphor lies in the semantic interaction between two small units of discourse, two disparate frames of reference, and the surprises and effects of that encounter. Here, the encounter between two distant frames of reference is not metaphorical, but the freshness of the surprise and the semantic interaction are as effective. A special kind of indirection, encoded in the structure of Yiddish idioms, presents an extension of a hypothetical situation which might embody the issue at hand. The common expression, "Was your father a windowpane maker?" implies: "Did he make you from glass?" Hence: "Do you think I can see through you?" instead of the direct "Why are you standing here and obstructing my view?" Halpern loved this form of *hypothetical* or *analogue situation* as a substitute for poetic metaphor.

All these modes of translogical discourse common in Yiddish communication have three major principles in common: (1) associative digression; (2) resorting to a canonized textual store; and (3) assuming that all frames of reference in the universe of discourse may be analogous to each other.

Yiddish has embraced all these forms of speech. Its folklore is fond of short units—rhymed proverbs, idioms, anecdotes, jokes, "stories," and tales of great people—embedded in longer discourse; they may be ready-made and quoted in conversation or made up ad hoc from material of personal experience or imagination. When Martin Buber excerpted such stories from Hasidic books and popularized the Hasidic world in the West, he lost the double-directed tension between the embedded story and its free-flowing, talkative, and moralizing framework; that is, he sacrificed the impurity of the text to the isolation of an "aesthetic" object, imitating Oriental rather than Jewish genres. In Yiddish storytelling—and in the

Hebrew form in which it was recorded—the tale was not an abstract vignette or parable of Oriental wisdom but a story situated in the messy Jewish reality and in the library of texts, all at the same time.

In sum, it is not the systematic essay but the concatenation of an associative chain that characterizes Yiddish discourse and its Hebrew sources. This mode of discourse was captured by James Joyce in the characterization of Bloom and is typical of Bellow's writing. (In both cases, this style is motivated by modern psychological theory.) In this mode, the small units of language and thematic motifs are not strung on one narrative string and made subordinate to the unfolding of plot or an architectonic structure, but are relatively independent and episodic; they can easily relate to their contextual neighbors in several directions and, more important, they are related to a total universe of discourse outside the particular context. That is, they become emblematic or symbolic. At the same time, such a unit clashes with and relates to its discontinuous neighbors, creating mutual reinforcement, semantic density, stylistic play, and irony in this tangle. Mendele and Sholem Aleichem understood and foregrounded this property of Jewish discourse; they used it as a major tool for characterization, for providing symbolic dimensions to any trivial incident related by their naïve characters, and, above all, for the composition of their quasi-"medieval" but actually protomodernist prose.

Poetry is a different matter. Modeling its language on Russian and European examples of "pure" symmetrical and monologue-oriented strophic verse, Yiddish poetry avoided, at first, this rambling, "unstructured," and "undisciplined" dialogue-oriented discourse. However, poets like Jacob Glatshteyn [Glatstein], whose work was closer to the "dramatic monologue" from the beginning, and Moyshe Leib Halpern in his later poetry, broke the symbolist poetic conventions of "conciseness" and symmetry and discovered the possibilities inherent in Yiddish communication, in what Glatshteyn called "the wise prosaic smile of Yiddish." They used Yiddish as an unusual tool of talk-verse, which may be as fresh, effective, and surprising as the language of metaphorical imagery in Western verse (though perhaps less familiar to its readers). Naturally, the reader has to imagine the character who does the talking, to reconstruct him from his speech, as in the fiction that the Russian Formalists called *skaz*. The talk and the inverse characterization of the talker create a double-directed semantic dependence, ironized further by the narrator or the poet standing above the text. Talk-verse is often a dramatic projection of the poet's voice, as in Glatshteyn's cycle of monologues by Rabbi Nahman of Bratslav. Moyshe Leib Halpern raised this art—almost to a parodic degree—in his long, aggressive, and politically charged monologue to himself (with his year-and-a-half-old listener), "This I Said to My Only Son at Play—and to Nobody Else" (*American Yiddish Poetry,* 490–505).

Associative talking—a national sport in Yiddish—is a long, exuberant, and rambling affair. To its participants, it is a joy, too. When Glatshteyn's Rabbi Nahman of Bratslav turns up in Heaven, losing all his words, he complains: "What will you do from now to eternity?/ No tales, no melodies./ Poor soul, you are naked./ You are a mute in heaven." Eventually, he awakens from his dream, is back on earth, and says: "May I be damned if I'd like/To sit on a heavenly rock./ Here, in the sinful world—/To talk and talk and talk" ("Hear and Be Stunned," *American Yiddish Poetry,* 293–97).

Precisely because it is devoid of clear-cut narrative structure or metaphorical density, the value of such associative talking lies in the many "asides" it can have. Anything may be linked with anything else. From every situation one can shift to another situation that does not explicitly relate to the problem at hand, but is rich in new experiential detail. In principle, every chain developed in a text may link it with the whole universe of discourse. Thus, every trivial anecdote may attain "metaphysical" dimensions. Indeed, the principle of universal analogy, derived from "Talmudic" thinking and domesticated in Yiddish, is typical of Freud's method, as well.

Two major devices puncture this discourse: the ironic interplay between the component-languages of Yiddish, employing its double nature of *fusion* and *openness* (as described above), and the abundant use of quotations, proverbs, and idioms. Both quotations and proverbs subsume the case at hand, the individual and concrete situation, under some general law or some distilled wisdom, using the authority of a holy text or of a folk convention. It was a highly codified society and it used codified situations and evaluative "bricks" of experience to describe the world. Anecdotes, quotations, and proverbs also provided a tactic of evasion: in a bind, or in a puzzling situation, instead of answering specifically, there was a readymade phrase or exemplary "story." Tevye the Milkman, that quoting animal, evades the direct response to any new event or question by referring to an existing "holy" text or proverb. He thus subsumes every experience under some universal "way of the world," turning any trivial detail into a "philosophical" issue about the order of the universe and God's reason.

Sholem Aleichem's "Tevye the Milkman"

Let us observe one complex example of such Yiddish speech as registered by Sholem Aleichem (1859–1916). His book, *Tevye the Milkman,*[7] is constituted as a series of monologues by the main character, who tells the narrator how his daughters left home for a tailor, a revolutionary, a Christian boyfriend, a rich man, and so on. The chapters represent the various solutions of centrifugal movement of Jews out of the *shtetl* world, which Tevye's beloved daughters implemented, breaking their father's heart in the process. As Victor Erlich has pointed out, these are monologues in a dialogue situation: though the listener, Sholem Aleichem himself, never speaks, Tevye fills his monologues with devices to catch his listener's attention or to counter his possible arguments: "How did we get to this point?"; "And as to what you say: children nowadays" (Sholem Aleichem, of course, did not say anything); "In short, let us leave alone—how do you say it in your books?—the prince, and deal for a while with the princess" (which actually has nothing to do with Sholem Aleichem's writing, in which there are no princes or princesses).

This monologue-in-a-dialogue situation has embedded within it a second level of dialogues. Events are not presented directly, but through Tevye's rambling, roundabout associative chains telling not about events proper but about other, similar dialogues in the past; often those embedded dialogues are themselves arguments about hypothetical situations in which the speaker imagines a happy outcome for an imminent event, and the dialogues ensuing from it, and then is surprised by an unhappy outcome, or vice versa. Sometimes there are even hypothetical arguments about such hypothetical situations. This is not just a literary structure of a frame story with embedded stories; rather, the embedding is intertwined in every sentence and phrase, often by constant interpolations of "says I," "says she," "says I." This double network of dialogues provides ample room for the internal narrator's (Tevye's) meditations, quotations, and metaphysical and metadiscourse remarks, and for the overall narrator's (Sholem Aleichem's) distancing and irony. Unfortunately, this double-layered mediation of talk gets lost in any dramatization of the book which presents the "events" themselves. What remains in that case is the sentimental internal story alone, as in the film *Fiddler on the Roof*, or in some translations that subdue the mediating dialogue and foreground the internal dialogue as a scenic presentation.

This ironic interplay and multidirectional prism breaks up the events and situations into small splinters reflected in talk and, reciprocally, reflects rather than describes them. At the same time, the book is a parody of a world based on talking and of a culture steeped in quotations and commentaries of texts rather than in facing realities. When a wave of pogroms sweeps Russia, Tevye refers to it with his typical historiosophical complacency: "when the time came *to talk* about pogroms" (emphasis added).

Let us take a specific example in its complex entanglement. The chapter "Tevye Goes to *Eretz* Israel" begins with the following associative chain. After years of not having seen him, Tevye meets the writer again, not in

Boyberik but on a train, is amazed to see him alive and, in turn, introduces himself: can Sholem Aleichem recognize him? —Tevye is dressed in a festive coat—how come? —He is going to the Holy Land. —Why such an ambition? —A long explanation follows. I shall use, as far as possible, a literal translation to convey a sense of the original:

> In short, I must tell you, first of all first-of-alls, that I was left, may it not happen to you, a widower, my Golda, may she rest in peace, died. A simple woman she was, with no tricks, no big headlines, but a great saintly woman, may she intercede there for her children, she suffered enough for them, and perhaps because of them she left this world, couldn't bear that they were all scattered, one to Lissy one to Strissy.

In the first sentence Tevye says, "I was left a widower" and explains, "my Golda died"; what follows are either explanations on the mode of the discourse ("I must tell you," "first of all first-of-alls") or evaluations ("may it not happen to you," "may she rest in peace"). The second sentence is a mere unfolding of the last formula, with Tevye saying good words about the deceased in a traditional manner (that the deceased was a modest person), then superseding his statement with its opposite ("but"), then using the new quality of saintliness to ask her to intercede in heaven for her children (still a formulaic move), then explaining the opposite (that she suffered plenty for them), and thus shifting back to reality and de-automatizing the formulaic style. A statement in five words, "I was left a widower," has thus acquired a chain of embellishments in the irrational folk manner of talking but in the process has introduced a whole tangle of essential motifs.

Thus, in one paragraph, we come from the meeting in a train, to a voyage to the Holy Land, to Golda's death, to her simple and good nature, to a conversational formula used for the deceased (a plea for her intercession for her children), to an aside de-automatizing this formula ("she suffered enough for them"), to her children having left home, to Golda's complaint that her life makes no sense without the children. In response to this, Tevye argues with her in his usual way, quoting some pseudo-holy phrase, thus raising the personal issue to a matter of the order of the universe, and then explains it in his own words. The two levels of dialogue—present and past—which intersect with each other are foregrounded by the frequent use of "says I" in one breathless chain:

> "Eh, I says to her, Golde dear, there is a verse, says I, *if as sons or as servants*—as it goes with children, so it goes without children, I say. We have, says I, a great God, says I, and a good God, and a strong God, says I, and nevertheless, says I, may I have the number of blessings as the number of times The-Master-of-the-Universe, says I, comes up with a piece of work

that better, says I, that all my enemies should have such a year" . . . But she, may she forgive me, is a female, so she says: "You're sinning, Tevye. You must not, says she, sin." "Look at this new thing, says I, did I say something, says I, bad? Would I, says I, go, God forbid, against the ways of the Lord, says I? Because if, says I, He already, says I, created such a beautiful world, says I, that the children are not children, says I, and father-mother are mud, says I, so He probably knows what He has to do." But she does not understand what I say and answers me out of the blue: "I'm dying, says she, Tevye, who will cook your supper?"

As usual, Tevye leaps from the concrete issue of their own children's dispersion to a general "philosophical" statement about children (a poor excuse, though an escape into language), and from "philosophy" to "theology," ruminating about God, who thus arranges His world. The sentence about God, broken up after every few words by the second level of dialogue ("says I"), begins with formulaic blessings ("we have . . . a great God . . . and a good God, and a strong God") and breaks it to their opposite, using the slang and curses of artisans. Golda climbs one level higher, to a metadiscourse about the permissibility of referring to God in such a manner. Tevye retells it in the present with a further level of metadiscourse, explaining that her talk is that of a woman and, on an additional level, asking forgiveness for even using the expression "female" in conjunction with male talk ("but she, may she forgive me, is a female"). But, Tevye adds, in the dialogue in the past, she understood nothing and, "out of the blue" (in Yiddish: "out of the attic"), she inserted such a mundane matter as her death. Indeed, true to her feminine role, she brings down the discourse from textual citations and "theology" to concrete detail: "Who will cook your supper?" The super-narrator, Sholem Aleichem, thus inverts the relationship between who is and who is not sticking to the point and, at the same time, through a subtle shift, brings us back from several levels of deviations and metadiscourse to the real issue: Golda's death.

The whole chain of associations is accompanied by several levels of metalingual remarks and evaluative interjections accompanying almost every expression ("may I have the number of blessings as the number of times"; "better, says I, that all my enemies should have such a year"; and so forth). Thus, an incident is presented not through a realistic description but through talk about talk about it, in the course of which the incident itself and the ways of talking are linked to the metaphysical questions of human existence which preoccupy our hero and are conveyed in the manner of Yiddish folklore with quotes, generalizations, blessings, and proverbs—all de-automatized—and with metadiscourse about the ways of talking about such things.

This concatenation may be represented in the following simplified diagram. In the left column, we climb with Tevye, in an associative chain, until the woman interrupts his chatter; in the right column, he goes down the same steps, this time in brief clauses, until we reach the crucial event.

What does a woman understand	[What does Tevye understand]
The woman protests	Tevye denies
Tevye criticizes God	Tevye praises God
Tevye praises God	Tevye criticizes God
God's order in the world	God's order in the world
The children have left	Children have left
His wife has died	Golda is dying
Tevye travels to *Eretz* Israel	
Tevye in a Sabbath coat	

The associative chain is Tevye's irrational mode of discourse. The author himself creates a carefully controlled text in which every element and every order of elements is functional. The second half of this chain mirrors the first half precisely. (As to the unfulfilled symmetry of our diagram, concerning Tevye's travel to the Holy Land, the rest of Sholem Aleichem's chapter will be devoted to explaining that.)

The associative chain of Tevye's rambling chatter thus enables Sholem Aleichem to introduce a whole *kaleidoscope* (to use a key term of the Introspectivist poets) of central motifs omnipresent in the book and his hero's consciousness. Tevye's *kaleidoscopic* visions result from the Yiddish folk ethos in which all things are linked with all things in one, transhistoric destiny, prefigured in the Holy Scriptures, and are compositionally motivated by his "Jewish" way of talking. All these—the kaleidoscope, the folk ethos, and the associative composition—are ironized at the same time.

Questions

A whole array of semiotic moves may be said to characterize "typical" Jewish behavior, though none is exclusive to the Jews. Let us examine one such "Jewish" mode, namely, starting and advancing a conversation by asking a question and answering with a counter-question.

One reason for asking questions is the need to make contact with strangers on the road, to get acquainted quickly—acclimatized, as it were—to look for allies or for business possibilities. Sholem Aleichem, who was a master at catching and distilling the essence of Yiddish talk, imitated a train conversation between strangers:

"It looks like you're traveling to Kolomea?"
"How do you know I'm going to Kolomea?"
"I heard you talking to the conductor. Are you really from Kolomea or only traveling to Kolomea?"
"Really from Kolomea. Why do you ask?"
"Nothing. Just asking. A nice city, Kolomea?"
"What do you mean, a nice city? A city like all cities in Galicia. A pretty town, a very pretty town!"
"I mean, are there any nice people, rich ones?" [etc., etc.]
—from "It's a Lie: a Dialogue in Galicia"

The proverbial riddle asks "Why does a Jew answer a question with a question?" And the answer, appropriately, is "Why not?" In reality, however, the answer is even less straightforward: "Why do you ask?" or "Who says he does?" or "Who answered you with a question?" or "Wasn't I the first one to ask?"

Questions have a variety of purposes: to understand the world; to search out information; to avoid revealing too much by passing the ball of affirmative description to the interlocutor; to know one's interlocutor as quickly as possible; to question his motivations for asking that particular thing; to question his general assumptions; to question his assumptions about one's own motivations; beyond that, to inquire about other possible alternatives to the given situation; to question the nature of the words used—that is, to leap from object-language to metalanguage; and even further, to question the reasons and forms of using them—that is, to shift to metadiscourse.

One other obvious source for such a mode of conversation is the Talmudic argument. The structure of the Talmud is not that of an essay or a systematic treatise but a juxtaposition of oral arguments, pro and con, concerning sentences from the Mishnah. The text advances by raising all possible questions and solutions to a problem or interpretation of a legal sentence, calling up quotations from the Bible, reinterpreting those, and arguing out the alternatives. In the learning process, too, the same questioning method is used for the Talmudic text itself, by evoking later writings as well as the holy texts and the student's own ingenuity. Asking questions and questioning the answers is encouraged. The Talmudic term *kushiya* (or *kashe*, frequently used in Yiddish) means a "question" (such as the "four questions" a child asks at the Passover Seder) but, more profoundly, it means "a difficulty in an argument," "a contradiction." A modern Hebrew dictionary defines it as "a difficult question, a contradiction, an objection to an opinion or to a law with the purpose of proving that they are wrong."[8] That is, asking a question is equivalent to questioning, raising a difficult or problematic point in an argument. Indeed, the expression *shtelt zikh a kashe* (literally: "[if so,] a question poses itself"; that is, "that raises a question" or "One may ask, why . . .") followed by a question is a conventional opening for an explanation, in talmudic learning as in Yiddish discourse.

Asking questions, raising alternative possibilities to a situation, or questioning the interlocutor's assumptions that such an alternative was contemplated, was a usual mode of Jewish conversation from early childhood. The very first word in the first sentence of the Bible that a child learned, *Bereyshis*, "In-the-beginning (God created the heaven and the earth)," is accompanied by Rashi's commentary challenging God's structure of the text: "He should not have started the Torah other than with 'this month is for you,' which is the first good deed that the Israelites were ordered to do; then what is the reason that He started with 'In-the-beginning'?" As if to begin with "in-the-beginning" was neither logical nor natural!

Via Yiddish, this mode traveled to Jewish behavior in other languages. It is enough to leaf through Henry Roth's *Call It Sleep* (1935), describing a Jewish childhood in New York, to see the hundreds of question marks that cover the text. They serve both the child's curiosity about the world and his mother's "positive" guidance. They also underline the clash between the immigrant mother and the American child. For example:

> "You don't seem to be hungry?" she inquired. "You've hardly touched the oatmeal. Would you like more milk?"
> "No. I'm not hungry."
> "An egg?"
> He shook his head.
> "I shouldn't have kept you up so late. You look weary. Do you remember the strange dream you had last night?"
> "Yes."
> "How did such a strange dream come to you?" she mused.[9]

Here, even the affirmative sentences imply questions about possible alternatives: "I shouldn't have kept you up so late."

In comparison, in Joyce's "Eveline," when a Dublin girl is about to leave her home and is pondering, "Was that wise? She tried to weigh each side of the question," there are no question marks in the text, just the evocation of situations to be judged by the reader himself.[10]

Whether the source lies in religious learning, in the precarious Jewish existence—the question marks it raises, or the need for evasive behavior—

in the relativism of a marginal group, in the skepticism of a people exposed to bitter experiences throughout the ages, in foreign influences, or in some combination of all of these, a set of attitudes has crystallized and become typically "Jewish," incorporated into typical Yiddish speech. It seems that these attitudes, transferred to secular situations and to other languages, became the basis for what could be seen either negatively as the Jewish "inquisitive" or "argumentative" behavior, or positively as a questioning, "scientific" attitude, challenging any authority.

An example of the latter kind can be found in the story about Nobel Prize-winning physicist Isador Rabi: when he returned from school as a small child, his mother would ask him: "Did you ask any good questions in school today?" This is not just encouragement to learn actively and successfully, but a question that prods the child to ask questions.

The negative side of this discourse pattern in the eyes of European behavioral norms was observed in Jewish literature itself. Mendele Mokher Seforim (1835–1917) introduces himself, the persona of the narrator, at the opening of his novel *Dos kleyne mentshele* (*The Little Man*):

> What's your name? The first question one Jew asks another, a total stranger, whenever he meets him and stretches out his hand to greet him. It would never occur to anyone that you could respond, for example: "What's it your business, buddy, what my name is? Are we going to marry off our children? My name is the one they gave me and leave me alone." On the contrary, the question, "What's your name?" is quite natural. It lies in the nature of things, just like feeling a guy's new coat and asking how much a yard; like asking for a cigarette when a guy opens his tobacco pouch; like sticking your fingers in somebody's snuffbox and helping yourself to a pinch of snuff; like poking your finger into a guy's tub, dipping a greasy handkerchief in it and rubbing your body; like walking up to two people talking to each other, cocking your ear and listening to their conversation; or like throwing a question at someone out of the blue about his business and jumping on him with advice though he doesn't need it at all and can get along without it. Things of that kind and similar things are quite usual. This is the way the world has been since time immemorial and raising your voice against it would just sound strange, wild and crazy, an unnatural act. Not only in this world but even over there, in the next world, Jews believe that, as soon as you set foot in it, the greeting angel's first question is, "What's your name, buddy?" The angel that wrestled with our father Jacob, even he didn't change the order of the world, asked him right away what's your name. Not to mention a man of flesh and blood. I know very well that as soon as I enter Yiddish literature with my stories, the first question of the crowd will be, "What's your name, uncle?"
> My name is *Mendele*! [. . .]
> But I can't get away with this. After the first question, Jews really start pouring all sorts of question on you, like: Where does a Jew come from?

Does he have a wife? Does he have children? What is he selling? And where is he going? And more and more such questions, as it is the custom in all the Diaspora of the Jews to ask if you want to appear in public as an experienced man and not a benchwarmer and that it is only human to answer just like you answer "A good year!" to a greeting of "Good Shabbos!" or "Happy Holiday!" I don't want to quarrel with the whole world and I'm ready to answer these questions, too, as short and as fast as possible.

I myself was born in Tsvyatshitsh, a small town in the region of Teterivke . . . .

Mendele understands that this is as ingrained a mode of communication among Jews as saying "Good Shabbos!" Franz Kafka, in his "Letter to His Father," imitated this mode of pushing by asking:

An admonition from you generally took this form: "Can't you do it in such-and-such a way? That's too hard for you, I suppose. You haven't the time, of course?" and so on. And each such question would be accompanied by malicious laughter and a malicious face.

But Kafka's own writings are filled with the protagonist questioning every move he makes, usually after the fact. And in "Investigations of a Dog," which is but a veiled allegory on the Jewish condition, he brings questioning itself into the center of his investigation and into the center of Dog's existence. And he does it, again, very often through questions. As the typical Yiddish speaker, he asks questions about asking questions and shifts the questioning to the central existential problem: Who am I? Who are we? What is the meaning of our asking questions? Here are a few excerpts from the story:

And all really because of my questions, my impatience, my thirst for knowledge (289).

. . . but you are yourself a dog, you have also the dog knowledge; well, bring it out, not merely in the form of a question, but as an answer. If you utter it, who will think of opposing you (290)?

To be precise, is it in the hope that they might answer me that I have questioned my fellow dogs, at least since my adult years? Have I any such foolish hope? Can I contemplate the foundations of our existence, divine their profundity, watch the labor of their construction, that dark labor, and expect all this to be forsaken, neglected, undone, simply because I ask a question (291)?

Every dog has like me the impulse to question, and I have like every dog the impulse not to answer. Everyone has the impulse to question. How otherwise could my questions have affected my hearers in the slightest— and they were often affected, to my ecstatic delight, an exaggerated delight, I must confess—and how otherwise could I have been prevented from achieving much more than I have done (293)?

Moreover, who but is eager to ask questions when he is young, and how, when so many questions are going about, are you to pick out the right questions? One question sounds like another; it is the intention that counts, but that is often hidden even from the questioner. And besides, it is a peculiarity of dogs to be always asking questions, they ask them confusedly all together; it is as if in doing that they were trying to obliterate every trace of the genuine questions (297).[11]

This penchant for questioning was recognized in psychoanalytic circles, as well. Peter Gay quotes Isidor Sadger's talk at the Wednesday Psychological Society in Vienna in 1907:

> . . . the disposition of Jews to obsessive neuroses is perhaps connected with the addiction to brooding—*Gruebelsucht*—characteristic of them for thousands of years.
>
> —Peter Gay, *A Godless Jew*[12]

It seems to me that *Gruebelsucht* here, as pronounced by a Galician Jew, is used not in its German dictionary sense ("brooding") but in its Yiddish meaning, where *zikh griblen* is almost a technical term for "talmudic inquisitiveness," the exaggerated tendency to delve deeply, dig and upturn any piece of ground, uncover hidden motivations and alternatives.

To be sure, questioning is merely one of a whole array of semiotic attitudes internalized in Yiddish discourse and in the behavioral patterns of Jews from both the tradition of learning and the predicament and mythology of their historical existence.

Notes

1. Saul Bellow, *Him with His Foot in His Mouth and Other Stories* (New York: Harper and Row, 1985), 16.
2. Saul Bellow, *Herzog* (New York: Viking, 1961). Though the text refers explicitly to Herzog's notes rather than to language, there is the implicit metonymical connection to the language of his "long-dead" mother (again, a metonymy to mothertongue).
3. A new translation by Hillel Halkin, entitled *Tevye the Dairyman,* was published by Schocken (New York, 1987).
4. Roman Jakobson and Peter Bogatyrev, "Folklore and Literature," in *Readings in Russian Poetics,* ed. L. Matejka and K. Pmorska (Cambridge, Mass.: MIT Press, 1971), 91–93.
5. This may be used in continuation to (and may have been transformed from) such expressions as *Kh'vel dir makhn oys-tsu-drey-yen; kh'vel dir oysdreyen di kishkes!* meaning "I shall twist you [like a wet floor-mop], I shall wring your guts."
6. This was richly described in James A. Matissof's *Blessings, Curses, Hopes and Fears: Psycho-Ostensive Expressions in Yiddish* (Philadelphia: ISHI, 1979).
7. See my Hebrew paper, "Deconstruction of Speech: Sholem Aleichem and the Semiotics of Jewish Folklore," in *Tevye the Milkman and Other Monologues* [Hebrew], by Sholem Aleichem (Tel Aviv, 1983).

8. A. Even-Shoshan, *Ha-Milon he-Hadash* (Jerusalem: Kiryat Sefer, 1988) [editor's note].

9. Henry Roth, *Call It Sleep* (New York: Farrar, Straus and Giroux, 1991), 57.

10. Asking questions is hardly a universal value, as can be seen, for example, from the works of Mr. Betteredge in Wilkie Collins's novel, *The Moonstone*: "'How do you come to know about the jugglers, sir?' I asked, putting one question on top of another, which was bad manners, I own. But you don't expect much from poor human nature—so don't expect much from me." (New York: Penguin, 1966), 61.

11. Franz Kafka, *The Basic Kafka*, Erich Heller, ed. (New York: Pocket Books, 1984).

12. Peter Gay, *A Godless Jew* (New Haven, Conn.: Yale University Press, 1987), 135.

IV.
Individual Voices, A Common Tradition?
Four Case Studies

GERSHON SHAKED

Shadows of Identity:
A Comparative Study of
German Jewish and American Jewish
Literature

I

What is Jewish literature in non-Jewish languages? Is it any literature written by Europeans, Americans, or other nationals who happen to be of Jewish origin? Until what generation? Shall we define these writers according to Jewish law, or the racial laws of various nations, or is the genetic definition valueless and meaningless? Can a person of any religious or ethnic origin whatsoever be categorized according to the language of his literary loyalty?

Another approach to the questions is to define Jewish thematics and then ascertain whether, and to what degree, these themes are manifest or implied by the works under discussion. Accordingly, those who best represent these themes are Jewish writers, and those whose works are most distant from it must live, die, and be buried outside the walls.

Yet another alternative, a semiotic definition, is rather easy to adduce, claiming that Jewish literature is any literature in which a portion of the existential rites to which it refers are connected to forms of behavior derived from the Jewish social group.

I would argue that these definitions and their refutations are of little practical import, for the answer lies in an empirical realm: Jewish literature in non-Jewish languages is, most fundamentally, that written by individuals who define themselves as having a dual identity. They write for publications that have dual identities; and their work employs subjects and forms that respond to the national and the Jewish needs of their addressees in all the areas mentioned above: origins, thematics, and semiotics. A sampling of those binational publications that embody the contrast between (non-Jewish) linguistic identity and (Jewish) social identity reveals the implicit self-consciousness of both the contributors and their audiences.[1]

The German Jewish periodical *Sulamith*, published in German between 1806 and 1833, was the heir, as it were, of the Hebrew journal *Ha-meassef* (1783–1811) and a contemporary of *Bikurei ha-itim* (1821–31). After *Sulamith*, many other German Jewish periodicals appeared, from the *Allgemeine Zeitung des Judentums* (1837–88) to the Zionist *Der Jude* (1916–24), edited by Martin Buber. Alongside the vast number of Hebrew and Yiddish periodicals in Russia, there were Jewish Russian-language publications, such as *Razsvet* (1860–61) and the *Voskhod* (1881–1906).

In the United States, Jewish magazines were published in English from the mid-nineteenth century. The *Asmonean* first appeared in New York in 1849, and *The Hebrew Leader* lasted from 1856 to 1882. Since then a large number of American Jewish magazines have been published, the best known of them being *Commentary* and *Midstream*. Today, these periodicals are of course far better known and more widely distributed than Hebrew magazines in America, such as *Hadoar* and *Bitzaron* (which have led a precarious existence since their establishment) and than Yiddish newspapers, of which the *Jewish Daily Forward* (1897–) is the only one still in existence.[2]

What emerges from even this superficial survey is that a culture with a dual identity is not simply a theoretical creation of historians of literature[3] but, rather, an empirical entity. Its literature is a highly complex embodiment of both identities.

II

Critics have long recognized the existence of a dual-identity literature created by Jews who wrote in German. As early as 1922, Gustav Krojanker published a collection of articles in which Jewish literary critics discuss such writers as Franz Werfel, Franz Kafka, Albert Ehrenstein, Jakob Wassermann, Otto Weininger, Martin Buber, Else Lasker-Schueler, Peter Altenberg, Arnold Zweig, Arthur Schnitzler, Carl Sternheim, Max Brod, and others.[4] Since then many others have written about this body of literature. Harry Zohn, for example, has researched the Viennese writers,[5] and Hans Tramer has dealt with selected poets.[6]

In the United States, a number of Jews—American by birth or choice—have tried to define Jewish literature for themselves. Some have tried to free themselves from the stigma of dual identity; others have approached the problem sarcastically and critically;[7] yet others have provided us with literary meditations. The efforts at definition are often provocative, and the examples of Ludwig Lewisohn, Max Schulz, and Cynthia Ozick indicate the dimensions of the problem.

Lewisohn, one of the founders of American Jewish literature, answers the question head on: A Jewish book is one written by someone who is well aware that he or she is Jewish.[8] Jewish literature, therefore, consists of all the works—written in every age and language—whose creators knew they were Jewish. To paraphrase the sixteenth-century English poet Sir Philip Sidney: They looked in their hearts and wrote. Taking a different approach, Schulz writes of the Jewish imagination that it "has been stirred by the aesthetic possibilities of a radical sophistication, which simultaneously entertains contrary intellectual systems: the secular view of man alienated in an absurd universe and the religious view of man enthroned by divine fiat in God's earthly kingdom."[9] Whether or not this definition fits the Jewish paradox and correctly characterizes American Jewish literature, Schulz's remarks certainly indicate the concern of writers and scholars with the nature and function of that literature.

Ozick, our third example, takes an original approach to this issue.[10] She seeks to justify both the author's identity and that of other American Jews in the golden exile. Again, although a number of the arguments are questionable, they are indisputable evidence of a deep need to come to grips with the realities of a dual identity. "Gentile readers," Ozick writes, "may or may not be surprised at this self-portrait of a third-generation American Jew (though the first to have been native-born) perfectly at home and yet perfectly insecure, perfectly acculturated and yet perfectly marginal."[11]

Ozick argues that American Jewry, a latter-day Yavneh, will create a new exilic Jewish culture that is the heir of the rabbis of the Talmud and of the authors of the Golden Age of Spain. It will do so because the aesthetics of the Jewish novel is different from the aesthetics of many contemporary American novels: Whereas the latter worships the idols of art, the former, as always, "passionately wallows in human reality."[12] Taking her argument yet further, she contends that only those who wrote as Jews are remembered as Jews by Jews. Those who attempted to be universalistic are quickly forgotten. "The fact is that nothing thought or written in the Diaspora has ever been able to last unless it has been centrally Jewish. If it is centrally Jewish it will last for Jews."[13] To ensure its survival, then, American Jewry must create a culture and language of its own (English as a New Yiddish), a sort of new Yavneh, with imaginative literature assuming the role once played by Talmud. Ozick concludes with the challenge: "From being envious apes we can become masters of our own civilization—and let those who want to call this 're-ghettoization,' or similar pejoratives, look to their own destiny."[14]

Ozick's hope for a "new Yavneh," however, seems to be more wishful thinking than reality. I am not persuaded by her basic assumption that Jewish literature "passionately wallows in human reality" whereas non-Jewish literature is coldly aesthetic. Surely, it is belied by exceptions: the Gentile whose work is "Jewish" in spirit, and the converse. Nevertheless, a convincing message does emerge from her essay. By making "feeling" into a doctrine, she turns a shortcoming into an advantage, an indefinable situation into a defined one. Many of the Jewish writers in Germany and America (the two non-Jewish cultures with which I am most familiar) have grappled with that experience. Indeed, one may say of their work that the issue of identity itself is its most important characteristic.

III

Although this essay deals with the problem of identity in Jewish literature written in non-Jewish languages, the same problem challenged Hebrew and Yiddish writers as well. It is appropriate, then, to bring into our analysis the very intense and pointed words of M.Y. Berdyczewski's Hebrew story "The Stranger" (1908):

> He left his people! What did he leave? Shattered bodies, shadows, just shadows. What do you see in the Jews except shadows? But those shadows dwell in his spirit, in his essence, and in everything within him. They say, "The seed of Abraham has passed away," but they have not passed away. The individual is finished, but they are stronger than the individual. You and your thoughts will wither away in inactivity, and they will not die out. They will mock and deride you.[15]

There is a pervasive sense that the protagonist wishes to rid himself of his Jewish heritage but understands very well that he is pursued by it. Thus, the powerful, irrational powers of the shadows within overcome the rational forces of light in the souls of his characters.

For all that this formulation expresses the consciousness of the authors and the heroes in Hebrew literature, and often in Yiddish literature, as well as in the literature of Jews writing in other languages—the actual existential situation of the authors was in fact different. Those writing in a Jewish language *identified* with the shadow powers. The language itself spread over them like a shadow, providing refuge from one Jewish culture but at the same time offering itself as a substitute. Those who wrote in Hebrew (and to some extent in Yiddish) *chose* their identity. They may have struggled against it, criticized it, and resented it, but they did so from within. They expanded and deepened it with every expression of love, envy, and hatred.

That is not the case with writers who chose another language. Although a writer may have opted for the path of "spirit and light" (to use Bialik's phrase), the shadow is always a present, if latent, antagonist. We may ask: What character did that struggle between the shadow and (what appears to be) the linguistic "powers of light" assume? In what ways was the struggle modified when it passed from the hostile cultural environment of Germany to the welcoming pluralistic cultural environment of America?

IV

In addressing these questions, I shall begin with an author who occupied an intermediary place between linguistic cultures and ideological positions: Ludwig Lewisohn (1882–1955). Born in Berlin, he immigrated to the United States with his parents in 1890. After a rather thorough assimilation, Lewisohn returned to Judaism (in the national sense), so much so that in the 1920s he became an avowed Zionist.

The Island Within, first published in 1928, is a kind of novel of repentance, in which an assimilated Jew (Arthur) has a relationship with a Gentile woman (and with the world she represents) but ultimately returns to his Jewish roots. This book by a Jew from Germany, written in English in the United States, is quite typical of much of German Jewish fiction as well as of some American Jewish fiction. In these works the problem of identity (for both the characters and their creators) derives mainly from the struggle against an outside world that is unwilling to accept the Jews as completely German or completely American. One copes in one of two ways: by bearing Jewish identity as a tragic destiny or by turning this disadvantage into an advantage.

Jewish literature in Germany sought to accommodate itself to the tension between a minority with a dual identity and a majority with a single one. The majority stigmatizes the minority. Worse, in general, the minority internalizes that stigma by frequently accepting those assumptions— believing that it lives in the foreign, alienating environment by sufferance, not by right.[16] That internalization frequently took on pathological proportions, as in the case of Otto Weininger, whose theoretical work *Sex and Character* (1903) presented the most extreme expression of the existential condition of persecution: someone pursued from all sides who has internalized the rationale of the pursuers and thereby justified his own fate as the victim.[17] That condition often influences the literary form of the works. Many, for example, are similar in plot to *The Island Within*, in which the protagonist confronts his identity after encountering barriers to erotic (or other) self-realization in the foreign world that both attracts him with its charms and repels him with its hatred. In many of the writers of that generation (1900–40), the problem of identity was repressed, only to reappear in metamorphosed guise.

From a literary standpoint, the weaker examples tend to be those offering an overt treatment of the problem of Jewish identity, with manifest use of Jewish, generally Eastern European, semiotics. This category would include not only Lewisohn's novel but also Max Brod's *Reubeni, Furst der Juden* (*Reubeni, Prince of the Jews*, 1925), which depicts a Jew's path from assimilation to Zionism. This rather trivial work recounts the life of David Lemel of Prague who, assisted by an assimilated Jew named Hirschel, rebels against his father, falls in love with a Gentile woman, and runs away with her. After she leaves him, he returns, repentant, to his people, as David Reubeni, a "false" messiah—"false" in the eyes of the people, who are unable to recognize the truths he imparts.[18] The message is unambiguous: The Jews must become a nation like all others by returning to their ancient homeland; but they refuse to be redeemed. Much of the book is a conventional piece of German Jewish literature, the erotic attractions of the alien world providing the ideological justification for the abandonment of family, tribe, and religion and Lemel-Reubeni's rejection by the alien world ultimately leading him to repent. Brod distinguishes himself from most of his contemporaries in his presentation of a messianic Zionist ideology that seeks to liberate the Jews from dependence on that alien world.

Such a simplistic and rather overt approach to the topic of identity also characterizes the "Jewish" works of Arthur Schnitzler, *Professor Bernhardi* (1912) and *Der Weg ins Freie* (1908). The former is an apologetic play about a Jew who seeks to defend himself against intolerance, prejudice, and the irrational hatred of the anti-Semites (a kind of response to a small-scale blood libel); the latter is a novel about two Jews, one assimilated Jew who struggles with the problem of identity and another who seeks a Zionist solution to an otherwise hopeless problem. Such rather simplistic ideological works fail to penetrate the problem of existence very deeply.

V

Much more significant are the works of writers who tackle the problem of identity on a subtler, implicit level. It is, moreover, often the case that such writers display a gap between their direct expressions of Jewish consciousness in journals, essays, and letters and the absence of such explicit expressions in their fiction. We find implicit and profound depiction of the problem in the works of three very different German Jewish writers: Joseph Roth, Franz Kafka, and Jakob Wassermann.

Roth was born into an Eastern European family.[19] But, after leaving his hometown, he assimilated to such a degree that he fabricated a fictional identity for himself as the son of an Austrian officer with whom his mother had had an illicit romance. In the late 1920s, he became a Hapsburg monarchist, idealizing the empire as the model of an international, pluralistic paradise in which Jews, too, could find a safe haven, unencumbered by their identity. Roth lavished praise on his subjective utopia (which, of course, had never existed) both in his imaginative works, such as *Die Buste des Kaisers* (1935)[20] and in his essays and travel writing, *Juden auf Wanderschaft* (1927), in which he describes various centers of Jewish life. There he comments on the situation of the Jews:

> They have no fatherland, the Jews, but every country where they dwell and pay taxes demands patriotism and a heroic death from them and reproaches them for not being pleased to die. In that situation Zionism is really the only way out: as long as there must be patriotism, it might as well be for one's own country.[21]

But one must not conclude on the basis of that passage that Roth was a Zionist. He was not. Indeed, he was, to my knowledge, the first to compare Zionism with Nazism—that in 1935 in a letter to Stefan Zweig.[22] He rejected all nationalism as narrow and believed in deracinated supranationalism, universalistic and free from all national obligations. He tried to give a political dimension to "positive deracination"—an idealized incarnation of the defunct Habsburg empire.

That issue concerned Roth throughout his life. But his works are less an expression of the *joy* of the universalist existential situation than they are, if one may say so, the dreadful misery of one resigned to it. His novella *Die Flucht ohne Ende* (1927) gives voice to this sentiment. Tunda, a half-Jew, fights in World War I and, following his imprisonment by the Russians, wanders across various landscapes and ideologies. He leaves his cosseted, bourgeois Viennese home (and his conventional fiancée) to travel through Soviet Russia (with his Communist mistress), to postwar bourgeois Germany, and from there on to cosmopolitan Paris. The deracinated hero, it seems, is at home everywhere and nowhere, always marginal, exceptional, and expelled. Wherever he finds himself, the pattern repeats itself, and so the novel finishes with the following description:

> It was 27 August 1926, 4:00 P.M.: The shops were full, in the department stores women shoved, in high fashion boutiques models spun about, in the patisseries idlers chattered, in the factories wheels whirled, on the banks of the Seine beggars picked at their lice, in the Bois de Boulogne couples kissed each other, in the parks children rode on the carousel. It was at this hour. There stood my friend Tunda, thirty-two years old, healthy and chipper, a strong young man with all sorts of talents, in the Place de la Madeleine, in the middle of the capital of the world, and he

didn't know what to do. He had no profession, no love, no desire, no hope, no ambition, and not even any egotism. No one on earth was more superfluous than he.[23]

This marvelous description emphasizes the impossibility of living in the abstract: without place, without time, without defined identity. The primary, unconscious, psychological processes of fiction, in other words, admit what the lips otherwise never dare to utter—that the universal, pluralistic ideal is empty, that living without a shadow exacts a dreadful price. The flight from identity leads into a cul-de-sac of dismal despair.

Kafka imbued the problem with metaphysical and metapsychological significance. It is not by chance that although his protagonists have appellations similar to that of their creator (K. or Joseph K., for example), most of them lack an identity. Letters stand for humans, who are mere ciphers symbolizing universal, utterly deracinated man. Born into emptiness, they occupy neither historic time nor geographic space. (Only *Amerika*, of all the novels, is still populated with characters from the Austro-Hungarian empire.) Kafka's works are the most complex internalization in "foreign-language" Jewish fiction of the feelings experienced by characters whose identity is determined by persecution and ambiguity: accused of a sin they did not commit and yet justifying the verdict (*The Trial*); expelled from their society, which does not recognize their identity (*The Castle*). As marginal subtenants, they are exposed to false accusations.

Kafka's protagonists are not pursued by external forces or accused by courts that hold real jurisdiction. Rather, they embody the psychological and existential dimension of their social predicament. The universal Jew—persecuted and having no identity or place in space and time—typifies the modern "human condition"; the Jewish plot, in other words, is actually a universal human metaplot.

Our final example in German is the work of Jakob Wassermann. His *Die Juden von Zirndorf* (1897) is a *Bildungsroman* like many Hebrew novels of the *Haskalah* (Jewish Enlightenment) period, such as Brod's *Reubeni*. The metamorphoses of the topic of identity, persecution, and guilt are given splendid expression in *Der Fall Maurizius* (1928), which actually does not treat a specifically Jewish topic. Like Roth and Kafka, however, Wassermann frequently dealt with the tension between his Jewishness and his Germanness in his journalistic and documentary writing, and like them he preferred the authentic Jew, whom he called "Oriental" (referring to Eastern Europe), to the assimilated Jew.

It should come as no surprise that these three assimilated Jews, who were ashamed of their identity or viewed their dual identity as tragic, admired those Jews who, rather than concealing their identity, exhibited it conspicuously. Wassermann relates to them in terms taken from the lexicon of German romantic nationalism as "a noble consciousness, a blood consciousness" that "lives with the matriarchs."[24] They, it seems, are the true *nation*. Those authentic Jews are to be admired because they are almost "non-Jewish" in that they have a nationality—in total contrast to the Wassermanns, Kafkas, and Roths, who have none. In fact, Wassermann vehemently rejects German Jews such as himself. He vacillates between these two identities, most poignantly expressed in his work *My Life as German and Jew* (1921), a kind of dismal monologue by a jilted lover who blames his rejection upon his identity: "You may try in vain to die and live for them [the Germans]; they will always say, 'He's a Jew.'"

This, in essence, is Wassermann's predicament: All his life he tried to be completely German and failed abjectly. Like Roth's Tunda, he stands at a spiritual crossroads, with no idea which way to turn. Toward the end of his life Wassermann had planned a novel to be called *Ahasuer*—its protagonist, the wandering Jew.[25] And in *Der Fall Maurizius* he had taken up that theme. Waremme-Warschauer, one of the central characters, is reminiscent of Judas Iscariot and Ahasuerus. By his perjurious testimony he brings about the unjust condemnation of his friend Maurizius and from that time is doomed to wander throughout Europe and the United States, like Ahasuerus. Waremme-Warschauer tries to hide his past by pretending to be a German nationalist. But by the end of his life, he acknowledges that the attempt to mask his identity had failed. With the destruction of all his Germanic illusions and hopes, only his miserable Jewish identity remains. He wishes to convert his handicap into an advantage and travel to Eastern Europe, to his daughter and the Hasidim, as a positive response that emphasizes one-half of his dual identity.

It can be said of all the writers considered here that the attempt to return to Jewish identity provided a spark of hope, although none of them realized that hope on either the fictional or biographical level. Roth opened various gates to repentance for his Eastern European protagonists. In *Job* (1930), the main character immigrates to America. He despairs after the death of his wife and children but finally emerges into a new life. Roth's novella *Der Leviathan* (1940) tells the story of Nissen Piczenik, a coral merchant who sinned by selling artificial corals. He repents by plunging into the sea to seek the Leviathan, the father of all corals; and there, in the ocean, he finds his own death. At the end of his own life in Paris, Roth formed deep bonds of friendship with a rabbinical scholar, Joseph Gottfarstein, and in attendance at his funeral was a grotesque mélange of characters: a rabbinical scholar, a rabbi, a Catholic priest, and a deputation of the Habsburg royalist party.[26]

In Kafka's work one finds, in my opinion, no optimistic Jewish message at all. That was not so in his life, for throughout it he sought to form a bond with the Jewish world. He studied Hebrew, he was in sympathy with Zionism, he contemplated a visit to Palestine, and at the end of his life a Jewish woman, a Zionist named Dora Diamant, cared for him.

Wassermann, of the three, was the most personally ambivalent, although he remained a member of the Jewish community of Gratz until his death.[27] In his later years he became extremely sensitive to the fate of the Jews, and he planned, as noted, to write a novel about the fate of the wandering Jew, Ahasuerus. According to one of Wassermann's letters to his publisher, that work was to encompass the turning points in the history of the Jewish people over two thousand years, to be presented in the form of tableaux and dialogues, some of which he had already written.[28] There would be conversations with St. Paul, Julian the Apostate, Charlemagne, Pope Innocent III, Isabella of Spain, Spinoza, Richelieu, Cromwell, Catherine II of Russia, Frederick the Great, Maria Theresa, Napoleon, Karl Marx, Bismarck, Lenin, and Hitler. He promised, in addition, scenes of persecution and expulsion, of *yeshivas* and the formation of religious sects. Thus we see that (before his premature death) he wished to write what he thought was *the* Jewish book of his generation. That project is a convincing expression of the trauma of the wandering Jew: In the wake of events in Germany, Wassermann had to take up *his* own wanderer's staff.

Generally speaking, then, German Jewish literature was a literature of flight from identity, a burdensome identity that was imposed on the victims as a stigma and then internalized by them. The conflict between identities, as well as the experience of lacking an identity, was negative and destructive, to such a degree that it could not be resolved by our authors' literary plots.

VI

Although American Jewish literature and German Jewish literature have similar origins, it must be emphasized that American Jewish literature today is prouder of its dual identity than any other "foreign" Jewish literature has ever been. Daniel Walden's anthology, *On Being Jewish*, documents three stages in the literary embodiment of the American Jewish experience: (1) immigration, (2) Americanization, and, finally, (3) Jewish Americans and American Jews.[29] Among the books belonging to the first stage (though in fact Walden places it in the second) is Henry Roth's novel *Call It Sleep* (1934), doubtless the most interesting of them all.[30]

Still permeated by the world of Eastern Europe, this work describes *shtetl* life as it is transplanted from Eastern Europe to the United States. Roth details the inner disintegration of the community in America—the collapse of paternal, divine, and communal authority. In its wake there arise problems of the individual's identity and his [or her] relations with the non-Jewish world. The author successfully gives his characters authentic linguistic and behaviorial identities by conveying Yiddish conversation within the family in correct English and conversation outside the family in broken English. *Call It Sleep* is close in its materials, semiotics, and thematics to the Hebrew and Yiddish literature of Eastern Europe, in many respects closer to Sholem Aleichem's *Motl peyse dem khazns* (the story of the immigration to America of an Eastern European Jewish family told from the child's point of view) than to many American and American Jewish novels of its generation.

Roth's tale focuses on young David, who discovers his human identity through unraveling a dark family secret, the roots of which reach down deep into its country of origin. Genya, his mother, had been seduced by a Gentile lover and married her Jewish husband as a last resort. Having committed the original sin, the shaken family tumbles from the *shtetl* in Europe to its crumbling reincarnation in New York, where Genya's past overshadows her present, determining her fate and that of her son. Because of her deep feelings of guilt, she submits to all her husband's caprices; and the boy feels rejected by the father. Roth's themes—the loss of paternal authority and the Oedipal tension between fathers and sons; the opposition between erotic sin (the hidden secret underlying the family relations) and the norms of family existence; the opposition between the house as a shelter and the external world as a primal forest arousing fears— are all subjects and motifs typical of Hebrew literature (M.Y. Berdyczewski, J.H. Brenner, Y.D. Berkowitz) and Yiddish writing (Chaim Grade, Isaac Bashevis Singer). In this sense, *Call It Sleep* is a Hebrew or Yiddish novel written in English that tries to imitate Yiddish. Like Joseph Roth's *Hiob*, it is a Yiddish novel in its use of language, in its behavioral norms, and in the Jewish identification of the protagonists. Similarly, the Yiddish and Hebrew works set in America attempt to find an equivalent for English.[31] This phenomenon is in evidence elsewhere as well. Hebrew novels such as *Hayyei nissuim (Married Life*, 1929–30) by David Vogel or *Shaul ve-yohannah* (1956–67) by Naomi Frankel are, in that sense, German novels written in Hebrew. *Vengeance of the Fathers* (1928) by Yitzhak Shami is an Arabic novella written in Hebrew. And Isaac Bashevis Singer's *Enemies, A Love Story* (1972) is a novel written originally in Yiddish whose linguistic materials are Yiddish, Polish, and American. In all of these works, even though the characters explicitly identify as Jews, one can already discern the first stages of the collapse of identity that would lead to the works of "American Jewish" writers.

Chaim Potok's *The Chosen* (1967), written thirty years after Henry Roth's novel, is close to it in several respects.[32] It, too, is based on the language and semiotics of the American Jewish *shtetl* society. In the American context, it raises the very issues of the conflicts among Enlightened Jews, Hasidim, and Zionists that had been familiar to Hebrew and Yiddish readers decades earlier. Both of Potok's protagonists, different as they are, have their roots in their Jewish heritage. Danny Saunders, the son of a Hasidic rebbe, yearns for secular education; Reuven Malter, the son of a traditionalist Zionist intellectual, seeks the light within Judaism. Yet, despite their conflicting ambitions, neither has doubts about his identity as a Jew—which places this work closer to the Hebrew and Yiddish literature of the turn of our century than to German or American Jewish literature of this century. The characters' Jewishness per se is not in question, despite its yearning for spirit and light.

For *assimilated* American Jews, however, as for their European parents and brethren, the problem of identity arises with its full gravity— surprisingly, since America as a host society differs in its pluralistic character from European societies in general and from German society in particular. Yet subjects, motifs, and conflicts that had been common in German Jewish literature appear in American Jewish literature, albeit in rather strange guise. American Jewish literature also features the paranoid who flees from himself and from his environment because of external pressures; but some of the works, unlike their German predecessors, hint that the pressure is merely superficial and that the situation being described is actually a parody of the former one, which had inner justification.

Such a parody of the experience of anxiety and flight is found in Bruce J. Friedman's novella *Stern* (1962), the story of the existential fear of a Jewish anti-hero who cannot stand his own identity and tries to escape from it and from people who seek to impose this burden upon him. Stern, drafted into the Air Force, blames his Jewishness for his not being a pilot: "Somehow Stern connected his nonflying status with his Jewishness, as though flying were a golden, crew-cut, gentile thing while Jewishness was a cautious and scholarly quality that crept into engines and prevented planes from lurching off the ground with recklessness."[33] He hates his Jewish identity, which contrasts with his positive image of the true American. (And, according to Friedman, the true Israeli is the Jew who embodies that same positive image.)

Apparently Friedman, in parodying self-hatred, has himself internalized an anti-Semitic doctrine: the Jew as anti-warrior. Friedman's protagonist flees because one of his neighbors insulted his family with the word "kike." That flight (like the stigma), arising out of persistent European anxiety, in Friedman's view, lacks any objective justification in the American context. Paranoia has become empty, a psychosis with no empirical basis.[34]

We can see from this example that American Jewish literature partakes of the legacy of German Jewish literature. The state of having a dual identity is unaltered—although the outer pressure has abated, at first slightly, then much more so. There are works by Bernard Malamud, Philip Roth, and Saul Bellow that are far closer to their German Jewish kinsmen than one might first imagine. One striking example is Roth's "Eli the Fanatic." It concerns Eli, who has been asked by his community to prevent recently arrived European Jewish refugees from flaunting their identity, which has been an embarrassment to their American brethren. Instead, to the astonishment of the community, Eli dons the traditional Jewish garb. The refugees, it seems, are more authentic to him than the people he represents. Thus, Philip Roth, like Joseph Roth and Jakob Wassermann, uses the image of Eastern European ultra-Orthodox Jews—their language, costumes, and customs—as a model of authentic Judaism that is opposed to the assimilated, shallow version of the American suburbs, which he vigorously rejects. This strange nostalgia for a foreign world that no longer exists grows out of the perception that the world that has replaced it is far worse.[35] In that respect, then, Philip Roth evidences his affinity with the German writer who consciously and unconsciously chose the Jewish world of yesterday, with its single identity, over their contemporary world of dual identity.

About this point Cynthia Ozick offers an ambivalent and ironic thesis. We have noted that she calls for the creation of a "New Yiddish," claiming that the world of American Jewry, with its dual identity and single language, can exist as an autonomous cultural realm. Its drawbacks must be converted into advantages, since its duality is inherent, a fact of life. For one thing, even Hebrew and Yiddish culture has lost its singleness of identity today. An emphasis on the opposite and complementary aspect of a Jewish dual identity can be found in Ozick's story "Envy; or, Yiddish in America."[36]

It tells of the envy felt by the Yiddish poets Edelshtein and Baumzweig toward the Yiddish novelist Ostrover. They write poems in Yiddish and remain within the pathetic, moribund confines of a backward language; he writes stories that are translated into English to become treasures of American literature. It is no startling revelation that the prototype for Ostrover seems to be Isaac Bashevis Singer. What is important in this story is not so much the acute description of the writer or the sarcastic portrayal of the wretched poets but, rather, the implication that *shtetl* culture has no future in America: Anyone seeking to create a secular culture cannot do it with a dead language, and anyone writing in that language comes to life only if he is translated from the idiom of the *shtetl* into that of the city and suburb.

In this work of fiction, Ozick, who attacked "universalism" with such vehemence, comes out against the wretched "localism" of the representatives of Yiddish culture who seek to break through the walls of the ghetto. In other words, Yiddish "culture," if it is not to be embalmed as a living cadaver, must cross the border and put on local, American clothing. And, in fact, the refugees themselves know they must assimilate in order to survive; they are as eager to fit in as the culture is open to accommodate them. It is only through translations—that is, the readership of strangers who are also relatives—that Isaac Bashevis Singer, for instance, achieves any sort of literary identity. Ozick senses the depths of the conflict of the cultural refugees—the writers, who, in contrast to physical refugees, are liable to swear themselves to silence because they have lost their natural environment—unless they succeed in passing from their original language to that of their potential readership. Ozick makes it clear that there is no room for nostalgia: The one and only possible identity in the American Jewish world is a dual identity. Her work implies that the best the Jews can hope for is that their authors not ignore the duality in their deep desire to abandon their Jewishness and become uniquely American in identity.

The relation between the original identity and the target identity is, as noted, a subject that has preoccupied American Jewish literature, although it has apparently been freed of external pressure, far more than one might first suspect. Still, it could almost be said that, as with German Jewish literature, that topic of identity defines the Jewishness of the literature.[37]

The more traditional issue of an identity forced upon a person against his will is the main theme of Bernard Malamud's *The Fixer* (1966), which recounts the case of Yakov Bok. (This book, which purports to be a historical novel, is a reflection of the Beilis affair, one of the most notorious blood libels in czarist Russia. To the post-Holocaust American Jewish audience, the Russian blood libel seems like a harbinger of the horrifying spectacle to come.) Bok relates to his Jewish identity as a cruel fate: "From birth a black horse had followed him, a Jewish nightmare. What was being a Jew but an everlasting curse? He was sick of their history, destiny, blood guilt."[38]

In Malamud's "Last Mohican," one of a volume of stories about Fidelman, the artist with a dual identity, the protagonist tries to escape the curse of Zusskind, an "authentic" Jew who appears as a miserable *schnorrer* (leech), arousing guilt in Fidelman's heart.[39] The two figures—ego and alter ego—are bound to each other like Siamese twins and no one can sunder them. In other stories by Malamud, and particularly in "The German Refugee" or the pathetic, allegorical tale "The Jewbird," Jewish identity is conceived as something imposed on a person like the sword of Damocles.[40] As with their counterparts in much of German Jewish literature, these characters would prefer to separate the ego from the alter ego, the image of American light from the Jewish shadow.

The nature of Jewish identity and the status of Jews in America is one of the major issues in Saul Bellow's novel *The Victim* (1947). Leventhal, the main Jewish character, assumes indirect responsibility for the firing of his friend, Albee, and for his nephew's death, although he is guilty of neither. What we have is the metaphysical and existential experience of guilt and persecution that typified the work of Kafka, here reduced in dimension (almost parodically) to fit the narrower, concrete scale of human society. It is astonishing that the subjective experience of the protagonist or, implicitly, that of the author who resented that character, has been transferred, unaltered, from a closed, non-Jewish society to one that is open and pluralistic. Leventhal's antagonist, Albee, makes anti-Semitic statements that are reminiscent of Germany: The Jews pollute the culture; they are children of Caliban; they seek to destroy the foundations of the American upper class.

In fact, this anti-Semitism is a domesticated version of the ingrained European anti-Semitism of the past. The model for persecution has independent existence as a suprapersonal entity embodied in various trivial events, and it is not connected with the changes that took place in the host country.

VII

Although several German Jewish literary models—in terms of character, plot, and subject—recur in strange fashion in American Jewish literature, without doubt great changes have taken place in the depiction of Jewish dual identity. Philip Roth formulated the difficulty of depicting the new Jew.

> *Jews are people who are not what anti-Semites say they are.* That was once a statement out of which a man might begin to construct an identity for himself; now it does not work so well, for it is difficult to act counter to the ways people expect you to act when fewer and fewer people define you by such expectations. The success of the struggle against the defamation of Jewish character in this country has itself made more pressing the need for a Jewish self-consciousness that is relevant to this time and place.[41]

Roth argues, further, that it is ridiculous to pretend to be a victim in a country where no one forces you to be one if you choose to live otherwise.

Three major writers of American Jewish literature, Bellow, Malamud, and (Philip) Roth, have struggled with the problems of identity. Implicitly, they ask time and again: What is the "Jewish identity" of one who is not persecuted yet feels persecuted?—in Malamud's *The Assistant* (1957); in Bellow's *Herzog* (1964) and also in *The Adventures of Augie March* (1953) and *Mr. Sammler's Planet* (1970); and, of course, in Roth's *Portnoy's Complaint* as well as his other books. In *The Assistant* the question is asked outright by the rabbi who eulogizes Morris Bober: Who is a Jew and in what way was Morris Bober Jewish? His (not particularly convincing) answer, essentially, is that a Jew is a good person. For Malamud, a "Jew" is someone—who need not be Jewish—for whom achievement is not the ultimate value. The novel's protagonists do not flee from their Jewish identity; in fact, the Jew and even the Gentile (Frank Alpine) embrace it. Malamud respects this identity, in contrast to the typical American Jewish, achievement-oriented way of life. The individual who fails by those standards gains in the spiritual realm what he loses in the material world.[42]

Thus, Malamud converts defeat into moral victory and translates the historical failure of the Jews as a persecuted minority into the economic failure of a ne'er-do-well minority. Bober remains an authentic Jew because he does not wish to leave the confines of the local *shtetl*; as a consequence, he does not fit like the majority of his brethren into the American way of life economically or socially. But by virtue of his economic failure, the character preserves his identity (and integrity); conversely, economic success entails losing it. Malamud seems to suggest a connection between economic upward mobility and cultural assimilation. One infers from the overall structure of the work that the author values the existence of some kind of Jewish identity in pluralistic American society, this in contrast to German Jewish writers, whose characters wished to rid themselves of their identity.

Bellow approaches this issue in more complex fashion, removing the problematics from the area of relations between Jews and non-Jews. The structure of relations he describes in *Herzog* is mainly intra-Jewish. The two main characters of the novel are both Jews: Herzog, the refined, aristocratic intellectual, on the one hand; the plebeian, vulgar Gersbach, on the other—two faces of a new generation of Jews. They vie, as creators and purveyors of the spirit, for influence in American society; and their competition for the same woman represents a kind of struggle for the "world."

Much has been written about the persona of the *schlemiel* in Jewish literature.[43] But Herzog is certainly *not* this type: Women are fond of him, and he has a position in the academic establishment. Still, he takes Madeleine's betrayal as a kind of absolute treachery, isolating him and making all his activities in the world seem unreal. Instead of taking action to influence the realities of human life, he composes political and philosophical epistles. He lives in a fictional world of his own creation, enjoying his role as a tortured romantic, whereas his friend and his divorced wife take pleasure in worldly vanities.

Bellow's view of the romantic in a mass society is very ambivalent.[44] Herzog struggles for his identity against a society that blurs identities but, to a great extent, he enjoys his plight of weakness and isolation. He has been separated from the one social group that might have protected him: the Jewish family. Having left its protective embrace, he is exposed to the ravages of American society and to the intellectual battles that mark the quest for achievement in the cultural sphere. This uprooted Jew endures the struggle as best he can until he becomes overwhelmed and his brother and sister come to the rescue.

So Bellow, like Malamud, feels nostalgia for the identity of the primary matrix, the family, which welcomes the hero unconditionally and does not demand that he prove himself in an erotic and pseudointellectual war in which the talented but vulgar survive. In other words, "modern" society splits his uprooted identity, and he must constantly prove himself anew. Only in the world of his parents, the world of yesterday, does his identity exist as an unshakable wholeness.

In *Portnoy's Complaint*, Roth presents the Jew whose identity is not defined with the "assistance" of outside pressure but who nonetheless struggles with it (similarly in the work of Roth's followers and imitators, such as Alan Lelchuk and Erica Jong). The protagonist, like his German Jewish counterparts, gets no pleasure from his Jewish identity and, along with his father, is smothered by the embrace of his mother, who demands complete identification with the tribe. He is expected to remain an infant all his life and yet to serve as a substitute for his impotent father. Moreover, on the one hand, he is called upon to open the gates to the non-Jewish world that were closed to his father, whereas on the other he is expected to remain loyal to his mother and the family.

Lying on his psychoanalyst's couch, Portnoy recognizes his predicament. This awareness, however, does not alter the experience. Indeed, he seems to enjoy it: fleeing from his mother to the bosom of strange women (although he never takes the decisive step and marries one), both hating the mother's tribal Jewish identity and experiencing revulsion for the Gentile women and their families. Whereas that ambivalence is certainly a source of pain, the hero nevertheless revels in his use of psychoanalytic rhetoric. His story amuses him, filled as it is with jokes and puns and memories. Recounting his experiences, he relishes every relived moment; indeed, the analyst's couch itself seems to be the source of his greatest pleasure.

The tale finishes without offering a solution. Rather, its conclusion is its beginning: In response to the protagonist's monologue, the analyst proposes that they begin! Thus, the author signals that this is a circular process that has no termination: Portnoy's "complaint" will go on and on forever. Just as the hero has enjoyed his own cleverness up to now, so the enjoyment will endure; just as he enjoyed reviling his mother and father, so he will also continue to make ironic fun of the WASPS. As he is revolted by his family's weakness, so he is revolted by the qualities of his Gentile "hosts," who stand for the good, the marvelous, and the enlightened everywhere and at all times. Roth's *Portnoy's Complaint* sings the praises of abnormality. Rather than "Lucky me, I'm an orphan" (as Sholem Aleichem wrote), he says, "Lucky me, I'm neurotic; lucky me, I suffer from a dual identity." When he encounters a Jewish woman with a healthy, integrated personality in Israel, he loses his bearings and becomes impotent because he is not equipped to deal with normality.

There is a pathology in Malamud's and Bellow's characters, who take pleasure in their peculiar identity as self-persecutors. Roth's Portnoy enjoys his neurosis and derives his satisfaction from being psychoanalyzed, not from the possibility that he may find fulfillment outside the analyst's office.

VIII

The German Jewish authors I have discussed took their identity as imposed and absolute, a cruel fate against which they all rebelled. Nonetheless, they viewed those who reject it with contempt, as miserable antiheroes, hopeless and pitiful. American Jewish writers place less emphasis on pressure from the outside and emphasize the positive-negative bond between the characters and their identity. They choose it even though all gates seem to be open before them in their pluralistic country: Frank Alpine converts; Moses Herzog flees to the bosom of his family in his hour of need; Alex Portnoy does not marry a Gentile woman. How can we explain the pleasure that the characters take in ambivalent situations and in pain and suffering? It is, of course, possible to offer universal (psychological and philosophical) interpretations. But American Jewish literature of the 1960s formulated its explanations in openly tribal and ethnic terms, whereas in the German Jewish literature of the 1920s (but before then and afterwards too), the tribal and ethnic terms were implicit.

European Jewish culture was almost completely destroyed during the Holocaust, including both the society that had produced German Jewish authors and the authors themselves, who left no local heirs. Thus, the postwar period has seen no comparable "European" Jewish literature. If European Jewish literature in general, and German Jewish writing in particular, have any heirs, they are on the other side of the Atlantic. The culture with its dual identity has passed, in modified form, from one place of exile to another. The identity of its Jewish readership has changed, as have the authors. Yet the problem of Jewish identity plagues Jewish writers, their characters, and their readers as much as ever.

Notes

1. For a very sensitive example of conspicuous concern for the definition of Jews and Judaism in literature, see Hans Mayer, "Comrade Shylock" and "Jewish Figures in the Bourgeois Novel," in *Outsider: A Study in Life and Letters*, trans. Denis M. Sweet (Cambridge, Mass.: MIT Press, 1982).

2. See *Encyclopaedia Judaica* (1972), s.v. "Press."

3. Dov Sadan, Introductory essay [Hebrew], in *Avnei-bedek* (Tel Aviv: Ha-Kibbutz ha-Meuhad, 1962), especially 16–25.

4. Gustav Krojanker (ed.), *Juden in der deutschen Literatur* (Berlin: Weltverlag, 1922). Arnold Zweig, *Bilanz der deutschen Judenheit* (1933; repr. Cologne: J. Melzer, 1961), is a particularly interesting book, mentioning all the varied achievements of German Jewry and discussing their literary activities with enthusiasm (238–63).

5. Harry Zohn, *Wiener Juden in der deutschen Literatur* (Tel Aviv: Editions "Olamenu," 1964).

6. Hans Tramer dealt with the problem of identity in the poetry of Karl Wolfskehl, in particular, and also discussed several other poets in "Uber deutsch-judisches Dichtertum: Zur Morphologie des judischen Bekenntnisses," *Bulletin des Leo Baeck Instituts* 2 (1957): 88–103.

7. For example, see the essays by Philip Roth, "Some New Jewish Stereotypes," "Writing about Jews," and "Imagining Jews," in *Reading Myself and Others* (New York: Farrar, Straus and Giroux, 1975).

8. Ludwig Lewisohn, *What is this Jewish Heritage?* (New York: B'nai B'rith Hillel Foundation, 1954), 81–83.

9. Max F. Schulz, *Radical Sophistication: Studies in Contemporary Jewish American Novelists* (Athens, Ohio: Ohio University Press, 1969), 26.

10. Cynthia Ozick, "Toward a New Yiddish," in *Art and Ardor: Essays* (New York: Knopf, 1983), 155–77, first presented as a lecture at the Weizmann Institute in Rehovoth, Israel, in 1970; reprinted in this volume.

11. Ibid., 156.

12. Ibid., 165.

13. Ibid., 172.

14. Ibid., 180–81.

15. M.Y. Berdyczewski, "The Stranger" [Hebrew], in *Kol kitvei Berdishevski* (Collected Stories) (Tel Aviv: Devir, 1951), 67. First published in *Revivim* 1 (1908).

16. The term "self-hatred," coined by Theodor Lessing in *Der judische Selbsthass* (Berlin: Zionistischer Bucher-Bund, 1930), is appropriate here. Hans Mayer gives a brilliant account of the connection between self-hatred and Jewish identity: "Jewish integration in Europe proceeded from the assumption that Jewish language and history were to be sacrificed, just as Moses Mendelssohn taught; that there would be no Jewish nation. Everything was to be 'adopted' from the host country and people: language, culture, region. That failed." (Mayer, *Outsider*, 363).

17. See Hans Kohn, *Karl Kraus, Arthur Schnitzler, Otto Weininger: Aus dem judischen Wien der Jahrhundertwende* (Tubingen: Mohr, 1962), especially 34–37. Some of Kohn's remarks contrasting Weininger's relations with his father to those of Kafka (36) are not always persuasive. A Hebrew author, David Vogel, wrote a novel (*Hayyei nissuim*, 1929–30) based on Weininger's doctrine.

18. Max Brod, *Reubeni, Furst der Juden: Ein Renaissanceroman* (Munich: K. Wolff,

1925). Brod's presentation of Reubeni resembles Hayim Hazaz's depiction of Yuzpa in *The End of Days,* trans. Dalia Bilu (Tel Aviv: Institute for the Translation of Hebrew Literature, 1982). See Gershon Shaked, "The End of Days and the Expressionist Play," in Hazaz, *The End of Days,* 131–58.

19. David Bronsen, *Joseph Roth: Eine Biographie* (Cologne: Kiepenheuer and Witsch, 1974).

20. Joseph Roth, *Die Büste des Kaisers* in *Werke,* vol. 3, ed. Hermann Kesten (Cologne: Kiepenheuer and Witsch, 1975–76), 192.

21. Roth, *Juden auf Wanderschaft,* in *Werke,* 3:304. Translations from German are by J. Green.

22. Joseph Roth, *Briefe 1911–1939,* ed. Hermann Kesten (Cologne: Kiepenheuer and Witsch, 1970), 419–22. I refer to the letter dated August 8, 1935, in which he makes rather harsh remarks about Zionism, such as: "A Zionist is a National Socialist; a Nazi is a Zionist" (420). And he continues: "Therefore I cannot fathom how it is that you wish to start the fight against Hitler, who is merely an imbecilic brother of the Zionist, using a brother of the National Socialist, i.e., a Zionist, even the most ingenious of them. Perhaps you can protect Jewry in that way. But I wish to protect both Europe and mankind from Nazis *and also* from Hitler-Zionists. I don't wish to protect the Jews, except as the most endangered vanguard of all mankind." In these remarks, addressed to another assimilated Jew, Stefan Zweig, pathological universalism reaches its apogee.

23. Roth, *Die Flucht ohne Ende,* in *Werke,* 1: 421.

24. Jakob Wassermann, *Lebensdienst* (Leipzig: Grethlein and Co., 1928), 177.

25. I have seen Wassermann's handwritten notes on Heinrich Graetz's *History of the Jews* and on other sources, made in preparation for this novel. The manuscripts are in the Schiller German National Archive for German Literature in Marbach am Neckar. I am grateful to that archive for allowing me to examine those materials.

26. Bronsen, *Biographie,* 598–608.

27. Two of Wassermann's letters are highly instructive about his ambivalent attitude toward his dual identity. One, to the Jewish community of Gratz dated May 15, 1933, informs them that he cannot pay the amount demanded of him for membership in the community because his books are no longer sold in Germany. (On the other hand he is bound to the community, but on the other hand he slips away from it.) The second, rather pathetic letter, dated August 1, 1933, is addressed to the Association of German Writers. He retracts his letter of resignation from that organization, claiming that he had left the organization after seeing an announcement in the press stating that any non-Aryan author would be expelled; not wishing to be expelled, he submitted his resignation first. In the meanwhile, he says, he has learned from his German friends that the announcement was in error and that only new non-Aryan members would be rejected. Therefore, he withdraws his resignation and encloses his membership dues. That letter is in the Schiller German National Archive for German Literature in Marbach am Neckar. It shows the humiliating self-abnegation to which Wassermann brought himself in order to belong to the institutions of the German people.

28. The précis is given in a letter, dated August 25, 1933, to Klement, apparently the intended American publisher of the proposed book. That letter is also in the archive at Marbach.

29. Daniel Walden (ed.), *On Being Jewish: American Jewish Writers from Cahan to Bellow* (Greenwich, Conn.: Fawcett Publications, 1974).

30. Henry Roth, *Call It Sleep* (1934; repr. New York: Avon, 1969).

31. I refer to the novels and stories about Jewish migration to America written in Hebrew by writers such as Reuben Wallenrod, *Ki fanah yom* (1946), *Be-ein dor*

(1945); Simon Halkin, *Yehiel ha-hagri* (1928), *Ad mashber* (1945); Samuel Leib Blank, *Mr. Kunis* (1934), *Al admat Amerikah* (1958); and the Yiddish novels of Joseph Opatoshu, *Lost People* (1922), *Die tentserin* (1929), and others.

32. Chaim Potok, *The Chosen* (New York: Simon and Schuster, 1967).

33. Bruce J. Friedman, *Stern: A Novel* (New York: Simon and Schuster, 1962), 54.

34. It appears to me that the interpretations of Friedman's novel and of Edward Wallant's *The Pawnbroker* (New York: Harcourt, Brace, and World, 1961) offered by Schulz are no less symptomatic than the works themselves. Schulz ignores the problem I have raised almost completely and even disregards the fact that Friedman intended to parody Jewish fears. See Schulz, *Radical Sophistication*, 186–94.

35. Roth himself discusses a series of letters to the editor that protest the "anti-Semitic" character of his works (the writers refer to stories such as "Defender of the Faith"). See Roth, *Reading Myself and Others*, 149–69.

36. Cynthia Ozick, "Envy; or, Yiddish in America," in *The Pagan Rabbi and Other Stories* (New York: Knopf, 1971).

37. I believe that the struggle for identity and doubts about it are part of that desperate striving for historical continuity that is typical of contemporary secular Jewish culture. Here is Robert Alter's formulation: "I would suggest that Jewish life since the entrance of the Jews into modern culture may be usefully viewed as a precarious, though stubborn, experiment in the possibilities of historical continuity, when most of the grounds for continuity have been cut away." See Robert Alter, *After the Tradition: Essays on Modern Jewish Writing* (New York: E.P. Dutton and Co., 1969), 10–11.

38. Bernard Malamud, *The Fixer* (New York: Farrar, Straus and Giroux, 1966), 187.

39. Bernard Malamud, *Pictures of Fidelman: An Exhibition* (New York: Farrar, Straus and Giroux, 1969).

40. Bernard Malamud, *Idiots First* (New York: Farrar, Straus and Giroux, 1962).

41. Roth, *Reading Myself and Others*, 165.

42. Robert Alter links the figure of Bober to the *schlemiel* (as does Ruth Wisse in her book on the *schlemiel* as a modern hero). In Alter's opinion the main image in *The Assistant* is that of the prison: "The prison, like the *schlemiel* who is usually its chief inmate, is Malamud's way of suggesting that to be fully a man is to accept the most painful limitations; those who escape these limitations achieve only an illusory, self-negating kind of freedom, for they become less than responsible human beings" (*After the Tradition*, 122). Cf. Ruth Wisse, "Requiem in Several Voices," in *The Schlemiel as Modern Hero* (Chicago: University of Chicago Press, 1971), 108–24.

43. Wisse describes Moses E. Herzog as the spoiled child of a Jewish mother, trying to attain some great marvel, although he progresses toward it in ironic fashion, like a *schlemiel*, and, regarding the desire to advance in life, as he knows, childhood is decisive. I agree with Wisse's remarks about the central role of the Jewish family in the hero's life. See Wisse, "The *Schlemiel* as Liberal Humanist," in *The Schlemiel as Modern Hero*, 92–107.

44. That view of Herzog as a romantic in mass society is common among the critics. See Malcolm Bradbury, *Saul Bellow* (London and New York: Methuen, 1982), 71.

SASSON SOMEKH

Lost Voices:
Jewish Authors
in Modern Arabic Literature

T HROUGHOUT THE MIDDLE AGES, the Jews of Arab lands did not participate *as Jews* in the mainstream of Arabic literature. The Andalusian poet Ibn Sahl al-Isra'ili (1208–51), for instance, does not reflect motifs and concerns that are specifically Jewish in his *qasidas* or *muwashshahs*, and we are always reminded by Arabic sources that he converted to Islam. There are a few exceptions, most prominent of which is Maimonides, whose medical writings and career received some acclaim in Arab bibliographic literature. However, most Jewish theologians, poets, and literary scholars who operated in the world of medieval Islam were rarely heard of in Islamic circles.[1]

It is a well-known fact that medieval Jewish writers in Arabic-speaking regions wrote profusely in Arabic, but they did so in Hebrew script. Some of them, for example, Saadia in tenth-century Iraq and Yehudah Halevi in twelfth-century Spain, were widely conversant with Arabic literature and theology. Moreover, the language of their own Arabic writing was at times remarkably rich in style and far removed from the casual, semicolloquial Judeo-Arabic that we often find in the *Geniza* correspondence. Nevertheless, their literary production was meant exclusively for a Jewish audience.

As contrasted with, for instance, Christian participation in medieval Arab Islamic letters (for example, Hunayn Ibn Ishaq), Jews, whether by choice or by force, led their own, self-contained, literary life. Their Arabic works never came to be regarded as part of the history of Arabic literature. Parenthetically, one might make mention at this point of the sixth-century Jahili poet al-Samaw'al b. 'Adiya', whose Jewish identity is acknowledged by the Arabic sources. He is lauded as one of the greatest Arab poets of all times. But then we are talking about the pre-Islamic era.

In modern times we find a somewhat different picture. Since the middle of the nineteenth century, Jews of the Near East and North Africa began breaking out of their isolation and exploring new areas of material and intellectual life. In a few countries (especially in the Levant and Iraq), they gradually became proficient not only in classical Arabic but also in some European languages. Here and there we come across a Jew taking part in politics and national causes. The Egyptian Jew Ya'qub Sanu' (James Sanua, 1839–1912) was even known to be a member of the circle of Jamal al-Din al-Afghani, the famous Islamic activist; and it was apparently with the latter's blessings that he launched a series of anti-British journals. Furthermore, Sanu' was the first Egyptian dramatist of modern times and was fond of viewing himself as the "Egyptian Moliere."[2]

Sanu''s theatrical activity and his numerous plays are in fact the first "Jewish participation" in modern Arabic culture, and contemporary Egyptian literary historians acknowledge his crucial role in the development of a local dramatic tradition. His plays do not reflect Jewish concerns, although the editor of these plays, Professor Najm, assures us that his dramatic works reflect Jewish social issues.[3] The life and career of Sanu' were exceptional in more than one way, but he was the only Jew of note who pursued a literary and journalistic career during the formative decades of modern Arabic literature. Another minority played a crucial role in that development. As is well known, it is the Lebanese Christians who can be credited with the establishment of a modern Arabic press. They were also the chief translators of European literature into Arabic in the late nineteenth century and well into the twentieth. It was thanks to their efforts in Lebanon, Egypt, and the American diaspora that Arabic literature acquired many of its distinctive modern features.[4]

I now move to the twentieth century, in which the phenomenon of Jewish participation in Arabic literature and in the Arabic press became more pronounced.[5] That is true, however, only of certain Arab lands, especially Iraq, and to a certain extent Egypt and Palestine. In Syria and Lebanon, in contrast, Jewish participation in modern Arabic culture is comparatively marginal. In the Yemen and North Africa, we find no such activity whatever, although in some North African countries a few Jewish authors appeared who wrote in French rather than in Arabic. In each of these regions the extent of Jewish involvement in modern literary life was the outcome of local conditions, which I will not go into here. Instead, I would like to concentrate on the two most active centers of Jewish literary life in our century, Egypt and Iraq. My remarks will concentrate mainly on the literary careers of two of the most prominent Jewish writers in those two countries.

Egypt

The Egyptian Jewish community in the last two centuries was not pre-dominantly Arabophone; neither were its members entirely of Egyptian origin.[6] A sizable number of the Jews of modern Egypt settled there with the waves of immigration that swept in during the second half of the nineteenth century and the first decades of the twentieth. Many of them spoke languages other than Arabic at home (Ladino, French, Italian, Yiddish, and Turkish), and their communal schools were for the main part French-oriented. Nevertheless, certain sections of that community, especially the native Egyptians, imbibed Arabic culture. Certain Egyptian Jews were prominent in theater, cinema, Oriental music, the printing industry, and occasionally the Arabic press.[7] That was especially true of the Karaite Jews, who constituted a substantial part of Egyptian Jewry and were well integrated into the local culture.[8]

From among the Karaite subcommunity comes the most prolific Jewish writer and poet of modern Egypt. He was Mourad Farag (Murad Faraj), who was born in Cairo in 1866 and died in that city in 1956.[9] Farag wrote mainly in Arabic, and while some of his books address specific communal concerns and legal issues, the bulk of his writing was meant for the general reading public and was most definitely regarded by him as part of the modern Arabic literature of his country. Three volumes of his *Diwan* are proudly prefixed by lines of praise written by the leading Egyptian poet of the day, Ahmad Shawqi; and the second edition of his book *al-Shu'ara' al-Yahud al-'Arab* (Cairo, 1939) opens with a copious introduction by the Turkish-Egyptian scholar, Isma'il Ahmad Adham.

In fact, the very title of the book just mentioned, *The Jewish-Arab Poets*, is indicative of a most basic theme in his writing. Throughout his long literary career, which spans some sixty years, he left no stone unturned in his effort to demonstrate the long tradition of Jewish-Muslim cooperation in the lands of Islam. The Jews are an integral part of Arab Islamic culture, he repeatedly asserted. They participated in the past in the creation of medieval Arab civilization, and they are willing and able to lend a hand in its rejuvenation. It is to be noted, however, that this theme received a somewhat different coloring in different periods of his life. In his writings published around the turn of the century, we find pro-Ottoman sentiments and a clear interest in the Young Turks. The stress at that stage was on the Jewish-Muslim brotherhood.[10] Later on, his main concern shifts to the idea of nationhood, and the word *watan* (*patrie*) becomes central. The accent now is on the brotherhood of all Egyptians: Muslims, Christians, and Jews. In the late 1920s we detect in his writings a certain disillusionment regarding the prospects of national unity, coupled with a greater attention to biblical and linguistic studies rather than to public affairs.

A growing interest in the Zionist enterprise in Palestine also manifests itself in his poetry and prose of the 1920s and 1930s. He viewed Zionism not as an alternative or foreign allegiance, but most emphatically as being in keeping with Egyptian patriotism. He firmly believed that the two national movements, the Egyptian and the Jewish, could work hand in hand toward securing a better future for the inhabitants of the region. The dream of a Jewish-Muslim cooperation was therefore finally transformed into an idea of a possible link between the two national movements. Both movements, he felt, were his own. Three poems published in the third volume of his *Diwan* aptly demonstrate his concept of identification with both nations. These poems were originally composed in 1926 to mark the Cairo visit of a group of Jewish professors from Palestine, a group that was given a lavish reception by the Egyptian government. The first two poems extol (in the traditional neoclassic fashion) the Hebrew scholars and welcome them on behalf of the Egyptian nation; the third is written in the name of the visiting Jewish scholars upon their return to Palestine and opens with the following hemistich: *'afi-l-firdawsi kunna am bi-misra,* "Was it Egypt that we visited or was it paradise?"[11]

No wonder, then, that in subsequent years the growing hostility of Egypt toward Zionism and Egyptian involvement in Pan-Arab affairs dismayed Farag and prompted him to abandon national issues for communal ones, such as promoting a greater measure of understanding between Karaite and Rabbinite Jews. In the last two decades of his life, the flow of his literary production became markedly slower. He devoted all his efforts to the conclusion of his multivolume etymological dictionary of Hebrew and Arabic (*Meeting Points of Hebrew and Arabic*)[12] and the translation of some sections of the Hebrew Bible into versified Arabic.[13] His presence on the Egyptian Arabic literary scene became increasingly imperceptible, and at the moment there is hardly an Egyptian literary historian who is aware of Farag's unique literary legacy. In all he published some forty books on a variety of topics: poetry (five volumes), essays, translations, and philological and legal studies. It would seem that because of his preoccupation with Jewish affairs, his voice as a poet was lost in the context of Arabic literature. The vision of Jewish-Muslim cooperation that he so passionately preached was absolutely shattered by new realities of the Middle East, especially after the establishment of the State of Israel.

Let us, however, go back some seventy-five years and browse briefly through the volume of Farag's collected essays entitled *Maqalat Murad* (titled in French *Essai sur la morale*). This volume, published in Cairo in

1912, contains fifty-five essays on various topics: literature, philosophy, language, moral and social issues, education, and so forth. The essays originally appeared in different Egyptian journals, including the epoch-making newspapers *al-Mu'ayyad* (edited by Shaykh 'Ali Yusuf) and *al-Jarida* (edited by Ahmad Lufti al-Sayyid).

One essay, "The Struggle of the Motherland" ("Harb al-Watan"),[14] deals with the interreligious tensions in contemporary Egypt and is of special interest to us. Originally serialized in *al-Jarida* around 1908, this essay represents the young, ambitious Farag at his best. He is fairly optimistic concerning the possibility of an Egyptian nationhood based on equality and fraternity. He passionately advocates the adoption of a constitution under which Egyptians of all faiths can work together for the good of their country. However, he reproaches his Muslim countrymen, gently but forcefully, for certain prejudices that their language betrays. Those prejudices are highly detrimental to the coveted national unity *(al-jami'a al-wataniyya)*. For instance, a non-Muslim acquaintance is addressed as *Khawaga*, whereas Muslims are addressed as *Effendi*. That practice was prohibited by the Ottoman government, but much to Farag's dismay it was still in evidence in Egypt. Furthermore, Muslims refrain from using the word *rahma*, "divine mercy," and its derivatives in conjunction with a non-Muslim. Egyptian newspapers, with the exception of *al-Jarida*, even refuse to apply the expression *Rahimahu Allah*, "May God have mercy on . . . ," in death announcements concerning non-Muslims. Likewise, Muslims would never address their non-Muslim friends with the locution *Al-salamu 'alaykum*, "Peace be on you." Some of them even concocted a special form of greeting for non-Muslims: *Naharkum sa'id*, "Have a pleasant day." "I am writing this," recalls Farag, "because the other day someone called on me and began to address me with *al-salamu 'alaykum* but he stopped short in the middle, and corrected himself by saying *naharak sa'id*. However, he went on addressing other men with the full *al-salamu 'alaykum*. I admit that I was mortified."

Farag vehemently denounces these discriminatory practices, dubbing them unpatriotic and a violation of the true spirit of Islam. He argues that they were based, in fact, on a misreading of the Koran and marshals a variety of quotations from the Koran and its commentators to prove his point. One is indeed impressed by his amazing familiarity with Islamic sources.

Iraq

Iraq was another important Arab center in which Jews were active in literary circles.[15] In a recent book about the rise of the short story in his country, an Iraqi literary scholar shows that the first modern short story to be written in the interwar period by an Iraqi author was "Shahid al-Watan wa-Shahidat al-Hubb" (loosely translated, "He Died for His Country, and She Died for Love"). It was published in 1922 in *al-Mufid* and its author was Murad Mikhael.[16] The fact is that Mikhael (1906–86) was a prominent Jewish educator, poet, and scholar, who died in Kiron, Israel. Among other things, Murad Mikhael was the headmaster of the Baghdad Jewish secondary school Shammash. He published several volumes of poetry and prose, and in his youth he was a close friend and disciple of the well-known poet Jamil Sidqi al-Zahawi. In the late 1940s he immigrated to Israel, and there wrote a doctoral thesis on the Geniza documents under the late Professor S.D. Goitein and also continued publishing literary works in Arabic.[17]

Mikhael was by no means the only Jewish author in modern Iraq. In the interwar period we find in that country a considerable number of Jewish writers, journalists, and translators of European literature into Arabic. In fact, it is possible to distinguish two or three successive "waves" or "generations" of such authors. The first generation made its debut in the early 1920s, and it included, alongside Murad Mikhael, such writers as Anwar Sha'ul (to whom I shall presently return) and Ezra Haddad (1903–72), who in subsequent years translated *The Travels of Benjamin of Tudela* into Arabic. A second generation came to the fore in the late 1930s and included such authors as Shalom Darwish (1912–), Meir Basri (1912–), and Ya'qub Bilbul (1920–). A third and final generation was taking its first steps when the war in Palestine interrupted its activity.

About 1950, most of these authors emigrated to Israel and other countries. Most who have pursued literary careers in recent years have tended to write in languages other than Arabic, for example, Sami Mikhael (1926–), a prominent Israeli novelist who now writes in Hebrew, and Na'im Kattan (1928–), who settled in Quebec and writes in French. However, a few Israeli authors of Iraqi origin still write in Arabic, including two novelists, Yitzhak Bar-Moshe (1927–) and Samir Naqqash (1937–). Their Iraqi background figures prominently in their works.

A few remarks are in order here regarding the three generations of Iraqi Jewish authors. It is interesting to note that members of the first wave of Iraqi Jewish authors were by and large apolitical. They were Iraqi patriots, who earnestly hoped for the emergence of a "new Iraq," a modern, democratic, and open state. However, they normally refrained from dabbling in political affairs. Most of their works were published in newspapers and journals that had no distinct political coloring. Some of them launched their own cultural journals, but these were also distinctly nonpolitical. By contrast, the second wave was more involved in Iraqi politics, and some of its members joined those political parties that admitted Jews into their ranks (for example, Shalom Darwish, who was an active member of the moderately leftist National Democractic party).

The post-World War II generation presents yet another set of allegiances. They were divided between those who leaned toward Zionism and those who were attracted to communism (or, as Sami Mikhael put it on one occasion: "There were those who opted for a short-range cure [Zionism] and those who sought an all-embracing solution [communism]. Obviously, it was the latter individuals who espoused Iraqi causes, and some of them assumed leading positions in the outlawed Iraqi Communist party.")[18] It is only natural, therefore, that many of the members of the last generation of Iraqi Jewish writers were at one time or another pro-Communist.

Another point worth making is that unlike the Egyptian Mourad Farag, whose literary output was marked by a distinct neoclassic style, the Iraqi Jewish authors were fairly modern. That is true of all three generations, including the first, whose members (thanks to the Alliance Israelite Universelle schools, which had operated in Baghdad and other major Iraqi cities since the second half of the nineteenth century) were exposed to French Romantic and pre-Romantic authors. Their writings were by and large far more individualistic in their approach and simpler in their language than the works of other contemporary Iraqi writers and poets. In fact, the very title of the previously mentioned story by Murad Mikhael ("He Died for His Country, and She Died for Love") is indicative of the romantic-sentimental predilection of his group. The second generation boasts one of Iraq's first realistic storytellers (Darwish), as well as one of the first experimental poets (Bilbul). Broadly speaking, they played an important role in the development of a modern Iraqi literature, and it is not because of their insignificance that most of them are today all but forgotten in their native homeland.

A third and final point is that, unlike Farag, the Iraqi Jewish authors usually refrained from raising specifically Jewish issues in their writings. Even such a clearly autobiographical story as Shalom Darwish's "Qafila min al-Rif" ("A Village Caravan") presents no distinctive Jewish features, and its protagonists are made to speak the Baghdadi Muslim, rather than the Jewish, dialect.[19] That would be understandable in the case of the Communists, whose interest was in all-Iraqi problems. But many of the members of the first two generations of writers were deeply involved in Jewish communal affairs. The fact that their Jewishness is hardly evident in their literary works can be explained by their desire not to project an image of a minority literature. Alternatively, avoiding Jewish issues might be ascribed to the lesser degree of openness of Iraqi society, which, unlike

Egypt, was not ready as yet to tolerate a distinctly Jewish expression in the interwar period.

Anwar Sha'ul belongs to the first generation of modern Iraqi Jewish writers. He was born about 1904 in the city of Hilla in southern Iraq. Early in his life he settled in Baghdad, became a teacher and a lawyer, and pursued a literary career that spanned a full half-century. He stayed in Iraq after the exodus of its Jewish communities in 1950–51, but he too was finally obliged to leave the country in 1971. The last fourteen years of his life were spent in Israel, where he died in 1986. In Israel he published a retrospective volume of poetry[20] as well as a sizable autobiography, to which I shall presently return.

In Iraq, Anwar Sha'ul engaged in a variety of literary activities. His books include poetry, prose fiction, and translations. In 1929 he launched his own weekly cultural journal, *al-Hasid*, which he was able to sustain for ten years. *Al-Hasid* hosted many leading Iraqi writers and also promoted young authors, Jewish and non-Jewish alike. Anwar Sha'ul was highly esteemed by his Muslim and Christian fellow writers and in 1932 was elected a member of the committee that was designated to welcome the Indian poet Rabindranat Tagore, who visited Baghdad that year. Owing to his presence in Iraq after the emigration of most of its Jews, he is lucky enough to be mentioned occasionally in Iraqi literary histories.[21]

He wrote his autobiography, *Qissat Hayati fi Wadi al-Rafidayn (My Life in Iraq)*,[22] after he had immigrated to Israel, and it was published in Jerusalem in 1980. It records memorable events in his life and literary struggle. I would have liked to dwell upon this fascinating book at some length. In the context of this paper, however, I shall have to confine myself to summary remarks concerning two motifs that are paramount in the work as a whole and that determine its literary structure: that of the author's self-image and that of the rise and fall of the ambition of Iraqi Jews to add their voice to the fledgling modern Arabic literature of their country.

A literary autobiography is never a spontaneous flow of recollections. It is a well-established literary genre, involving selection, organization, and focus. Certain episodes, especially those related in the opening chapters, tend to assume a symbolic value in autobiographies, often reflecting the author's self-image and life philosophy.

The first five chapters of Anwar Sha'ul's autobiography are highly indicative of his sense of identity. Chapter 1 tells us that he was born in the city of Hilla, which he identifies as the site of ancient Babylon on the Euphrates. It is to that site that the exiles of ancient Israel were said to have been deported, and it was there that they chanted, "By the rivers of Babylon, there we sat down, yea, and wept, when we remembered Zion."

Thus, the author's connection with his biblical roots is forcefully evoked.[23]

Chapter 2 intimates that the author is a scion of Shaykh Sasson, the patriarch of the famous Sassoon family. Here the word *Shaykh* is significant, because it denoted that special type of Jewry that is rooted in the world of Islam. In Chapter 3 the author discloses that his mother, who died shortly after his birth, was in fact the daughter of an Austrian tailor, Hermann Rosenfeld, who had settled in Iraq and married into the family of Shaykh Sasson.[24]

Further, in Chapter 5, we learn that the author's wet nurse (Arabic *umm bi'l-rida'a,* "mother by nursing") was a Muslim woman named Umm-Husayn. For fifteen months she breastfed the baby boy together with her own son, 'Abd al-Hadi. The two "brothers by nursing" meet in Baghdad many years later, and an emotional reunion ensues.[25]

The author's identity as projected in these chapters is, therefore, that of a Jew with biblical origins—part of the modern Jewish people but retaining deep roots in the Arab Islamic ethos, an Arab Jew who is proud of being both Jewish and Iraqi.

It is significant, then, that the book does not betray a spiteful or bitter tone, although it was written *after* its author had to desert Iraq for good. To be sure, the bulk of the autobiography records fond memories rather than a sense of disappointment. The non-Jewish personages whom Anwar Sha'ul recalls are mostly portrayed as positive characters. In fact, the only unpleasant ones in the book are those Iraqis who were in one way or another pro-Nazi. The German ambassador in Baghdad during the 1930s, von Grobba, is singled out as a major factor in the deterioration of Jewish-Muslim relations; and the anti-Jewish pogrom of June 1941 (often referred to as the *farhud*) is seen, here as in many other Jewish sources, as the beginning of the end of a community that had lived in Mesopotamia for three millennia.

Admittedly, the rise of modern Zionism and the establishment of the State of Israel proved to be detrimental to the dream of integration and harmony that Anwar Sha'ul and his generation nurtured. But anti-Jewish prejudices, as is evident in this autobiography, antedate the involvement of Iraq in the anti-Zionist struggle. Thus, the 1920 disturbances in Iraq were not devoid of an anti-Jewish element, although the question of Palestine played no part in it. Fascist and Hitlerite ideas were becoming fashionable in some Iraqi circles as early as the mid-1920s.[26] At times modern Iraqi intellectuals would reflect in their words and conduct some deep-rooted anti-Jewish sentiments. Anwar Sha'ul records an incident that occurred in Baghdad in 1928: A Muslim writer and lawyer, Tawfiq al-Fukayki, buttonholed him one day to express his admiration for a poem that the young Anwar had recited at a reception held in honor of a visiting Tunisian patriotic leader. Al-Fukayki, however, added wistfully, "It's a pity, though, that you are Jewish"—to which Anwar Sha'ul retorted, "Why 'pity'? I am quite happy to be a Jew."[27]

In the face of such sentiments, Anwar Sha'ul's efforts to assert his Iraqi identity and his Jewish Arabness were bound to encounter some insurmountable obstacles. *My Life in Iraq* is a sad book, in spite of the basically sanguine outlook of its author. His poetry and prose written after his departure from Iraq still entertain that noble but elusive notion of Jewish-Muslim and Jewish-Arab symbiosis. Yet, his labor of love, as well as that of his fellow Jewish Arab authors in Iraq and in other countries, was unrequited. Their voices were lost.

Notes

1. Arab writers often claim that Maimonides, too, converted to Islam. However, the modern Egyptian scholar, Shaykh Mustafa Abd al-Raziq, describes Maimonides as "one of the philosophers of Islam" because he regards all those philosophers who operated in the Muslim milieu as "Islamic philosophers." See his introduction to Israel Wolfenson, *Musa Ibn Maymun: Hayatuh wa-Musannafatuh* (Cairo, 1935), 4.

2. See Irene L. Gendzier, *The Practical Visions of Ya'qub Sanu'* (Cambridge, Mass., 1966).

3. Muhammad Yusuf Najm (ed.), *Al-Masrah al-'Arabi/Dirasat wa-Nusus III: Ya'qub Sanu'* (Beirut, 1963), iv.

4. See H.A.R. Gibb, *Studies on the Civilization of Islam* (Boston, 1962), 245ff.

5. For details about these authors, see Itzhak Bezalel, *The Writings of Sephardic and Oriental Jewish Authors in Languages Other Than Hebrew* (Tel Aviv, 1982), 279–310; see also Shmuel Moreh's bibliography, *Arabic Works by Jewish Writers, 1863–1973* [Arabic] (Jerusalem, 1973).

6. See Jacob M. Landau, *Jews in Nineteenth Century Egypt* (New York: New York University Press, 1969); Shimon Shamir (ed.), *The Jews of Egypt in Modern Times* (Boulder, Colo.: Westview Press, 1987).

7. See Sasson Somekh, "The Participation of Egyptian Jews in Modern Arabic Culture," in Shamir, *Jews of Egypt*, 130–40.

8. On Egyptian Karaites, see Rabbi Yosef al-Gamil, *Toledoth ha-Yahduth ha-Qara'ith [A History of Karaite Jewry]*, vol. 1 (Ramla: The National Council of Karaite Jews in Israel, 1979).

9. On the life and works of Farag, see Leon Nemoy, "A Modern Karaite-Arabic Poet: Mourad Farag," *Jewish Quarterly Review* 70 (1980): 195–209. Nemoy lists Farag's dates as 1867–1955.

10. Articles expressing these sentiments can be found in Farag's book *Maqalat Murad* (Cairo, 1912); as well as in many poems included in the first two volumes of his *Diwan Murad*, published in Cairo in 1912 and 1924, respectively.

11. Mourad Farag, *Diwan Murad*, vol.3 (Cairo, 1929), 48.

12. Mourad Farag, *Multaqa al-Lughatayn al-'Arabiyya wa'l-'Ibriyya*, 5 vols. (Cairo, 1930–50).

13. The last of these was a translation of the Book of Job, published in 1950.

14. Farag, *Maqalat Murad*, 200–23.

15. On the Jews of Iraq in modern times, see Nissim Rejwan, *The Jews of Iraq: 3,000 Years of History and Culture* (London: Weidenfeld and Nicholson, 1986). On

the literary life of this community in recent decades, see Shmuel Moreh's introduction to his anthology, *Al-Qissa al-Qasira 'inda Yahud al-'Iraq, 1924–1978* (Jerusalem: Magnes, 1981).

16. 'Abd al-Ilah Ahmad, *Nash'at al-Qissa wa-Tatawwuruha fi 'l-'Iraq, 1908–1939* (Baghdad, 1969), 85. The collected poetry of Dr. Murad Mikhael was published posthumously as Murad Mikha'il, *Al-A'mal al-Shi'riyya al-Kamila* (Tel Aviv and Shafa 'Amr, 1988).

17. Other authors who emigrated to Israel from Iraq and continue to write and publish in Arabic include Abraham Ovadya (1924–), Shalom Katav (Salim al-Kataib, 1931–), Salim al-Bassun (1927–), and David Semah (1933–).

18. On Jewish participation in the Iraqi Communist Party, see Hanna Batatu, *The Old Social Classes and the Revolutionary Movements in Iraq* (Princeton: Princeton University Press, 1978), 650–51, 699–701, 1190–92.

19. Shalom Darwish's story is included in his book *Ba'd al-Nas* [*Some People*] (Baghdad, 1948); on the dialect of the Jews of Baghdad (the *qeltu* dialect) as well as on other Baghdadi dialects, see Hayim Blanc, *Communal Dialects in Baghdad* (Cambridge, Mass.: Harvard University Press, 1964).

20. Anwar Sha'ul, *Wa-Bazagha Fajr Jadid: Diwan Shi'r* (Jerusalem, 1983).

21. See for instance, Ahmad, *Nash' at al-Qissa*, 237–51.

22. Anwar Sha'ul, *Qissat Hayati fi Wadi al-Rafidayn* [*My Life Story in Mesopotamia*] (Jerusalem, 1980).

23. Ibid., 12.

24. Ibid., 12–14.

25. Ibid., 22–23.

26. Ibid., chap. 17.

27. Ibid., 111–18.

SIMON MARKISH

The Example of Isaac Babel

Isaac babel fits perfectly into the landscape of Soviet literature of the 1920s. Thematically, his collection of short fiction, *Red Cavalry*, takes its place alongside the stories of Vsevolod Ivanov, Dmitri Furmanov's *Chapayev*, Alexander Fadeyev's *The Rout*, and innumerable other works on the civil war. The naturalism of *Red Cavalry*—its brutal depiction of elemental forces unleashed by the revolution—is not more remarkable or more terrifying than what can be found in Vsevolod Ivanov or Artem Vesely; its style is not more colorful than the bewitching verbal tissue of Andrei Platonov, or the inimitable palette of Mikhail Sholokhov's *And Quiet Flows the Don*. As for the exotic underworld of Babel's *Odessa Tales* and of his play, *Sunset*, both of which reflect a general interest in criminal life (as well as in subjects related to the borderlands and "aliens," Jews included), it finally parallels such works as V. Kaverin's *The End of Khaza*, or Leonid Leonov's *The Thief*. Even Babel's notorious silence, his catastrophically low output after *Sunset* (1928), and the relative weakness of that work compared with his other work of the 1920s, are merely an extreme form of the disease and crisis that afflicted all of Soviet literature at the turn of the decade.[1]

It was no slip of the tongue and no exaggeration when Stalin called 1929 the "year of the great breaking point." That year marked the threshold not only of great economic and social upheavals—the destruction of the peasantry, industrialization, the beginning of the new autocracy and of a new terror—it also signaled the fundamental reconstruction of the young Soviet culture. For all the blindness and randomness of the Great Purges, which struck out right and left indiscriminately, there is no denying them a certain logic, which can be discerned in their results: everything was liquidated that stood out from the rank and file, that did not blend with the general mass, or that was unable to fall into line behind the party leadership, without hesitation or complaint. Naturally, there were exceptions, but it was not by chance that Titian Tabidze or Pavel Vasiliev disappeared, while Nikolai Tikhonov and Alexander Prokofiev were spared and allowed to flourish. Nor was the destruction of Babel a matter of chance. Soviet literature of the 1940s and 1950s had no place for the likes of him.

And yet Babel does stand out obviously and sharply among his contemporaries. The reasons for this preoccupied critics during his lifetime, and have done so since his posthumous rehabilitation. Some have spoken simply about his talent and its uniqueness. Others have offered explanations based on his experiments in genre, his special brand of romanticism, the peculiarities of his character, and his personal fate. Without rejecting any of these arguments, I would like to concentrate exclusively on one circumstance of fundamental importance, Babel's tie to Russian Jewish literature.

I do not mean Babel's Jewish origin or his Jewish mentality. Others have written on that before, and continue to do so. Thus, we read in an article by Pavel Novitskii, published in 1928:

> Babel has a passionate, dry, precise Jewish mind . . . . A solemn serious-ness and concentrated severity make his work true and sharp . . . . He is wearied by the dense melancholy of memory. The past (in his phrase, "the rotted Talmuds of his memories") holds him fast in its grip. He is incapable of drastic action.[2]

More recently, the French critic Judith Stora-Sandor has similarly stressed Babel's Jewishness: his religiosity, his knowledge of Yiddish, his youthful study of Hebrew, the Bible, and the Talmud; his loyalty to Jewish traditions, both familial and social; his passion for Hasidism, which, in Stora-Sandor's view, led him on to Tolstoyanism. Her conclusion:

> It was precisely due to his Jewish interests that Babel, the *Soviet* writer, became also a *Jewish* writer. In making himself the mouthpiece of his fellow Jews, without locking himself up within the close confines of their restricted community, as the Yiddish writers did, Babel tried to demon-strate the practical possibility of uniting two souls, the Jewish and the Russian.[3]

Where Novitskii connects the Jewish "past" with weakness and inde-cisiveness, and with these alone, Stora-Sandor wraps her definition of what makes a "Jewish" writer in an equally dense fog of half-under-standing or even total misunderstanding. Babel, in fact, did not "become" a Jewish writer—he had always been one. He did not choose to write in a particular language, as did Mendele Mokher Seforim, or Hayim Nahman Bialik; for him, the Russian literary tradition was natural, organic, and the only one possible. As for the supposed opposition between Yiddishist ex-clusivity and Babel's "universality," that is as senseless as the notion of his striving to unite the Jewish and Russian "souls."

By the time of Babel's first literary efforts, a Russian Jewish literature already existed. It had arisen immediately after the first shoots of Jewish Enlightenment (*Haskalah*) appeared on Russian soil in the nineteenth century. This movement, which aimed at bringing the Jews out of their isolation in the ghetto, had as one of its main objectives the introduction of the Jews to the culture and especially to the language of the indigenous population. In Germany, where the movement originated, the German language was assimilated quickly and successfully, owing partly to its closeness to Yiddish and partly to the greater material well-being of the Jewish population. In the Russian empire, the followers of Moses Mendelssohn, the father of *Haskalah*, encountered enormous difficulties. Yet, despite the appalling poverty and congestion of the Jewish masses; despite the inconsistency of government policy, first fostering the enlightenment of the Jews, then obstructing it, first hoping for their assimilation, then fearing "Jewish domination"; and despite the decisive turn to repression and restriction under Alexander III, Russian Jewish literature did indeed develop, and it generated its own growing readership.

Already by the turn of the twentieth century, then—or, at any rate, by the eve of World War I—Russian had become one of the languages of the Jewish Diaspora. Notwithstanding the unquestionable predominance of Yiddish, a certain section of the Jewish intelligentsia, notably in Odessa, Kiev, and St. Petersburg, had become Russian-speaking; there was widespread and accomplished Russian Jewish journalism, historiography, and belles lettres; periodicals and books were being published in large numbers. The rise of Russian Jewish literature at the beginning of the twentieth century was enhanced by emergent Zionism, which rejected Yiddish and adopted Russian as a stepping-stone to Hebrew, a language undergoing its own renaissance.

The Russian Jewish literature of the pre-revolutionary period was a literature written in Russian by Jews for Jews, and one way or another charged with Jewish themes. Even if Russian Jewish writers succeeded in attracting the attention of the Russian-reading public—as was the case with the poet Semyon [Shimon Shmuel] Frug or, later and with greater significance, David Aizman and Semyon Iushkevich—he still remained outside the bounds of Russian literature proper, and was perceived as an alien or exotic phenomenon. And so indeed he was.

The Revolution changed things fundamentally. Leaving aside the social and political changes which turned the life of Russian Jewry inside out, let us consider one circumstance of a general nature which seems not yet to have received the attention it merits. Since the Revolution, the Soviet regime has in truth created a new, unified culture—not "socialist in content, national in form," as the official formula has it, but an imperial

Russian culture which continuously absorbs the best (by whatever standard) that is created in the provinces. Only translation into Russian, performance on the Moscow stage, exhibition on the Moscow screen or in Moscow galleries confers real life on an artistic production. And that, with very few exceptions, is what every artist works for. This has produced a curious analogy to the imperial culture of ancient Rome, which was created by the united efforts of the Italians, Gauls, Spaniards, Africans, and Greeks—and in which, with the passage of time, the proportional contribution of the provinces became more and more significant. Thus, Soviet literature today is inconceivable without Vasil Bykov (a Byelorussian), Okudzhava (a Georgian), Faizul Iskander (an Abkhaz), or Genghis Aitmatov (a Kirghiz), all of whom either write in Russian or translate their own work into Russian. Another parallel with ancient Rome: just as the label "provincial" covers Seneca (whose Spanish origins are undetectable in his work) and Apuleius (clearly a Hellenized North African, in literature as in life), so Okudzhava is Georgian in name only, while Oljas Suleimenov is a passionate Kazakh nationalist. In other words, the national markings of the alien who has entered imperial Russian-language literature fluctuate within very wide limits, so that in extreme situations new branches emerge; thus, in the case of Suleimenov, we are plainly dealing with a Russian Kazakh, or possibly Russian Turkic, branch of Soviet literature.

All this must be borne in mind in order to understand the fate of Russian Jewish literature and its role in the Soviet period. As an independent and isolated cultural phenomenon, it was liquidated along with neo-Jewish (Hebrew) literature. This was a politically motivated, violent action, one of the important moves in the Bolsheviks' struggle against Zionism and national-cultural autonomy, and it represented a systematic carrying out of the Bolshevik program as drawn up before the Revolution.

In the course of the 1920s, all the Russian Jewish periodicals were gradually closed down, and the leading figures of Russian Jewish literature either died, emigrated, or fell silent. But from the very beginning a considerable number of Jews had gone into Soviet-Russian literature. Many of them never in any way evinced any connection with Judaism, even in those far-off times when to be a Jew was positively encouraged. Examples are Benjamin Kaverin, the prose writer, and the poet Alexander Bezymenskii (the level of talent is irrelevant here); in a later period one might cite Emmanuel Kazakevich, who began writing in Yiddish but went over to Russian after the war and in the entire corpus of his Russian work betrayed not a hint of anything Jewish. Among Russian writers of Jewish origin, however, a fair number exhibited (and continue to exhibit) national characteristics, though in very varying quantities and forms, depending on general circumstances and personal situation. The 1920s and 1930s are particularly rich in examples of this phenomenon, revealing a freshness and directness in literary reminiscences of distinctively Jewish life, made possible by the absence of official anti-Semitism. By contrast, the last years of the Stalin regime, which saw the peak of anti-Semitic terror, are almost totally sterile. Then, in the second half of the 1950s and the 1960s, came a resurgence of a new kind, an explosion of a people's frustrated dignity (no matter that its positive self-awareness, its cultural "baggage," might be scant or even nonexistent).

However disparate the forms and quantities involved, works with a Jewish orientation do constitute a certain whole, for which two claims, at least, can fairly be made: they represent the first—and, up to now, the most significant—non-Russian branch of Soviet-Russian literature; and despite their inseparability from the imperial literature described above, they are the direct descendants of pre-revolutionary Russian Jewish literature, and can be studied and understood only in relation to the latter. (To these two claims a third might well be added: it is that Russian Jewish literature of the Soviet period might instructively be considered alongside such parallel phenomena as contemporary American Jewish, Anglo-Jewish, and Franco-Jewish literature from a whole range of standpoints.)

At the very headwaters of the Russian Jewish literature of the Soviet period stands Isaac Babel. Or perhaps one should say that he himself was its main source—to which its peculiarities, its development, and its role within Soviet literature are in large measure traceable.

The daily life and cultural background from which Babel came played an important role in his creative life. He grew up in Odessa, in a family that was economically comfortable. (It may be pertinent to note here that many details in his quasi-autobiographical Odessa stories are invented out of whole cloth, as, for example, the assertion, "I come from a poverty-stricken wreck of a family.") A substantial part of the Jewish population, which in the year of Babel's birth, 1894, formed one-third, and on the eve of the Revolution one-half, of the total population of Odessa, had left the old traditional and enclosed Jewish life far behind. Theirs was the path of assimilation—in the original and literal meaning of that term, "becoming like"; what they had in view was adaptation, perhaps even the first step toward integration. Despite pogroms, persecution, and discrimination, the situation in Odessa was not unlike that in America: a blending with the surrounding milieu, and at the same time a secure sense of group community, with the synagogue as spiritual and organizational (rather than purely religious) center. This situation was unique in Russia; there was nothing like it in any of the other centers of Jewish culture, not in St. Petersburg, in

Kiev, or in Vilna. That the contribution of Jewish Odessa to the nascent Soviet culture proved so large was thus no accident.

According to Babel's sister, at home the parents spoke Yiddish to each other and Russian to the children.[4] This may have been the case—it was typical enough in Odessa at the time. And yet (as we learn from his letters, published in English in 1964 as *Isaac Babel: The Lonely Years*), Babel knew Yiddish well enough to edit the collected works of Sholem Aleichem in Russian translation, expressed the desire to translate *Tevye the Dairyman*, and did in fact translate David Bergelson's tale, *Dzhiro-Dzhiro*. What is even more important, he read Yiddish not simply for professional reasons but for his own pleasure, sitting before the fire at his *dacha* outside Moscow; in one letter to his mother, he calls Yiddish "our language."

Babel studied at a commercial school, together, according to his *Autobiography*, with "the sons of foreign merchants, children of Jewish brokers, imposing Poles, Old Believers, and many overgrown billiard players."[5] In that motley place, and in the dockside cafes and billiard halls, he not only absorbed the language of the Russian classics, he also fell in love with that special Odessa dialect, half-Russian, half-Ukrainian, in which even today the strong Jewish intonation and phrasing are evident. In school he also learned French, so well that after only two years he was writing stories in that language. But during the same period, for about six years, from age ten to sixteen, he was studying biblical and talmudic teaching as well, and was thus able (in 1926) to approve the Hebrew translation of six of his tales.

Stora-Sandor asserts that Babel was religious. That seems not quite accurate; he is on record too often with public denials of God's existence (for instance, the end of his speech at the First [Soviet] Writers' Congress), and no one who knows his life and work would accuse Babel of hypocrisy. Yet, religious traditions were an inseparable part of his nature. He punctiliously sent greetings to his parents on the High Holidays in the fall and at Passover, always mentioning that he himself intended to celebrate as far as possible, and lamenting that his possibilities were so meager and poor. In his letters he asks his mother if she had been to the synagogue, and, after attending the synagogue in Odessa himself for the New Year service, he tells her how "everything was so painfully familiar, I am terribly glad I went and, as always, I prayed in my own way to my own, other God, above all for you both" (that is, his mother and his sister).[6]

The "above all" is not an exaggeration. Babel's love for and attachment to his family, which may seem surprising and excessive to the present-day generation, is an age-old and important tradition of the Jewish Diaspora, and Babel clearly understood the nature of his family feelings. So when he says that at every minute and every hour he is sharing in spirit the sufferings of his family, and would give everything to be able to do so physically, he adds the comment: "Look what a classic Jewish family-man I've become." Again and again in his letters he recalls his late father: he swears to carry out everything he had promised this father who had always expected success, not complaints, from his children; thus, thoughts of his father give him strength and drive away despair. In consciously accepting tradition, Babel was also trying to sustain it, if only symbolically, in the family that had been torn apart by his wife's emigration from Russia. When his daughter was born in Paris, he asked his wife to give her a real Jewish name—in vain: instead of "Judith," Natasha made her appearance in the world in 1929.

It is understandable that Babel should have loved Odessa as no other city in the world. He regarded it as the only place where he could really work, and he dreamed of returning there to live, traveling to Moscow only on business. It is understandable, too, that each visit, no matter how impoverished and provincialized the city had become, should bring him great pleasure. His spirit and his brain were refreshed. His ears were caressed by the Odessa accent. Newspaper boys, garbage collectors, janitors would greet him on the street and engage him in the most improbable conversations, of a sort that could only be heard in Odessa. After an evening at the theater, where he delivered a few utterly unmemorable remarks, thousands of young people lined the streets and blocked the path of his car. So it is understandable that he should have refused to emigrate with his mother, his wife, and his sister. Apart from his genuine Soviet patriotism—of which more later—the feeling was too strong in him of belonging to Russian Jewry, to that cultural milieu, in the broadest sense, which existed nowhere else in the world and of which the focus, the quintessence, was old Odessa. Even for so "poignant" a writer as Babel, the nostalgic lines he wrote about Odessa, in his brief note on Edward Bagritskii, sound unusually poignant:

> I remember our last conversation. We agreed it was time to get out of strange towns, time to go home, to Odessa, to take a little house on Blizhnie Melnitsy, to write chronicles, to grow old . . . . We saw ourselves as old men, sly, portly old men, warming ourselves in the Odessa sun, on the boulevard by the sea, and following the women with a long gaze . . . .[7]

Still, the Jewish background—Jewish traditions and emotional attachments—are not in themselves enough. The writer or artist may recall his Jewish youth with tenderness and yearning, he may prefer gefilte fish with red-hot horseradish above all other food and drink, he may indulge himself with *matzot* and even pop into the synagogue a couple of times a year, but none of that entitles him to a place in Jewish culture, or in a Jewish encyclopedia. This can only come when his entire creative life, or a good part of it, has taken form under the influence of Jewish self-awareness. Babel's moment of self-awareness and choice arrived rather early, and antedates his appearance in print. Two crucial pieces of work, written at the end of 1915, provide the evidence—"Childhood II: At Grandmother's" and a fragment, "Three O'Clock in the Afternoon"[8]— both of them entirely Jewish in theme and, more important, in the subjectivity that informs them.

The first is a sketch of a day spent at his grandmother's. House and grandmother together evoke this response in the boy: "Everything seemed strange to me. I wanted at the same time to run away from it all and to stay there forever." Here a familiar routine and atmosphere undergo an abrupt transformation, take on a piercing novelty, inspiring simultaneously horror (or perhaps revulsion) and a feeling for what is "one's own," ineluctable and permanent. Here we have essentially the whole Jewish Babel, the basis of his social and emotional values and the foundation of his aesthetics. Jewishness of whatever kind—the steadfastly traditional, the *shtetl*-Hasidic, or the urban-emancipated—is perceived dualistically. The heritage is at once accepted and rejected, a fact that precludes simple social realism along with apologetics and denunciation—the three characteristic stances of the old Russian Jewish literature. What appears in their stead is a fresh perspective from a new vantage point; sheer astonishment is no small part of it. Here is the source of that exoticism of the quotidian, that fantastic sharpness of line and violent emotionality that are the mark of Babel's style. But here, at the same time, is the source of his loneliness, dooming him to the role of outsider, always and with everyone.[9]

The fragment, "Three O'Clock in the Afternoon," was published in an obscure journal only in 1971, and is generally unobtainable.[10] It has been described by a Soviet critic, however, as a combination of "plotless lyrical narration saturated with precise psychological details which constitute a second level" and a vivid story "with heightened emphasis on individual speech."[11] Thus, long before *Red Cavalry* and the *Odessa Tales*, but at the time when his general position had crystallized (and, obviously, as a result of that crystallization), Babel discovers, at least in principle, the expressive means and the manner that were to become his hallmarks. The moment of registering this self-awareness is the moment of Babel's self-invention as a writer.

The novelty of his position involved a new approach to his subject matter. Until then it had not been possible to imagine a work of Russian Jewish literature on a non-Jewish subject. Now the author's attitude to his material acquires greater importance: his dual vision, from within and without, deepens his imagery and gives it a dimension which it had not and could not have known before.

But if the approach "from outside" had been construed only negatively, as synonymous with "not inside," if the phrase "I wanted to run away from it all" had simply signified flight, then we would not be able to speak of the dimension that comes from binocular vision. The Bolshevik Revolution gave Babel a second vantage point, another feeling of belonging, as indisputable as the first. I have already remarked that even the best and most famous Russian Jewish writers were alien beings to the non-Jewish reader. But these writers felt themselves to be aliens in Russian literature, guests at best. For Babel, however, Soviet-Russian literature was as much hearth and home as it was to Vsevolod Ivanov, and I am convinced that Babel's loyalty to the Soviet regime, his love for Soviet Russia, his importuning of his family to return from emigration, especially in 1934–35, are in many ways connected with this feeling. After returning from his first trip abroad, he wrote that he felt well in his native land, even if there was poverty and a great deal of misery; here he had his language and his material, the only things he found truly and inexhaustibly interesting. That disposition remained intact even during the 1930's—like the Jewish heritage, Soviet life was for him his rightful property, and more: his creation.

It follows that until this dual support was found, the real Babel did not exist. His first stories, published in 1916, are equally feeble, whether they have Jewish themes ("Ilia Isaakovich and Margarita Prokofievna") or non-Jewish ("Mama, Rimma, and Alla"). His first success, *Red Cavalry*,[12] was destined to prove his largest one as well—because here, as in no other work, he drew on *both* his supports with such assurance and strength.

Kirill Vasilievich Liutov, the narrator and protagonist of *Red Cavalry*, is not Babel, even though the writer gave him the name under which he himself had served in the First Cavalry Army as correspondent for a military newspaper. Liutov is half of him, the Jewish half that is frantically in quest of a complementary, revolutionary, Bolshevik half: "'Gedali,' I said, 'today is Friday and it's evening already. Where can I get hold of some Jewish biscuits, a Jewish glass of tea, and a bit of that pensioned-off God in the glass of tea?'"[13] Jewishness gives him his bearings in the savage and bloody, longed-for and unattainable, Revolution. Thus, although the death of the hero and pillager, Trunov, is not connected with the Galician village of Sokal, except geographically, Liutov nevertheless gives a detailed (detailed, that is, for Babel—two paragraphs) account of the ancient synagogues and torn gabardines, of the noisy wrangling of the Orthodox and Hasidim, and he concludes: "Heavy-hearted because of Trunov, I too went pushing among them, shouting along with them to ease my sorrow" (from "Squadron Commander Trunov").[14] The ending of the famous "Discourse on the Tachanka," which appears at first glance to have no connection with the rest of the text, is in fact a most important paragraph on the Jews of Galicia and Volhynia. The son of a Zhitomir rebbe, "the last prince of the dynasty," the Red Army man Bratslavskii, a party member who had prayed in his father's synagogue because he felt unable to leave his mother, comes to understand that "in the Revolution a mother is only an episode,"[15] and, sent by his organization to take charge of a combat regiment, dies of typhus on the filthy floor of the news correspondents' railroad car. The contents of his trunk are as mixed as those of his brief biography: "Agitator's orders and booklets of a Jewish poet, portraits of Lenin and Maimonides, pages from the Song of Songs, and bullets for his revolver." "He died, the last prince, amid verses, phylacteries, and leg windings. And I, barely able to contain the gales of my imagination within my ancient body, received the last gasp of my brother."[16]

The Red Army man Bratslavskii is more than Liutov's brother, he is his double. He sacrifices all, asking for nothing and claiming nothing, except revolutionary solidarity. Yet he dies in solitude, under the indifferent gaze of "Cossacks in red baggy trousers" and "two big-breasted typists in sailors' jackets," having been wrested by his "brother" from the mass of typhus-ridden peasants who "rolled before them the customary hump of a soldier's death" and "wheezed and scratched and flew on wordlessly."[17] He had been alone even in that crowd; indeed, his "brother" recognizes him by his solitude: He is the only one to reach out for a pamphlet, while all the others vie with each other to grab the potatoes Liutov is scattering from the wagon. The narrative of the story is addressed to an unknown Vasilii, whose name is mentioned insistently, almost importunately, five times in two pages. This persistence rests on the opposition of brother with stranger; to the latter, no matter how hard you try and how many times you call him by name, nothing can finally be explained.

Yet the rebbe, Motele Bratslavskii, the Red Army man's father, is one of Babel's own, albeit no "brother." The dialogue between him and Liutov, in the story "The Rebbe," is a conversation between people who understand each other intuitively. Joy, laughter, merriment are what Liutov craves as he wanders voluntarily through the convulsions and carnage of the class war, and the rebbe seeks the same with his pupils, as does the rag-and-bone man Gedali—which is why Gedali's praise of Hasidism has the ring of the author's own judgment. By contrast, the argument with Gedali (in "Gedali"), the champion of the "sweet Revolution" and the "International of good people," rings hollow. Liutov answers the ragman's "abstract humanism" with only two arguments, quite summarily presented: The Revolution "cannot help shooting, because it is the Revolution,"[18] and the International "is eaten with gunpowder and seasoned with the finest blood." In fact, these are something less than arguments. The principal refutation of

Liutov's position, however, lies elsewhere: immediately after his menacing reference to gunpowder and blood comes the plaintive request, quoted above, for some Jewish biscuits and a glass of Jewish tea. "There isn't any," Gedali replies, "there isn't any. There's a tavern next door, where good people used to do business. But people don't eat there anymore, they just weep there."[19]

Liutov has nowhere to go. The old world, from which he fled but that still retains its hold on him, has been destroyed by the new, toward which he is striving with all his heart, but that will not accept him, and repels him with its ugliness and blood lust. The loneliness and desperation of the intellectual in the Revolution, a frequent enough literary theme in the 1920s, are compounded by the loneliness of the Jew—the Jew, moreover, being of a particular kind, split down the middle in his attitude to Jewishness, as the intellectual is split in his attitude to the Revolution. As a result, in the strength and tension of the tragic principle, the insolubility of its conflict, *Red Cavalry* may well take pride of place among books on the civil war.

The sharpness of the conflict is intensified by a vision so unsparing in its precision as to suggest at times the moral indifference of an aesthete:

> Right in front of my windows, some Cossacks were executing an old silver-bearded Jew for spying. The old man yelped and struggled. Then Kudrya, from the machine-gunners, tucked the old man's head under his arm. The Jew fell silent and spread his feet apart. With his right hand, Kudrya took out his knife and carefully cut the old man's throat, avoiding the spurting blood.[20]

But this precision is itself the result of a sense of apartness and alienation that often borders on active hostility. (Simple compassion for "one's own," whether in ethnic kinship or common cause, would have blurred the vision and robbed the picture of its distinctive severity.) In the same story, "Berestechko," the Jewish way of life is delineated with a hostility that marks even the vocabulary ("the warm putrefaction of the old world"; "the stifling decay of Hasidism"; "the traditional wretchedness of this architecture"; and so on); and this hostility is underlined by contrast: "The village stinks, waiting for the new era, and instead of people, it is inhabited by fading schemata of frontier misfortunes. By the end of the day I was fed up with them and I left the town, climbed the hill, and found an entry into the ruins of the Raciborski castle."[21] Liutov is not shocked by the abomination of desolation in what was once the seat of a Polish aristocrat; his descriptive detail—the nymphs with their eyes put out, a fragment of a hundred-year-old letter—sounds, rather, elegiac.

But even sharper and more merciless is the vision he turns on his comrades-in-arms. Here, the alienation of an intellectual is augmented by ethnic alienation—and Liutov recoils in horror. He wants to admire and approve, and from this willed desire derive both the romantic phantasmagoria of landscapes and the infatuated portraits of his heroes, such as that of Savitskii, the divisional commander, in the opening paragraph of "My First Goose." But the romantic, technicolor film often snaps, and then one sees in the gaps the "raw fingers" and "fleshy, loathsome face" of another hero, another divisional commander, Pavlichenko in "Chesniki." The horror is even clearer in the stories told by narrators other than Liutov; between them and him lies an abyss of non-understanding and fear. With fear and bewilderment, the intellectual Liutov registers the dense and savage suspiciousness of the barbarian ("Betrayal"); but for Liutov the Jew, much more terrible is the fanatical savagery of the *goyim*, trampling the enemy to death ("The Life Story of Pavlichenko"), ready to kill for a bag of salt ("Salt"), capable of parricide and the murder of a son ("The Letter"). It would be wrong to see Liutov's reaction to all this as reflecting only a sense of moral superiority, millennia of living with the biblical commandment, "Thou shalt not kill," for it reflects as well millennia of passive martyrdom, the heritage of discrimination and intimidation.

On the whole, as I have already remarked, the author of *Red Cavalry* stands above his hero. His dual position is stable and productive. Despite his apartness, he is still his own man in both elements, in the old and in the new, in the Jewish and in the Soviet. He is not with the Liutov who is fed up with the Jews of Berestechko, or who confesses, "I am tired of living in this Red Army of ours."[22] He corrects Liutov through Gedali; and he cuts short Liutov's complaining with Galin's words:

> You're a ditherer, and it's our luck that we have to put up with ditherers like you . . . . We are taking the nut out of the shell for you. Soon you'll see the nut right out of its shell, then you'll stop picking your nose and start singing the praises of the new life in unusual prose. Till then, just sit quiet, you ditherer, and don't whine around our feet.[23]

This astonishing harmony-in-duality is what makes *Red Cavalry* a unique book, in Soviet as well as in Russian Jewish literature. It is Babel's best work, also his most Jewish—despite its non-Jewish subject matter—because at its center stands Jewish restlessness and yearning, gripped momentarily by the prospect of finding self-transcendence in the great common cause. That this hope was unrealizable, that the cause, "seasoned with the finest blood," would turn into an endless bloodbath, Babel did not know, and to indict him on this ground would be wrong.

Babel's works on purely Jewish subjects turn out, in a sense, to be less Jewish, precisely because in them the confidently sustained duality of position is weaker by comparison with *Red Cavalry*—when it is not, as in the early story "Shabbes Nakhamu" (1918), entirely absent. The latter is a rather pallid rendering of several anecdotes, or oral tales, about Hershele Ostropolier, the Jewish variation of the trickster-hero to be found in the folklore of almost every people. Babel, however, evidently gave this experiment (which, despite its subtitle, "From the Cycle, 'Hershele,'" he never continued) special significance, for in *Red Cavalry*, in reply to Reb Motele's question, "What does the Jew do?" Liutov replies, "I am rendering the adventures of Hersh of Ostropol into verse."[24]

Odessa Tales was probably written at the same time as *Red Cavalry*. They are marked, however, not only by different themes: the narrator is different, as is his relation to his material. Babel writes of the gangster life of Jewish Odessa in the first person, but at one point allows the narrative to pass to the synagogue beadle (*shames*), Arye-Leib, who refers to the narrator in rather disparaging terms: "You have spectacles on your nose, and autumn in your soul."[25] Nevertheless, the poetics and intonation, as well as the emotional background of all four tales, are identical. The narrator is as much in love with the fat, juicy, fleshy, full-blooded, expansive Odessa of robbers, rich men, and cemetery-gate beggars, as is Arye-Leib himself. Arye-Leib says of the rich man nicknamed "Jew-and-a-half": "Tartakovskii's got the soul of a murderer, but he's one of us. He started as one of us. He's our flesh and blood, just as if the same mother bore us."[26] *Mutatis mutandis*, Babel might have said the same thing about all of old Jewish Odessa—as old Odessa might about him. He is here at home among his own; of the urge to escape and the self-division, all that remains is the conventional pair of spectacles on the nose, contrasting with the eagle eyes of the horse-and-cart drivers, the thieves, and Tartakovskii.

None of this is intended to diminish the qualities of *Odessa Tales*. I merely mean to emphasize one thing: despite their stunning stylistic discoveries and innovations, despite their nostalgia for a recent but already irrevocable past, despite the utterly new and unexpected appearance of a bandit-hero in Russian Jewish literature, the *Odessa Tales* continue and perhaps crown the pre-revolutionary tradition of social observation in this literature, whereas *Red Cavalry* opens a new period and establishes a new tradition.

The four stories of the autobiographical cycle were written later than *Red Cavalry* and *Odessa Tales*. Two of them are dated 1925 and two 1930. These sad Jewish tales of sad Jewish childhood, with pogroms, penury, insane relatives—as I mentioned above, at least half of the events and details are imaginary—would not stand out among the childhood reminiscences in which Russian Jewish literature abounds but for the fact that here the author regards his past from a different, completely non-Jewish world. He has not broken with his former world demonstratively or noisily; he has simply left it, slipped away from it, into "nowhere," and he looks back with mixed feelings of nostalgia and fear, like the majority of children who have turned adult. Jewishness here is not the theme but the background against which the tragedies of childhood are reenacted: tragedies of love, deception, humiliation. Naturally, they are all strongly conditioned by the background, especially as, in the first two short stories, "The Story of My Dovecote" and "First Love," the background is a pogrom, but the tragedies themselves are universal, not linked to any one place or time or people. And the heart of each tale lies precisely in these universal tragedies; perhaps that is why the narrator, in focusing on his past sufferings, renders them with Babel-like tension and insight, observing everything else—the pogrom itself, his murdered grandfather Shoil, the Cossacks and their horses, the pogromists themselves—with a gaze that is clear, calm, and at times even admiring. That contrast represents not merely the special strength of Babel's autobiographical stories, but also an innovation of the greatest significance for the modern Jewish literatures of the Diaspora.

In 1935 Babel announced: "I would like to tell the world everything I know about old Odessa; after that I will be able to go on to the new Odessa." In fact he had undertaken to confront the new Odessa earlier, in 1931, when he published his story, "Karl Yankel." But the attempt was not a success—as Babel himself realized. In a letter written in February 1932, he expresses astonishment that the critics should pay any attention to such rubbish, and he calls the story simply bad. He cannot handle the new Odessa because he has no tender feeling for it. The scandal about the circumcision of the newborn Karl Yankel in the story of that name is inflated not merely in itself, but it is inflated and artificial for Babel, who is forcing himself and cannot disguise the fact. The same element of artificiality appears in the stereotype, Ovsei Belotserkovskii, who stockpiles farm supplies with the help of the Balta and Tiraspol district party committees. It appears in the feeding of the infant by the Kirghiz woman—a sugary vignette illustrative of the "indestructible friendship of the peoples of the U.S.S.R."—and in the pathos of the narrator's concluding exclamations. On the other hand, there is nothing false, despite some crude grotesque, in the "little operator" Naftula Gerchik; the page and a half devoted to him are Babel at his best.

Throughout the 1930s Babel was searching for a new style. Both his letters and his public speeches are full of complaints about the agonizing difficulties of the search. He was looking not only for new expressive forms but, above all, for another atmosphere, another milieu, new ground under his feet. Beyond the bounds of Russian Jewish literature, however, success would not favor him—even though he knew the Soviet Union very well, loved it devotedly, was himself loved and surrounded everywhere by friends. As I have said, the reasons for this are various and each has its own measure of validity; still, it would appear that the loss of his dual position, his dual vision, had a crucial effect. It is not in evidence—nor could it be—when he is regarding something entirely alien, as, for example, the high aristocracy (in the play *Mariia*), even if by the accident of revolution a Jewish speculator has managed to worm his way into its midst. Gorky, incidentally—who justifiably disliked *Mariia*—wrote to Babel: "I especially don't like Dymshits . . . . You make him too easy a target for the Judeophobes." I imagine such apprehensions had never occurred to Babel. The Jewish writer portrays a Jewish villain as naturally and unself-consciously as a Russian writer would a Russian villain, and neither would worry about what the Judeophobes or the Russophobes might say. Even so, there is no dual vision when one examines a thing of one's own making: In the two surviving fragments of a lost novel about collectivization ("Kolyvushka" and "Gapa Guzhva"), Babel is truthful—that is, true to himself—but he is unable to detach himself from the material, to stand to one side, and the sharpness, clarity, and depth of his account suffer in consequence.

Babel is the most important figure in Russian Jewish literature of the Soviet period, the model of the Jewish writer in Soviet-Russian culture. The Russian Jewish literature that was reborn after Stalin takes its bearings from him, and is measured against him. To imitate Babel is impossibly difficult, to repeat him impossible—just as his fate is unrepeatable, just as old Odessa and turn-of-the-century Russian Jewry are beyond recall. But one can compare, assess, learn. It is unlikely that anyone today will be tempted by Babel's second standpoint, the Russian Revolution. But his feelings and views suggest the possibility of another, much more attractive "bifurcation." I have in mind some such oppositions as these: insularity, rigidity, inhibition, hypertrophied rationalism—as against openness, emotional release, fullness of feeling, the joy of existence. That is what the dialogue in the bedroom of the old Kriks in *Sunset* is all about. Nekhama nags her husband: "Look how other people live. For supper, other people have ten pounds of meat, they make soup, they make cutlets, they make compote. The father comes home from work, everybody sits at the table, everybody eats and laughs. But what do *we* do?" And Mendel snarls back: "Pull out my teeth, Nekhama, pour some Yiddish soup into my veins, break my back . . . ." Here is the root of Babel's ill-concealed delight in his gangsters, in the violent, dangerous crank Simon-Wolf, in grandfather Levi Yitzhok, the ex-rabbi who lost his post for crooked dealing in currency, "the laughing-stock of the town, and its embellishment" ("In the Basement"; "Awakening"). Here also in the sense of the ending of "The Story of a Horse," is a remarkable paragraph that has been endlessly quoted: "Khlebnikov was a quiet man, like me in character. We were both rocked by the same passions. We both looked on the world as a meadow in May, a meadow where women and horses moved about."[27]

Not to reject tradition, not to turn away from one's own history, not to wallow either in the fruits of the Diaspora or in its rubbish, but instead, to leap into freedom, into open space, to burst free from one's chains, to know the taste, color, scent, texture of everything denied us by the ghetto wall, the Pale of Settlement, and that invisible pale which we put around ourselves and in which we suffocated for century upon century. And to find harmony in dichotomy.

That is not written in Babel's work, it is only implied. But the idea of that paradoxical harmony, which is not at all the same thing as peace and quiet and heavenly grace, comes to mind constantly when one looks at the old guard of the kibbutzim, the settlers of Palestine in the 1930s. It comes to mind with increasing frequency as one thinks of the Jews of Silence, who have now become the Jews of Courage.

Translated by Donald Fanger and Harry Shukman

Notes

1. In English, both *Red Cavalry* and *Odessa Tales*, as well as other stories, are available in *The Collected Stories of Isaac Babel*, ed. and trans. Walter Morison, with an Introduction by Lionel Trilling (New York: Meridian/NAL, 1960).

2. I.E. Babel, *Stat'i i materialy* (Leningrad: Academia, 1928), 46,48.

3. Judith Stora-Sandor, *Isaac Babel:L'homme at l'oeuvre* (Paris, 1968),20.

4. Stora-Sandor, 19.

5. Isaac Babel, *Izbrannoe* (Moscow, 1968), 23.

6. Isaac Babel, *The Lonely Years* (1964), 318.

7. Isaac Babel, *Izbrannoe* (Moscow, 1968), 314.

8. *Literaturnoe nasledstvo*. Vol. 74. (Moscow, 1965), 483–488.

9. This position afforded invaluable artistic advantages, and Babel made the most of them throughout his life; in this he anticipates the best American-Jewish writers, from Henry Roth to Saul Bellow and Philip Roth.

10. Now obtainable in (Ann Arbor: University of Michigan, 1989), 199–201.

11. N.A. Smirin, *Na puti k 'Konarmii* in *Literaturnoe nasledstvo*. Vol. 74 (Moscow, 1965), 472.

12. Isaac Babel, *The Collected Stories*, ed. Walter Morison (New York: World Publishing Company, 1960).

13. "Gedali," *The Collected Stories*, 72.

14. Ibid., 145.

15. "The Rebbe's Son," *The Collected Stories*, 193.

16. Ibid., 193.

17. Ibid., 192.

18. "Gedali," *The Collected Stories*, 71.
19. Ibid., 72.
20. "Berestechko," *Collected Stories*, 119.
21. Ibid., 120.
22. "Evening," *Collected Stories*, 129.
23. Ibid.
24. "The Rabbi," *Collected Stories*, 78.
25. "How Things Were Done in Odessa," *Collected Stories*, 90.
26. Ibid.,214.
27. "The Story of a Horse," *Collected Stories*, 114.

From Newark to Prague:
Roth's Place in the American
Jewish Literary Tradition

In *The Anatomy Lesson*, the central character of Philip Roth's trilogy *Zuckerman Bound* comes into his inheritance. Right after his mother's death of a brain tumor, her neurologist hands Nathan Zuckerman a white piece of paper on which one word appears in his mother's handwriting, her response to the doctor's request that she write her own name. The word is *Holocaust*, and Nathan notices that it is spelled perfectly.

> This was in Miami Beach in 1970, inscribed by a woman whose writings otherwise consisted of recipes on index cards, several thousand thank-you notes, and a voluminous file of knitting instructions. Zuckerman was pretty sure that before that morning she'd never even spoken the word aloud.[1]

As the neurologist is uneasy about throwing it away, he passes it on to Nathan, who cannot discard it either. It is a legacy alien to his experience and incomprehensible, a scrap of paper both portentous and incidental. His compelling need to preserve it serves as an emblem both of Roth's relationship to his Jewish tradition and of a significant portion of what has come to be called American Jewish literature.

Definitions of American Jewish literature abound, beginning with Malin's and Stark's landmark essay in 1964 in which the Jew is seen to be an existential hero and therefore a modern Everyman.[2] In a thesis that rapidly became a trend, Jews are singled out, because of their victimization, uprootedness, and history of suffering, as the most apt symbol for humanity in the twentieth century.[3] American Jewish fiction, argue Malin and Stark, tends to be about seeking home (as a result of mass immigration), about the conflict between fathers and sons (cast in terms of generation conflict brought on by immigration), about coming to terms with history (caused by the awesome scope of the Jewish past), about dualities (chosen by God and rejected by the Gentiles), about the heart (suffering as initiation into humanity), and about transcendence (through humanity, not God). Since all literature of the West tends to be about the longing for "home," the conflict between parents and children, the individual in the face of history, duality, suffering, and transcendence, the only conclusion that one can draw about Malin's and Stark's formula is that of Shylock: "If you prick us, do we not bleed?" If Jews are people, and all people are Jews, there seems to be little point in discussing American Jewish literature.

Several years later, Malin pursued the implications of his definition in a theological approach to the subject. American Jewish writers, he argued, "are made crusaders hoping for a transcendent ideal." Malin continued to see Jewish literature from a religious perspective: "Only when a Jewish writer, moved by religious tensions, shows 'ultimate concern' in creating a new structure of belief, can he be said to create 'Jewish literature'."[4] It would seem for Malin that a religious impulse linked with individualism and anti-traditionalism make for Jewishness. Continuity through discontinuity.

While not everyone agreed with Malin's stress on religion, other critics sought the Jewish elements in universal terms as well. Theodore Solotareff, for example, defined American Jewish writing in a thematic and moralistic framework. In Malamud, Roth, and Bellow, Solotareff identified the theme of suffering leading to purification: "There is the similar conversion into the essential Jew, achieved by acts of striving, sacrificing, and suffering for the sake of some fundamental goodness and truth in one's self that has been lost and buried."[5] As it would be problematic to argue that the ennobling of suffering is a Jewish concept, or that "the moral role and power of the human heart" are attributes distinguishing Judaism from other moral systems, the moral approach is hardly more enlightening than the religious one.

As early as 1964, when the sanctity of the melting pot was being replaced by pluralistic and ethnic ideals of American culture, David Daiches doubted whether American Jewish writing really amounted to a movement. "The American Jewish writer has been liberated to use his Jewishness in a great variety of ways, to use it not aggressively or apologetically, but imaginatively as a writer probing the human condition," he said, but he denied that extreme sensitivity was enough to qualify as a criterion for distinguishing American Jewish literature from any other corpus.[6] That same year Allen Guttmann limited American Jewish literature to a transient social and historical phenomenon, to documenting the immigrant Jews' conversion to other passions—communism, capitalism, and secularization. Assimilation, he argued, was inevitable and imminent.[7]

The most vociferous and sensible objection to existing definitions of American Jewish literature has been that of Robert Alter: "It is by no means clear what sense is to be made of the Jewishness of a writer who neither uses a uniquely Jewish language, nor describes a distinctively Jewish milieu, nor draws upon literary traditions that are recognizably Jewish."[8] For Alter, unless a writer's imagination is impelled by a consciousness of Jewish history, such as that of Kafka, there is no case for labeling him [or her] as Jewish. Admitting that there is "something presumptuously proprietary about the whole idea of sorting out writers according to national, ethnic, or religious origins," Alter sees American Jewish literature as one that informs the reader "of the precarious, though stubborn, experiment in the possibilities of historical continuity, when most of the grounds for continuity have been cut away."[9]

"Tradition as discontinuity," Irving Howe's summation of what constitutes the American Jewish novel, turns Alter's observation into a dictum. Howe's corpus for this genre has been the literature of immigration, and as he has tended to see immigrant neighborhoods as a kind of region, American Jewish literature is for him a "regional literature" focusing on one locale, displaying curious and exotic customs, and coming as a burst of literary consciousness resulting from the encounter between an alien group racing toward assimilation and half-persuaded that it is unassimilable. Drawing a parallel with American Southern writing, Howe has noted that a "subculture finds its voice and its passion at exactly the moment that it faces disintegration."[10]

By the time American Jewish fiction was legitimized to the extent that a full chapter was reserved for it in *The Harvard Guide to Contemporary American Writing* (in an ill-conceived project that distinguishes among Black Literature, Women's Literature, Experimental Fiction, and Drama), Mark Shechner had abandoned any attempt at defining what he went on to describe under the title of "Jewish Writers." Cautiously and defensively, Shechner admits that "neither 'Jewish writer' nor 'Jewish fiction' is an obvious or self-justifying subdivision of literature, any more than Jewishness itself is now a self-evident cultural identity." Nevertheless, Shechner chronicles a "historical fact"—that many American novelists happen to be Jews—and he invokes the Jewish writer as a "convenient shorthand for a feature of the literary consensus that we want to examine but are not yet prepared to define."[11]

American Jewish literature, then, has emerged as a recognizable corpus of work in the American literary tradition, although criteria for admission into this canon remain problematic, as recalcitrant as criteria for determining definitions of Jewishness itself. Where is Philip Roth in a tradition as tenuous and difficult to pin down as this one? For a large number of his

Jewish readers, Roth started out as an *enfant terrible* and matured into an informer. His writings have been called vulgar, vicious, and stereotypical of anti-Semitic lore. He has been accused of unfocused hostility and self-hatred. In his repeated self-defenses, Roth has portrayed himself as a victim of incompetent readers, philistines, impervious to irony and artistry. In his zeal for self-justification, declaring that he never received a thank-you note from an anti-Semitic organization or that his stories were not likely to start a pogrom, he occasionally became as single-minded about the processes of culture formation as his readers had been about the status of art. With implicit analogues to Joyce, Roth has depicted himself as an artist-rebel, unfettered by social retraints and collective anxieties. The task for the Jewish novelist, he has argued, "has not been to go forth to forge in the smithy of his soul the *uncreated* conscience of his race, but to find inspiration in a conscience that has been created and undone a hundred times over in this century alone."[12] Despite his resistance to the label of American Jewish writer, he has reviewed his own work in relation to other authors regularly included in that corpus. For example, he linked *Portnoy's Complaint* with Bellow's *The Victim* and Malamud's *The Assistant* as "nightmares about bondage." The novelistic enterprise in such books, he explained, "might itself be described as imagining Jews *being* imagined, by themselves and by others." In "Writing about Jews," Roth recorded what was "once a statement out of which a man might begin to construct an identity for himself: *Jews are people who are not what anti-Semites say they are*"[13]—from which one can deduce that Roth would see Jewish writing as literature that is *not* what American Jews say it is, namely, that renunciation, being Jewish, must be the inevitable subject of any Jewish literature.

Roth's early works, before he embarked on the long journey from Newark to Prague, are records of the last stages of the immigrant's assimilation into American life. From *Goodbye, Columbus* to *Portnoy's Complaint*, much of his writing documents the second and third generation of American Jews, well ensconced in the suburbs, the university, the army, and other American institutions, yet haunted by a tradition they do not understand and cannot abandon. "Defender of the Faith," set in the American army, is exemplary for measuring the distance between the Jewish literature of the immigrants and that of their children and grandchildren. Jewish immigrants from Eastern Europe would have regarded the army as does one of Sholem Aleichem's characters, Shalom Shachnah, in the comic story "On Account of a Hat." Borrowing from the tall tales of the Chelm repertoire, Sholem Aleichem describes a rattlebrained Jew on his way home for Passover who takes a nap in a railway station and, upon awakening, accidentally grabs the hat of a high-ranking army official instead of his own. When the conductor escorts him to third class, he reads his obeisance as mockery, as no Jew could be expected to be treated so deferentially. Only when he catches a glimpse of himself in the mirror does he realize what happened—the peasant boy he paid to wake him, he reasons, must have wakened the army officer instead! The story is spun around the *shtetl* Jew's anxiety at being mistaken for a Gentile and the impossibility of reconciling the army attire with Jewish identity. It brilliantly embodies the total separation of Shachnah's life from that of the Russian culture around him, the very unimaginability of assimilation.

In marked contrast, "Defender of the Faith," removed by several generations and set in America, records the anxiety of a Jewish army officer about being singled out as a Jew in the American army. One of Sergeant Nathan Marx's Jewish privates, Sheldon Grossbart, blatantly exploits his Jewishness to weasel out of his responsibilities in the army. As a result, Marx is caught between the expectations of Grossbart that he will abide by the collective loyalties of a minority and not betray him, and the expectations of his equally obnoxious superior Captain Barrett, who, in an anti-Semitic diatribe, praises Marx for his assimilation and loyalty to the army. When Grossbart invokes the persecution of the Jews and the invidious complicity of self-hating brethren in order to plead for a weekend pass on religious grounds, Marx relents. But when Grossbart brings back a Chinese eggroll from what was to have been a Passover Seder, Marx has Grossbart's sole exemption from the Pacific deployment revoked. Nathan Marx is "Defender of the Faith," but which faith? Did he defend the faith from the abuse of religious charlatans like Grossbart? As Grossbart and Barrett are equally reprehensible, Marx finds himself in a position of dual loyalty, and although one can argue that he sought a just position regardless of American or Jewish allegiance, it would not be interpreted as such by either Barrett or Grossbart, and the vindictiveness of his action, the exaggeration of his response to Grossbart's misdemeanor, is indicative of how excruciating it is for him to be on the cutting edge of these conflicting loyalties.

In "Eli the Fanatic," the smooth assimilation of second- and third-generation Jews into the upper-middle-class suburb of Woodenton is threatened by the infiltration of obtrusive Orthodox immigrants, including a yeshiva for orphaned refugees from the displaced persons camps after the Second World War. Eli Peck, appointed to represent the community in its campaign to keep this blight from their sanitized idyll, offers his tweed business suit to one of the black-garbed newcomers so offensive to Woodenton. Finding those black garments deposited at his doorstep, he cannot resist wearing them himself. Loping across the manicured lawns of his neighbors on his way to the hospital to see his first-born son, he vows that he will pass the same black garments on to the next generation. Treated like a madman by the hospital attendants, Eli screams "I'm the father!"—

an affirmation of both his familial role to the newborn and his role as purveyor of the ancestral line. But the response of suburban America to so far-reaching an outcry is to tear off the troublesome jacket and administer a sedative. "The drug calmed his soul but did not touch it down where the blackness had reached."[14]

These two early stories embody the Jewish elements in his fiction up to the publication of *Portnoy's Complaint*: they are both chronicles of the drama of assimilation several generations removed from immigration, and also tales of near-pathological allegiance to a collective past that has no meaning for Roth's protagonists other than an emotional kneejerk brought on by any reference to Jewish persecution, particularly the Holocaust. Both "Defender of the Faith" and "Eli the Fanatic" concern the Second World War, and each of these protagonists assumes extreme behavior to protect his only connection with the Jewish people, identification with their suffering. With the publication of *Portnoy* and Alexander Portnoy's endless and outrageously comic complaint about the crippling effects of Jewish psychic baggage on his sex life, Roth finally turned the "nice Jewish boy" into a pathological joke: "I am the son in the Jewish joke—only it ain't no joke! . . . who made us so morbid and hysterical and weak? . . . Is this the Jewish suffering I used to hear about?" By depicting narcissistic Portnoy, intent on blaming all of Jewish history, of which he is mostly ignorant, for his inability to lead a life of pure pleasure, Roth made himself vulnerable to moralistic attacks on his alleged self-hatred and vulgarity. The outburst of rage occasioned by the publication of *Portnoy* was a turning point in Roth's career. From then on, Roth's art began to turn inward so that the drama between the Jewish writer bent on freely expressing his desires in his art and his moralistic readers bent on denouncing him becomes the central subject of his fiction. And when his art begins to turn in upon itself, it also moves toward a more complex identification with Jewish life. Roth has himself admitted that this is the case: "Part of me wishes the misreading had never happened, but I also know that it's been my good luck; that the opposition has allowed me to become the strongest writer I could possibly have been. In fact, my Jewish detractors insisted on my being a Jewish writer by their opposition."[15]

How is that translated into his work? Roth has always been a comic writer with a moralistic streak, preoccupied with the relation between the carnal and the spiritual. Nathan Zuckerman, the writer-protagonist of Roth's most recent works, the *Zuckerman Bound* trilogy, is a comic author experiencing writer's block, exacerbated by his mother's legacy to him, the scrap of paper with the word *Holocaust* on it. Symptomatic of the relation of the American Jewish writer to recent Jewish history, it has a grip on the writer's consciousness disproportionate to its meager presence in his own life. One word on a scrap of paper invokes guilt and anxiety powerful enough to further paralyze Zuckerman. The Jewishness in Roth's more recent writings goes beyond chronicling the last stages of assimilation (as in *Goodbye, Columbus*), by taking the form of a vaguely felt duty to identify with the most recent Jewish past, namely, the Holocaust. Roth's work is marked by the discomfort of American Jews who have never suffered as a result of their Jewishness, but are heirs to a tradition that, from their point of view, is characterized by suffering. While he had already explored that theme in earlier works such as "Defender of the Faith" and "Eli the Fanatic," his more recent fiction has an additional dimension—the discomfort of American Jewish authors, particularly comic writers, committed both to their art and to some identification with the suffering of their fellow Jews.

Roth's artistic strategy for dealing with his dilemma begins to become evident in 1973 with "I Always Wanted You to Admire My Fasting; Or, Looking at Kafka." It is a daring essay in which he first documents Kafka's life, largely from the point of view of his "habit of obedience and renunciation," and then writes an imaginative life of Kafka as the road not taken, of Franz Kafka not dead of tuberculosis and enshrined as a worldwide synonym for modernism, but surviving the war as an unknown Hebrew school teacher in New Jersey, underpaid, and still practicing renunciation. It is told as a reminiscence from the point of view of the child who remembers him as the Czech refugee with the formal bow who courts his spinster Aunt Rhoda, but never marries her. When the courtship comes to a tearful end after a weekend trip to Atlantic City, the narrator's brother explains that his aunt's tears have something to do with sex. The story closes with a stormy confrontation between the adolescent narrator and his father, paralleling the reverse of Kafka's relation with his father: "Others are crushed by paternal criticism—I find myself oppressed by his high opinion of me!" Having left home, he receives a letter from his mother with Kafka's obituary thoughtfully enclosed that describes him as "a refugee from the Nazis" with no survivors, who died at the age of seventy in the Deborah Heart and Lung Center in Browns Mills, New Jersey. "No," reflects the narrator, "it is simply not in the cards for Kafka ever to become *the* Kafka—why, that would be stranger even than a man turning into an insect. No one would believe it, Kafka least of all."[16]

In this *tour de force*, Roth attempts to do what he strains for in all of his recent work, to strike a balance between the Jewish writer's moral impulse to draw on themes from his people's recent suffering, and the artist's insistence on creating in his own terms, in this case his comic mode; and furthermore, while he does draw on his own experience as an American Jew for his fiction, he also draws on the more compelling drama of his fellow Jews in Europe, which naturally overshadows his miseries, always threatening to belittle his own life and to render it pitifully inauthentic. One of his strategies is to bring that history closer to home, to rescue Kafka and place him on his own turf in New Jersey, thereby domesticating and deflating what is awesome in its own context. In one respect, this denial of the Holocaust, which always acts as a standard by which to measure American Jewish history of the same period, restores to the protagonist the legitimacy of his own family dramas and sexual problems. But by beginning his text with the actual recounting of Kafka's life, he insists on the fictionality of his comic alternative history, which is drawn from a background similar to his own and which pales beside the narrative of the "real" Kafka. In the juxtaposition of the two texts, "Looking at Kafka" elegantly sets forth the moral and artistic quandary of the comic Jewish writer in America.

Moreover, as the immigration experience ceased to be the Jewish element in his works, and his audiences began to blame him for betraying Jewish experience with his ribald comedy, Roth has continued to seek the artistic means to remain a Jewish writer without admitting to the charges leveled against him. To do so, he has had to see himself as part of a Jewish literary tradition. Without the benefit of writing in Hebrew or Yiddish, so that the language itself would be a purveyor of a literary tradition, he has identified in Kafka a literary father, his European alter ego, the writer who bridges both Jewishness and Western modernism and who is locked into a battle with his father that takes on mystical and mythical proportions in his art. But the real Kafka is an overwhelming father figure both in terms of the drama of his own life and the place he now occupies in the post-Holocaust view of that life and art. So Roth can claim him as a literary father and then minimize that threat by making Kafka an unpublished author, a pathetic elderly man with comic elements, the subject of mockery by his Hebrew school pupils. That leaves room for Roth's life and art, while also diminishing it.

Roth repeats this strategy several years later in *The Ghost Writer*, when he brings Anne Frank to New England, the road not taken had she not walked down that road to Bergen-Belsen. In *The Ghost Writer*, the first book in the trilogy *Zuckerman Bound*, Nathan Zuckerman's fantasies about a young woman named Amy Bellette as the real Anne Frank made up a story within the story, and those fantasies contribute to the self-referential theme of the young artist who must vindicate his life and art before his family and community. Nathan's two fantasies are:

1. Anne Frank, learning of her father's survival and the publication of her diary by a chance reading of *Time*, chooses not to be reunited with him because she is convinced that knowledge of her survival would diminish the power of her art and the message it brings to the world. She has

drawn this conclusion from sitting in the midst of a weeping matinée
crowd at a Broadway performance of *The Diary of Anne Frank*.
2. Amy, alias Anne, falls in love with Nathan, making it possible for
Nathan to be vindicated spectacularly by his family. "I'd like you to
meet my wife, the former Anne Frank."

The Ghost Writer, then, is a sophisticated and richly structured response
to those of Roth's critics who accuse him of betrayal in that he poses
questions about the nature of American Jewish identity through a tale
about the nature of art and life. Just as Roth has deliberately projected his
own problems onto Nathan, Nathan has projected his own wishes and
identity onto Anne/Amy. Nathan imagines that Amy is Anne in order to
be reconciled with his own father. But he also identifies with Anne, for she
is an artist who has willingly sacrificed her own bond with her father for
the sake of her art. Thus, Amy is the paragon of both Jewish suffering and
of renunciation at the holy altar of art. She is both artist and Jewish saint.
If Nathan married her, he would become an accomplice in her secret
scheme to preserve the memory of the Holocaust for readers like his own
parents, while they, ironically, could still consider him a traitor to the
Jewish community. Both Nathan and Anne, in his fantasy, are artists sacrificing personal happiness for their art, except that Anne's art is seen as
holy in his community and his as profane.

As in "Looking at Kafka," the implications of Anne Frank's life for the
American Jewish comic writer are neutralized by bringing her to the American scene and turning her into a college girl infatuated with her professor,
and as in the Kafka story, it has the opposite effect of dramatically contrasting the world of Roth's fiction with recent Jewish history, turning the
American Jewish writer's problem into the central issue of the fiction. Roth
raises the very complex issue of the morality of using the Holocaust, a
symbol of collective trauma, as a social tool, to bludgeon Jewish artists into
restraining their imagination for the sake of "the common good," or as an
artistic tool to invoke sympathy from a critical audience by offering up
one of its most sacred subjects.[17]

In *The Anatomy Lesson* and *The Prague Orgy*, the third novel and epilogue of his latest work, *Zuckerman Bound*, the search for a literary father in
the context of being an American Jewish writer is developed even further
as Nathan Zuckerman inherits that scrap of paper with the word *Holocaust*
on it. In *The Anatomy Lesson*, Nathan Zuckerman is incapable of writing
any more fiction, as he is suffering from severe pain of a mysterious origin.
His sole quest in that work is relief from his paralyzing and undiagnosed
ailment. Life under the influence of this disease is a parody of wish-
fulfillment: confined to a mat on the floor, Nathan is catered to and

entertained by a variety of beautiful women. Nathan begins to believe that his agony is self-inflicted, the product of his guilt about his writings, "penance for the popularity of *Carnovsky* . . . for the family portrait the whole country had assumed to be his, for the tastelessness that had affronted millions and the shamelessness that had enraged his tribe. . . . Who else could have written so blasphemously of Jewish moral suffocation, but a self-suffocating Jew like Nathan?"[18]

Nathan Zuckerman comes to the conclusion that he can no longer write because he has lost his subject: "A first-generation American father possessed by the Jewish demons, a second-generation American son possessed by their exorcism: that was his whole story."[19] In that summation, Roth has located his own movement away from the subject of American Jewish fiction that marked some of his own earlier work. Having left behind the fiction of immigration, he takes up the subject of the reception of that fiction, turning the drama between writer and audience into the moral dilemma of the Jewish writer in America, suspecting the legitimacy of his own private anguish when contrasted to that of his fellow Jews. Confronting the issue directly, Roth parodies Zuckerman's suffering while underscoring its debilitating effects. For a while Nathan considers basing his next fiction on the past suffering of his Slavic lover, Jaga (in a manner similar to *Sophie's Choice*, in which the American writer William Styron invents a Slavic World War II victim in order to write about experiences alien to his own life):

> But he couldn't get anywhere. Though people are weeping in every corner of the earth from torture and ruin and cruelty and loss, that didn't mean that he could make their stories his, no matter how passionate and powerful they seemed beside his trivialities. One can be overcome by a story the way a reader is, but a reader isn't a writer . . . Besides, if Zuckerman wrote about what he didn't know, who then would write about what he did know? Only what did he know? The story he could dominate and to which his feelings had been enslaved had ended. Her stories weren't his stories and his stories were no longer his stories either.[20]

To do penance and to bring about his own healing, he decides to abandon his writing career and become a healer himself. Viewed by the same audience that roundly condemned his writing, Nathan Zuckerman's desire to become a Jewish doctor would be supremely ironic and a posthumous victory for his parents, whose son's literary successes earned him what he believes to have been a deathbed curse from his father, and what surely would have been a blessing had he been a penitent medical student years before. But Roth does not give Zuckerman's community that satisfaction. On his way to medical school, Nathan launches what is first a practical joke and then an obsession—he presents himself to strangers as Milton Appel, pornographer. As Appel is the critic who has been most vociferous and persistent in his moral diatribes against the writer (Zuckerman's Irving Howe), Nathan can take revenge by the same tactic, public shaming. Nathan soon warms to the prank, however, and begins to identify with Milton Appel the pornographer, so that by the end of the book he is suspended between the two extreme identities that his community and family have forced upon him all along: the good doctor and the evil pornographer. Even a medical degree will not erase his having been the author of *Carnovsky*, nor is that necessarily what he wants.

The *Anatomy Lesson* ends with Nathan as a patient, not for the mysterious pain in his shoulder, but from the injuries incurred attacking a friend's father as the old man laments the end of his line because his adopted hippie grandson is "everything we are *not*, everything we are *against*." Zuckerman accosts Freytag with "What do you see in your head? Genes with JEW sewed on them? Is that all you see in that lunatic mind, the unstained natural virtue of Jews?"[21] His own father dead, Nathan lunges at Freytag, "the last of the fathers demanding to be pleased," intending to kill him. "Freytag! Forbidder! Now I murder *you*!"[22] Suffering takes on a different dimension for Nathan when he is recuperating in the hospital, for among the other patients he comes face to face with genuine physical pain and the disfigurement of disease. Zuckerman's craving for a real enemy and for a therapeutic mission peaks in what he perceives to be the universality and very literalness of disease—and he'd given his fanatical devotion "to sitting with a typewriter alone in a room!"[23] Yet the book ends without that resounding conviction, for Zuckerman roams the hospital corridors, "as though he still believed that he could unchain himself from a future as a man apart and escape the corpus that was his."[24] Zuckerman can escape neither the corpus of his own aging body, Yeats's spirit chained to a "dying animal," nor the corpus of his fiction, the testimony of his having set himself apart and undoubtedly a cause of his pain.

In Roth's fiction, the American Jewish writer cannot alleviate the anxiety provoked by his inheritance of that scrap of paper with the awesome word on it by relocating and neutralizing the Jewish past on his own territory ("Looking at Kafka" or *The Ghost Writer*), or by avoiding art altogether and redirecting his passion into the art of medicine. He will have to relocate himself, and since he cannot return to the past, he can only travel to the scene of that past, which for Roth is embodied in the city of Prague. This he does in the Epilogue to the trilogy, *The Prague Orgy*, although he had already made this journey in search of Kafka earlier in *Professor of Desire*. In the Epilogue, Nathan Zuckerman returns to a first person account of his experiences, as was the case in *The Ghost Writer*, and he travels to Prague on a mission to retrieve the Yiddish stories of a Jewish author allegedly killed by the Nazis. The Epilogue is both a finale to the Zuckerman trilogy and a coming together of Roth's central motifs. The goal of retrieving the fiction of a Jewish writer from anonymity and seeing to its publication is a most appropriate action for an American Jewish author anxious about his link to the Jewish history of loss and to Jewish literary fathers. It is also parallel to Roth's own goal of publishing the work of Eastern European writers in his "Other Europe" series.

A major effect of his helping to reconstruct a lost literary tradition is that it may provide a literary father for Zuckerman/Roth. The Epilogue is haunted by three literary fathers—Kafka, Roth's literary alter ego whose uncertain identification with his own Jewishness and comic treatment of alienation is most compatible with Roth's sensibility; Henry James, Roth's American predecessor, whose self-consciousness about the place of the artist and preoccupation with the interpretation and misinterpretation of fictional texts influenced Roth's exploration of the same motif; and Sisovsky, the lost Yiddish writer (in this case a fabrication of Roth's), whose absence haunts the post-Holocaust Jewish writer. The Jamesian influence in Roth's work is evident in his allusions to "The Middle Years" in *The Ghost Writer* and to the variation on the *The Aspern Papers* in *The Prague Orgy*. In neither James's nor Roth's tales about literary retrieval do the literary narrators actually get hold of the papers they are after, and in each case they court a woman in order to procure the manuscripts. But Roth's version is a reversal of James's, for in *The Aspern Papers* the woman rebuffs the narrator and destroys the papers; in *The Prague Orgy*, the woman propositions the narrator who rebuffs her, while she hands over the papers only to have them confiscated by the Czech police. In Roth's version, then, political forces come into play. Moreover, in James's version, the papers are letters and the narrator is a literary critic prying into the life of a poet, while in Roth's version, the papers are works of fiction and the narrator is a writer himself, torn loose from the kind of clear literary tradition that James enjoyed.

The Epilogue also draws on another of Roth's central motifs, that of trading places with another. In a new twist, Sisovsky remains in America and Zuckerman actually goes off to Prague to wrest the papers from the hands of the Czech author's wife, Olga. In an especially telling reversal of Roth's own fiction, Zuckerman contemplates making love to Olga as a means toward retrieving a bit of Jewish literary history, as opposed to Jewish history acting as a psychic obstruction when it comes to the goal of unrestrained sexuality. Sisovsky and Zuckerman both share the frustration of scandalous receptions of their books, and Sisovsky insists that the weight of stupidity, in the case of Zuckerman's readers, is heavier than the weight of banning. Zuckerman disagrees.

When the American Jewish writer trades places with the Czech Jewish writer in search of a literary father, he must finally skirt real danger. Apprehended by the Minister of Culture and deported as "Zuckerman the Zionist agent," Zuckerman is forced to turn over the shoe box full of manuscripts—"Another Jewish writer who might have been is not going to be; his imagination won't leave even the faintest imprint."[25] Each of the several crimes that Zuckerman is accused of committing is punishable by sentences of up to twenty years. For a moment, Zuckerman can feel what it might mean to have historical and political forces shape his life, but he is no martyr, and he only meant to trade places temporarily. While Roth explores the road not taken in America for Jewish figures like Kafka and Anne Frank, Nathan Zuckerman walks the road not taken only up to a hint of real danger. Like Bellow, who made his journey to Israel to record the drama and the price of Jewish continuity in *To Jerusalem and Back* without ever sharing the vulnerability he describes, it was time to go back. But back to where? Back to what he calls the "national industry of the Jewish homeland, if not the sole means of production (if not the sole source of satisfaction), the construction of narrative out of the exertions of survival."[26]

By the beginning of the twentieth century American literature was reflecting a change in national consciousness in its stories of returning East rather than heading westward. Philip Roth's long odyssey from Newark to Prague is also a turning point in the American Jewish literary tradition, for it marks the passage from a literature of immigration and assimilation into a literature of retrieval, of the desire to be part of a Jewish literary legacy alongside the European and American literary traditions. Roth's strategy for locating his fiction in such a tradition is to turn the denial of his work by many Jewish readers into his theme, to trace his own moral dilemma as an American Jewish writer compelled to treat recent Jewish history in his fiction (often by trading places), and to carve out a literary tradition by drawing on Eastern European predecessors. At the end of the *Zuckerman Bound* Epilogue, Nathan is left without a real or literary father, without a family, and without a home. Roth's intensifying preoccupation with the self-reflexive theme of his work's reception and with his own identity as a Jewish writer is narcissism turned moralism. These last works face the plight of the Jewish writer cut loose, as he is, from linguistic, religious, or cultural continuities, but seeking a literary tradition. They also signify, often elegantly, the impossibility of Philip Roth's *not* being a Jewish writer, given his need to document imaginatively every comic and tragic nuance of his own displacement.

Notes

1. Philip Roth, *The Anatomy Lesson,* in *Zuckerman Bound,* vol. 3 (New York: Farrar, Straus and Giroux, 1985), 477.

2. Irving Malin and Irwin Stark, "Introduction," in *Breakthrough: A Treasury of Contemporary American Jewish Literature* (New York: McGraw-Hill, 1964); reprinted in *Jewish-American Literature: An Anthology of Fiction, Poetry, Autobiography, and Criticism,* ed. Abraham Chapman (New York: New American Library, 1974), 665–90.

3. See Jeremy Larmer, "The Conversion of the Jews," *Partisan Review* 27 (1960): 760–68.

4. Irving Malin, "Introduction," to *Contemporary American-Jewish Literature* (Bloomington: Indiana University Press, 1973), 7.

5. Theodore Solotareff, "Philip Roth and the Jewish Moralists," in *Breakthrough: A Treasury of Contemporary American-Jewish Literature,* eds. Irving Malin and Irwin Stark (New York: McGraw-Hill, 1964) 359. Reprinted from *Chicago Review* Vol. XIII, 4 (Winter, 1959).

6. David Daiches, "Breakthrough," in *Contemporary American-Jewish Literature,* ed. Irving Malin. (Bloomington: Indiana University Press, 1973), 37. Originally in *Commentary* (August 1964).

7. Allen Guttmann, "The Conversion of the Jews," in *Contemporary American-Jewish Literature,* ed. Irving Malin.(Bloomington: University of Indiana Press, 1973), 39–57. Originally in *Wisconsin Studies in Contemporary Literature,* 6 (1965).

8. Robert Alter, "Jewish Dreams and Nightmares," in *After the Tradition* (New York: Dutton, 1961). See this volume, pp. 53–66.

9. Ibid.

10. Irving Howe, *World of Our Fathers* (New York: Harcourt Brace Jovanovich, 1976), 586.

11. Mark Shechner, "Jewish Writers," in *Harvard Guide to Contemporary American Writing,* ed. Daniel Hoffman (Cambridge, Mass.: Harvard University Press, 1979), 191–240.

12. Philip Roth, "Imagining Jews," in *Reading Myself and Others* (New York: Bantam, 1977), 221.

13. Ibid., 221, 150.

14. Philip Roth, *Goodbye, Columbus* (New York: Houghton Mifflin, 1959), 216.

15. Quoted in Clive Sinclair, "Why Philip Roth Says Goodbye to Columbus," *The London Jewish Chronicle,* March 2, 1984.

16. Roth, *Reading Myself,* 243–44.

17. See Hana Wirth-Nesher, "The Artist Tales of Philip Roth," *Prooftexts: A Journal of Jewish Literary History* 3 (1983): 263–72.

18. Roth, *The Anatomy Lesson* in *Zuckerman Bound,* 3:440.

19. Ibid., 446.

20. Ibid., 544.

21. Ibid., 668.

22. Ibid., 669.

23. Ibid., 697.

24. Ibid.

25. Roth, *The Prague Orgy,* in *Zuckerman Bound,* Epilogue: 782.

26. Ibid., 761.

Notes on Contributors

ROBERT ALTER is Class of 1937 Professor of Hebrew and Comparative Literature at the University of California at Berkeley. He has written on the history of the novel, on modern Hebrew literature, on modern Jewish writing in other languages, and on literary aspects of the Bible. Among his books are *Partial Magic, The Pleasures of Reading in an Ideological Age, Defenses of the Imagination, Necessary Angels, The Art of Biblical Narrative,* and, most recently, *The World of Biblical Literature.*

BAAL-MAKHSHOVES (pen name of Israel Isidor Elyashev, 1873–1924) was a pioneer in the art of Yiddish literary criticism and a major force in Yiddish culture. He wrote reviews and critical essays, served as editor of *Klal-Verlag* (Berlin), and translated Herzl's *Altneuland* into Yiddish. Born in Kovno, he later lived in Vilna, Riga, Warsaw, and St. Petersburg. Baal-Makhshoves brought European aesthetic approaches to his interpretation of Yiddish literature. His selected works appear in five volumes published between 1915 and 1929 and in a single volume published in 1953.

SAUL BELLOW is a Nobel Prize Laureate (1976) and author of many novels, among them *The Adventures of Augie March, Herzog* (winner of the Prix International de Littérature), *Mr. Sammler's Planet, To Jerusalem and Back, Dean's December, Him With His Foot in His Mouth and Other Stories, More Die of Heartbreak, The Bellarosa Connection,* and *Something to Remember Me By: Three Tales.*

BARUCH KURZWEIL (1907–72) was professor of Hebrew Literature at Bar Ilan University and an Israeli literary critic. Born in Moldavia, educated in Germany, and ordained as a rabbi, Kurzweil wrote regularly for the literary supplements, placing Israeli literature in the context of secular society's break with religious tradition. A major force in Agnon studies, he produced many other works, including readings of *Bialik and Uri Zvi Greenberg,* and his controversial volume, *Our New Literature: Continuation or Revolution?* [Hebrew].

BENJAMIN HARSHAV is Jacob and Hilda Blaustein Professor of Hebrew and Comparative Literature at Yale University, founding editor of *HaSifrut* and *Poetics Today,* and formerly Director of the Porter Institute for Poetics and Semiotics at Tel Aviv University. Professor Harshav has published widely in the areas of Hebrew and Yiddish literature and in semiotics, including *The Meaning of Yiddish* and *Language in Time of Revolution.* Among his translations are *American Yiddish Poetry: A Bilingual Anthology;* Yehuda Amichai, *Even a Fist Was Once an Open Palm with Fingers* (both with Barbara Harshav); and *Sutzkever—Selected Poetry and Prose.*

JOHN HOLLANDER is A. Bartlett Giametti Professor of English at Yale University. Both poet and literary critic, Professor Hollander was awarded the Bollingen Prize in 1983. Among his volumes of poetry are *Harp Lake, In Time and Place, Powers of Thirteen, Blue Wine and Other Poems, Tales Told of the Fathers, The Night Mirror,* and *A Crackling of Thorns.* His books of criticism include *Rhyme's Reason: A Guide to English Verse, The Figure of Echo: A Mode of Allusion in Milton and After,* and *Vision and Resonance: Two Senses of Poetic Form.*

SIMON MARKISH is Lecturer at the University of Geneva, Faculty of the Humanities. He is the author of several books published in Russian and French and has translated works of Erasmus into Russian. His most recent book available in English is *Erasmus and the Jews.* Professor Markish is at work on a history of Russian Jewish literature.

DAN MIRON is Leonard Kay Professor of Hebrew and Comparative Literature at Columbia University, Professor of Modern Hebrew Literature at the Hebrew University, and recipient, with Gershon Shaked, of the 1993 Israel Prize in Literature. He has published extensively on Hebrew and Yiddish literature, with essays on Bialik, Alterman, Sutzkever, Hazaz, and Scholem, among other writers (in Hebrew). His most recent book in English is *A Traveler Disguised: A Study in the Rise of Modern Yiddish Fiction in the Nineteenth Century.*

CYNTHIA OZICK is a novelist, essayist, and short story writer. Her books include *The Pagan Rabbi, Bloodshed and Three Novellas, The Cannibal Galaxy, The Messiah of Stockholm,* and, most recently, *Metaphor and Memory: Essays* and *The Shawl.*

YONATAN RATOSH (pen name of Uriel Halperin, 1908–81) was an Israeli poet, translator, essayist, and founder of the Young Hebrews movement, later coined "the Canaanites." In his controversial writings he advocated a separation between the nation of the Hebrews and the Jewish people as it evolved in the Diaspora. His volumes of poetry include *Black Canopy* and *Who Walks in Darkness.*

DAVID G. ROSKIES is Professor of Jewish Literature at The Jewish Theological Seminary of America. He is cofounder and editor of *Prooftexts: A Journal of Jewish Literary History* and author of two books on Jewish responses to catastrophe: *Against the Apocalypse* and a companion volume, *The Literature of Destruction.* He is also the editor of *A. Ansky, The Dybbuk and Other Writings* in the Library of Yiddish Classics Series. "The Story's the Thing," revised for publication in this anthology, outlines the thesis of his forthcoming book, *The Lost Art of Yiddish Storytelling.*

GERSHON SHAKED is Professor of Hebrew Literature at the Hebrew University in Jerusalem. A recipient of the Bialik Prize and, with Dan Miron, the 1993 Israel Prize in Literature, he has published widely in Hebrew, including *A New Wave in Contemporary Israeli Narrative Fiction, The Narrative Art of S.Y. Agnon,* and *No Other Place.* His most recent publications in English are *The Shadows*

Within: Essays on Modern Jewish Writers and *S.Y. Agnon: A Revolutionary Traditionalist.*

SASSON SOMEKH is Halmos Professor of Arabic Literature at Tel Aviv University and a former Fellow of the Annenberg Research Institute, Philadelphia. He has published several volumes on modern Arabic literature, among them *The Changing Rhythm: A Study of Najib Mahfuz's Novels.* His most recent book is *Genre and Language in Modern Arabic Literature.*

HANA WIRTH-NESHER, the editor of this collection, is Senior Lecturer at Tel Aviv University and Head of the English Department. She is the author of essays on Jewish literature, among them studies of Sholem Aleichem, Isaac Bashevis Singer, Franz Kafka, Amos Oz, Henry Roth, and Philip Roth, as well as publications on modern English fiction, on James, Woolf, Joyce, Conrad, and others. She is the editor of *New Essays on Call It Sleep* (forthcoming, Cambridge University Press) and author of *City Codes: Reading the Modern Urban Novel* (also forthcoming, Cambridge University Press).

RUTH WISSE is Professor of Yiddish Literature at Harvard University. She is the editor, with Irving Howe, of *The Best of Sholom* [sic] *Aleichem* and, with Irving Howe and Khone Shmeruk, *The Penguin Book of Modern Yiddish Verse.* She is the author of *The Shlemiel as Modern Hero, I.L. Peretz and the Making of Modern Yiddish Culture, A Little Love in Big Manhattan: Two Yiddish Poets,* and *If I Am Not for Myself: The Liberal Betrayal of the Jews.*

Suggested Further Readings

Aizenberg, I. "Latin American Jewish Writing." *Contemporary Judaism* 28 (Spring 1974): 66–72.

Alter, Robert. *After the Tradition: Essays on Modern Jewish Writing*. New York: Dutton, 1969.

———. *Defenses of the Imagination: Jewish Writers and Modern Historical Crises*. Philadelphia: The Jewish Publication Society, 1977.

Arendt, Hannah. *The Jew as Pariah: Jewish Identity and Politics in the Modern Age*. New York: Grove Press, 1978.

Baumgarten, Murray. *City Scriptures: Modern Jewish Writing*. Cambridge, Mass.: Harvard University Press, 1982.

Bloom, Harold. "The Sorrows of American Jewish Poetry." *Commentary* 53 (March 1972): 69–74.

———. *Kabbalah and Criticism*. New York: Seabury, 1975.

Budick, Sanford, and Geoffrey Hartman, eds. *Midrash and Literature*. New Haven, Conn.: Yale University Press, 1986.

Daiches, David. "Some Aspects of Anglo-American Jewish Fiction." In *Jewish Perspectives*, ed. Jacob Sonntag. London: Secker and Warburg, 1980.

Dembo, L.S. *The Monological Jew: A Literary Study*. Madison: The University of Wisconsin, 1988.

Even-Zohar, Itamar. "Aspects of the Hebrew-Yiddish Polysystem: A Case of a Multilingual Polysystem." *Poetics Today* 11 (Spring 1990): 121–131.

Ezrahi, Sidra. *By Words Alone: The Holocaust in Literature*. Chicago: University of Chicago Press, 1980.

Feldman, Yael. *Modernism and Cultural Transfer: Gabriel Preil and the Tradition of Jewish Literary Bilingualism*. Cincinnati: Hebrew Union College Press, 1985.

Fiedler, Leslie. "Master of Dreams, the Jew in a Gentile World" in *To the Gentiles*. New York: Stein and Day, 1971.

———. "The Jew in American Literature." In *The Collected Essays of Leslie Fiedler*. New York: Stein and Day, 1970.

Fried, Lewis, ed. *Handbook of American-Jewish Literature: An Analytical Guide to Topics, Themes, and Sources*. Westport, Conn.: Greenwood Press, 1988.

Gilman, Sander. *The Jew's Body*. New York: Routledge, 1991.

Goldin, Judah. "The Contemporary Jew and His Judaism." In *Spiritual Problems in Contemporary Literature*, ed. Stanley Romaine Hopper. New York: Harper & Brothers, 1952.

Gross, Theodore. *The Literature of American Jews*. New York: The Free Press, 1973.

Grossman, Allen. "'The Sieve' and Remarks Toward a Jewish Poetry." *Tikkun* 5 (1990): 45–48; 103–104.

Guttmann, Allen. *The Jewish Writer in America: Assimilation and the Crisis of Identity.* New York: Oxford University Press, 1971.

Halkin, Simon. *Modern Hebrew Literature from the Enlightenment to the Birth of Israel.* New York: Schocken, 1970.

Handelman, Susan. *The Emergence of Rabbinic Interpretation in Modern Literary Theory.* Albany: State University of New York, 1982.

Harshav, Benjamin. *The Meaning of Yiddish.* Berkeley: University of California Press, 1990.

Harshav, Benjamin, and Barbara Harshav. "Introduction." In *American Yiddish Poetry: A Bilingual Anthology.* Berkeley: University of California Press, 1988.

Hartman, Geoffrey. "On the Jewish Imagination." *Prooftexts: A Journal of Jewish Literary History* 5 (September 1985):201–220.

Howe, Irving. *World of Our Fathers.* New York: Harcourt, Brace, Jovanovich, 1976.

Jacobson, David. *Modern Midrash: The Retelling of Traditional Jewish Narratives by Twentieth Century Hebrew Writers.* Albany: State University of New York Press, 1987.

Kazin, Alfred. "The Jew as Modern Writer." *Commentary* 41 (April 1966): 37–41.

Malin, Irving, and Irwin Stark. "Introduction." In *Breakthrough: A Treasury of Contemporary American Jewish Literature.* New York: McGraw Hill, 1964.

Mintz, Alan. *"Banished from their Father's Table": Loss of Faith and Hebrew Autobiography.* Bloomington: Indiana University Press, 1989.

Miron, Dan. *A Traveler Disguised.* New York: Schocken, 1973.

Nadel, Ira. *Jewish Writers of North America: A Guide to Information Sources.* Detroit: Gale Research, 1981.

Niger, Samuel. *Bilingualism in the History of Literature.* Lanham, Md.: University Press of America, 1989.

Pelli, Moshe. "Jewish Identity in Modern Hebrew Literature." *Judaism* (1976): 447–460.

Prooftexts: A Journal of Jewish Literary History. Special Issue on International Jewish Writing from the Bellagio Conference, Vol. 4, no. 1 (January 1984).

Ragussis, Michael. "Representation, Conversion, and Literary Form: *Harrington* and the Novel of Jewish Identity." *Critical Inquiry* (Autumn 1989): 113–143.

Roditi, E. "The Great Tradition of Italian-Jewish Literature." *Midstream* 30 (November 1984): 53–55.

Rosenfeld, Alvin. *A Double Dying: Reflections on Holocaust Literature.* Bloomington: University of Indiana Press, 1980.

Roskies, David. *Against the Apocalypse: Responses to Catastrophe in Modern Jewish Culture.* Cambridge, Mass.: Harvard University Press, 1984.

———. "Jewish Literary Scholarship After the Six-Day War." In *The State of Jewish Studies,* ed. Shaye J.D. Cohen and Edward Greenstein. Detroit: Wayne State University Press, 1990.

Roumani, Judith. "The Portable Homeland of North-African Jewish Fiction:

Ryval and Koskas." *Prooftexts: A Journal of Jewish Literary History* 4 (September 1984): 253–269.

Shaked, Gershon. *The Shadows Within: Essays on Modern Jewish Writers*. Philadelphia: The Jewish Publication Society, 1987.

Shechner, Mark. *After the Revolution: Studies in the Contemporary Jewish American Imagination*. Bloomington: University of Indiana Press, 1987.

Wirth-Nesher, Hana. "Between Mother Tongue and Native Language: Multilingualism in Henry Roth's *Call It Sleep*." *Prooftexts: A Journal of Jewish Literary History* 10 (1990): 297–312.

Wisse, Ruth. *The Schlemiel as Modern Hero*. Chicago: University of Chicago Press, 1971.

Yudkin, Leon. *Jewish Writing and Identity in the Twentieth Century*. London: Croom Helm, 1982.

Annotated List of Authors

The following is an annotated list of most of the authors whose names appear in the essays in this collection. For authors who are known by their pseudonym, birth name is given in parentheses. The annotations contain brief, summary information only. They are intended to serve as a guide for further study.

ABRAMOVITCH, Shalom Jacob—see MENDELE MOKHER SEFORIM.

AGNON, Shai (Shmuel Yosef Czaczkes), 1888–1970. Hebrew writer, Nobel Laureate for Literature (1966), and a towering figure in modern Hebrew fiction. Among his novels, *The Bridal Canopy* (1937), *Temol shilshom* (1945), and *Shira* (1978, posth.) particularly distinguish themselves. He also published several collections of short stories.

AHAD HA'AM (Asher Hirsch Ginsberg), 1856–1927. Hebrew essayist, thinker, and leader of the Hibbat Zion movement. "Lo Zeh ha-Derekh" ("The Wrong Way," 1889) was the first of his articles concerning Zionism. His work includes the four-volume collected essays, *Al parashat drakhim* (*At the Crossroads*), started in 1895 and completed after 1922.

AIZMAN, David Yakovlevich, 1869–1922. Russian writer. His short stories deal with the Jewish poor and the revolutionary-minded Jewish intellectuals and their persecution by the czarist police—for example, "Savan" ("The Shroud," 1903). His later work was influenced by Russian symbolism. An eight-volume edition of his work was published in Russia in 1911–19.

AL-SAMAW'AL b. Gharid b. Adiya (Samuel Ibn 'Adiya), mid-sixth c. Poet in Tayma, Hejaz, Northern Arabia. He wrote Arabic poetry ranking with the finest Arab heroic poetry of the pre-Islamic period.

ALTENBERG, Peter (Richard Englaender), 1859–1919. Austrian author of fourteen volumes of prose vignettes, his major works include *Wie ich es sehe* (1896) and *Maerchen des Lebens* (1908).

ALTERMAN, Natan, 1910–1970. Israeli "imagist" poet who emigrated from Warsaw in 1925 to become one of the most influential poets of his time. He published verse (one of his major works being *Simhat aniyim*, 1941), satirical journalism, critical essays—*Mivhar ma'amarim shel yetsirato shel Alterman* (1971)—and drama translations.

AMICHAI, Yehuda, 1924– . Israeli poet and novelist. His volume *Akhshav u-ve-yamim aherim* (1955) marked the emergence of a new school of Hebrew poetry, whose language adopted modern idioms and an imagery reflecting the world of technology and law. His work includes *Love Poems* (1981), *Songs of Jerusalem and Myself* (1973), *Not of This Time, Not of This Place* (1973), and *The Selected Poetry of Yehuda Amichai* (1986).

AMIR, Aharon, 1923– . Israeli writer, translator, and editor (with Yonatan Ratosh from 1948–50) of *Alef*. His publications include the poetry collections *Kaddim* (*Sirocco*, 1949) and *Saraf* (*Fiery Angel*, 1957), the volume of stories *Ahavah* (*Love*, 1952), and the novel *Ve-lo tehi la-mavet memshalah* (*And Death Shall Not Rule*, 1955).

AMIR, Anda (née Pinkerfeld), 1902–81. Hebrew poet. Among her published books are *Ahat* (*One*, 1953), *Yamim doverim* (*Days Tell*, 1929), *Shirei yeladim* (1934, awarded the Bialik Prize in poems for children), *Gittit* (1937), *Dudaim* (*Mandrakes*, 1943), and *Kokhavim bi-dli* (*Stars in a Bucket*, 1957).

APPELFELD, Aharon, 1932– . Hebrew writer. His stories, mostly concerned with the Holocaust, were collected in volumes like *Ashan* (*Smoke*, 1962) and *In the Wilderness* (1963). Among his novels are *Badenheim, 1939* (1980), *Tor ha-pelaot* (*The Age of Wonders*, 1978), *For Every Sin* (1989), *Tzili: The Story of a Life* (1983), *The Retreat* (1984), and *To the Land of the Cattails* (1986).

ASCH, Sholem, 1880–1957. Yiddish novelist and dramatist. His volumes of fiction include *A shtetl* (*The Village*, 1904), the novel *Mitn shtrom* (*With the Stream*, 1904), and the trilogy *Farn mabul* (1929–31; *Three Cities*, 1933). *Got fun nekomeh* (1907; *God of Vengeance*, 1966) is one of his dramas.

AUERBACH, Ephraim, 1882–1973. Yiddish poet and essayist, associated for fifty years with New York Yiddish dailies. Some of his volumes of verse are *Oyfn shvel* (1915), *Karavanen* (1918), *Di vayse shtot* (1952), and *Vakh iz der step* (1963).

AVIDAN, David, 1934– . Contemporary Israeli poet. His published poetic work includes *Be'ayot ishiot* (1957), *Shirei lahats* (1962), *Shirim hitsoni'im* (1970), *Shirim shimushi'im* (1973), and *Sefer ha-efsharuyot* (1985).

AXENFELD, Israel, 1787–1866. Pioneering Yiddish novelist and dramatist. He completed thirty novels and plays in which he portrayed Jewish life. The largest part of his works, mostly anti-Hasidic in character, were circulated in manuscript and subsequently lost. Among those preserved is the novel *Dos shterntikhl* (1861) and a few plays.

BABEL, Isaac Emmanuilovich, 1894–1941(?). Russian writer. His work includes two collections of stories, *Red Cavalry* (1926) and *Odessa Tales* (1927), two plays, several tales and a few film scripts. Despite his relatively small literary output, Babel stands out as one of the greatest stylists and prose writers in twentieth century Russian literature.

BAECK, Leo, 1873–1956. German rabbi, religious thinker, and leader of progressive Judaism. His work includes *Wesen des Judentums* (1905; *The Essence of Judaism*, 1936), *Dieses Volk*, 2 vols. (1955–57; *This People Israel*, 1965), and *Judaism and Christianity* (1965). From 1954 he was the first president of the Leo Baeck Institute for the study of German Jewry.

BAGRITSKII, Eduard Georgiyevich, 1895–1934. Soviet-Russian poet, and one of the leading poets of the twentieth century. His best known work is the long poem "Duma pro Opanasa" ("The Lay of Opanas," 1926). Some of his best poetry appeared in *Yugo-zapad* (*South West*, 1928).

BAHUR, ben-Asher ha-Levi Ashkenazi (Eliyah Levita), 1468 or 1469–1549. Hebrew philologist, grammarian, and lexicographer. He taught Hebrew language and grammar to Christian humanists; wrote many Hebrew grammar books, as well as Hebrew and Aramaic dictionaries; did Masoretic research; and wrote secular literary works in Yiddish, based on medieval romances.

BAR-MOSHE, Yitzhak, 1927– . Israeli writer. A native of Baghdad who immigrated to Israel in 1950, he published several volumes of fiction in Arabic, including an autobiographical novel entitled *A House in Baghdad* (Engl. trans., 1982).

BASRI, Meir, 1912– . Iraqi author and economist. He published several volumes of poetry and fiction—notably the collection of short stories *Rijal wazilal* (*Men and Shadows*, 1955)—and a volume of essays on economics (1948). He has lived in London since 1974.

BELLOW, Saul, 1915– . American novelist, Nobel Prize winner for literature, 1976. Among his novels are the prize-winning *Adventures of Augie March* (1953), *Herzog* (1964)—an international bestseller that won the Prix International de Littérature, *Mr. Sammler's Planet* (1969), *Humboldt's Gift* (1975), *To Jerusalem and Back* (1977), and *Dean's December* (1982). See Notes on Contributors.

BENJAMIN, Walter, 1892–1940. German philosopher and literary critic. His writings, among them *Illuminations* (Engl. trans., 1961) and *Angelus Novus* (Engl. trans., 1966), were published mostly posthumously. He is regarded as one of the leading critics in the German language between the two wars.

BEN-YEHEZKEL, Mordechai, 1883–1971. Hebrew essayist and adapter of folktales. His multi-volume collection of folktales, *Sefer Ha-ma'asiyyot*, was published between 1926 and 1929.

BERDYCZEWSKI, Micha Yosef, 1865–1921. Hebrew writer and thinker. He wrote essays, fiction, folklore anthologies, and scholarly works. In his articles—for instance, "Reshut ha-yahid be'ad ha-rabbim ("The Individual and the Community," 1892)—he repeatedly attacked the accepted ideological positions represented mostly by the followers of Ahad Ha-am.

BERGELSON, David, 1884–1952. Russian Yiddish writer, co-editor of and contributor to Jewish journals from Berlin and Moscow to New York. His works of fiction include *Arum vokzal* (*By the Depot*, 1909), *Nokh alemen* (1913), *Baym Dnieper* (1930's), and *Naye dertseylungen* (1947).

BERKOWITZ, Yitzhak Dov, 1885–1967. Hebrew and Yiddish novelist, editor, and translator of Sholem Aleichem. He wrote stories, novels, and memoirs. He published the collected works of Sholem Aleichem (1933–48) and his own reminiscences of the latter under the title *Ha-rishonim ke-venei adam*.

BIALIK, Hayim Nahman, 1873–1934. One of the leading figures in Hebrew poetry in modern times, essayist, story writer, translator, and editor. He had a decisive influence on modern Jewish culture. His work includes lyrical poems, folk songs, poems on topical themes including "Mikra'ei Tsiyyon" ("Convocation of Zion," 1898) and "Ha-matmid" ("The Talmud Student," 1894–95), prose poems, and essays.

BILBUL, Ya'qub, 1920–). Iraqi writer, among the creators of the Arabic short story in Iraq. He is author of "Al-Jamra al Ula" ("The First Ember," 1937).

BIRNBOIM, Nathan, 1864–1937. Writer, philosopher, one of the originators of Zionist ideology, a leader of religious Judaism. He founded and edited the first Jewish nationalist journal in German, *Selbstemancipation*, where he coined the term "Zionism." Selections from his writings were published in *Ausgewaehlte Schriften zur Juedischen Frage* (1910) and *Et la'asot* (1938).

BREININ, Reuven, 1862–1939. Hebrew and Yiddish author. He published articles and sketches on contemporary Hebrew writers and artists, and monographs on writers of the *Haskalah* period. The central theme of his work was Hebrew literature in the context of world literature. His selected writings were published in three volumes (*Ketavim nivharim*, 1922–40).

BRENNER, Joseph Hayim, 1881–1921. Hebrew and Yiddish novelist, critic, philosopher, translator, and editor, he exercised a powerful influence on succeeding generations of writers. His work, characterized by self-probing, includes many articles and essays, the collection of short stories *M'emek akhor* (*From the Valley of Trouble*, 1901), the short novel *Bahoref* (*In Winter*, 1902), and the novel *Shekhol ve 'kishalon* (1920; *Breakdown and Bereavement*, 1971).

BROD, Max, 1884–1968. Czech-born German author and composer, known for his biography of Franz Kafka, as well as twenty novels, among them *Juedinnen* (1911), *Galilei in gefangenschaft* (1948), and *Die verbotene frau* (1960). His musical compositions include a piano quintet, songs, and Israeli dances.

BUBER, Martin, 1878–1965. Philosopher and theologian, Zionist thinker and leader. He published works on Hasidism (like *The Origin and Meaning of Hasidism*, Engl. trans., 1960) and translated the Bible and several works by Jewish writers into German. His philosophical works, among them, *The Knowledge of Man* (1965), are based on a dialogical theory of knowledge.

CAHAN, Abraham, 1860–51. Editor, author, and socialist leader. His Yiddish newspaper, *The Jewish Daily Forward*, which he helped found in 1897 and edited for almost fifty years, launched and sustained such authors as Sholem Asch and Isaac Bashevis Singer. His work includes *Yekl, A Tale of the New York Ghetto* (1896), *The Rise of David Levinsky* (1917), literary criticism, and stories.

CAHAN, Yaakov, 1881–1960. Hebrew poet. His poems are permeated by a longing for the revival of Hebrew culture and by a nostalgia for the distant, heroic Jewish past. He wrote lyrical poems (the cycle "Helvezyah"), dramatic poems ("Ha-Nefilim"), poetic dramas ("Yiftah"; "Aher"), ballads based on Jewish folklore, short stories, and plays.

CELAN, Paul (Paul Antschel), 1920–70. Romanian-born German poet and translator, whose work is shaped by the Holocaust and characterized by its Surrealism. His poetic works include "Der Sand aus den Urnen" (1948), "Mohn und Gedaechtnis" (1952), "Von Schwelle zu Schwelle" (1955), and "Die Niemandsrose" (1963). *Strette*, an anthology of his verse, was published in 1971.

DARWISH, Shalom, 1913– . Iraqi author. Among his short stories is the collection *Ba'd al-nas* (*One for the People*, 1948).

DER NISTER (Pinkhes Kahanovich), 1884–1950. Yiddish writer from the Ukraine. Der Nister composed fantastic tales based on the symbolic Hasidic tale created by Nahman of Bratslav. He is known for "Hekher fun der erd" ("Higher than the Earth," 1910) and his realistic novel *Di mispokhe mashber*, 2 vols (vol. 1, 1939; vol. 2, 1948). Arrested for his active support of the Yiddish language, he died in a prison hospital in the Soviet Union.

DICK, Isaac Meir, 1814–1893. One of the first popular writers in Yiddish fiction, author of over three hundred stories and short novels. He wrote in Hebrew and Yiddish and used literature to popularize the ideas of the *Haskalah*. His selected works were published in 1954 (*Geklibene verk fun I.M. Dick*).

D'ISRAELI, Isaac, 1766–1848. English writer. He wrote *Curiosities of Literature* (1791, and often reprinted) and *Amenities of Literature* (1840).

ETTINGER, Solomon, 1803–56. Yiddish poet and dramatist, influenced by the *Haskalah*. He wrote satirical and witty ballads, epigrams, poems, and dramas, of which the censors allowed only one short Hebrew poem to be published during his lifetime (1837). The definitive edition of his works, *Ale ksovim fun Dr. Shloyme Ettinger*, in 2 vols., was published in Vilna in 1925.

FARAJ, Murad, 1866–1956. Egyptian Karaite author and theologian. He published, in Hebrew and Arabic, some thirty volumes of poetry, religious works, and books on law. Among his books of poetry are *Diwan Murad*, 5 vols. (*Murad's Poetical Works*, 1912–29) and *Shir ivri mi-meshorer aravi* (*A Hebrew Song of an Arab Poet*, 1945).

FEIERBERG, Mordechai Ze'ev, 1874–99. Hebrew writer. Among the stories he published before his premature death are "Ya'akov ha-shomer" ("Jacob the Watchman," 1897), "Ha kame'a" ("The Amulet," 1897), "Ha tselalim" ("The Shadows," 1898), and "Leil aviv" ("A Spring Night," 1898). He also published articles, journalistic reports, and letters.

FELDMAN, Irving, 1928– . American poet. His poetry, frequently centering on Jewish themes, includes *Pripet Marshes and Other Poems* (1965) and *All of Us Here* (1986).

FICHMAN, Jacob, 1881–1958. Hebrew poet, critic, and literary editor. He was the editor of several journals in Palestine. His work includes the volume of poetry *Givolim* (1911), the collection of essays *Bavu'ot* (1911), prose poems, folk songs, idylls and sonnets, dramatic poems, and verse on national and biblical themes.

FIEDLER, Leslie Aaron, 1917– . American author and critic. He wrote short stories (*Pull Down Vanity*, 1962) and novels, including *The Second Stone* (1963) and *The Last Jew in America* (1966). But he is best known for his literary studies and critical essays, among which are numbered *The Art of the Essay* (1959), *Love and Death in the American Novel* (1966), *The Collected Essays of Leslie Fiedler* (1971), *Freaks* (1978), and most recently *What was Literature?* (1982) and *Fiedler on the Roof* (1991).

FOGEL, David, 1891–1944. Hebrew poet and writer, regarded as an important forerunner of Hebrew modernism. Among his published works are the volume of poetry *Lifnei ha sha'ar ha-afel* (*Before the Dark Gate*, 1923), and a collection of short stories, *Be veit ha-marpe* (*In the Sanatorium*, 1927), and the novel *Hayyei Nissu'im* (*Married Life*, 1929).

FRISHMAN, David, 1859–1922. One of the first major writers in modern Hebrew literature, author of short stories, ballads, tales (like the series of fictional biblical tales, *Ba-midbar*), essays, and lyric-satiric feuilletons. He was a literary critic and translator, as well as editor and publisher of several Jewish journals.

FRUG, Shimon Shmuel, 1860–1916. Yiddish poet. He was among the first poets to treat Jewish themes in Russian verse. A complete edition in three volumes of his Yiddish verse appeared in 1904 and 1910. Some of his lyrics, urging the Jews to labor on their ancestral soil, inspired the early Zionist pioneers. He also wrote ballads based on Jewish folklore.

GILBOA, Amir, 1917–76. Israeli poet. His volumes of poetry include *Le'ut (Fatigue*, 1942), *Shirim ha-boker ba-boker* (1953), *Kehulim va'adumim* (1963), and *Raziti likhtov siftei yesheinim* (1968).

GINSBERG, Allen, 1926– . American poet. *Howl and Other Poems* (1956) identified him with, and made him the acknowledged leader of, the Beat movement. Among his later works are numbered the volumes *Empty Mirror* (1961), *Kaddish and Other Poems* (1958), *Reality Sandwiches* (1963), and *Collected Poems* (1987).

GLANZ-LEYELES, Aaron, 1889–1966. American Yiddish poet and essayist. For over fifty years he contributed articles to the New York Yiddish daily *Der Tog*. In 1919 he was a cofounder of the In-Zikh movement of Yiddish introspectivist poetry. *Labirint* (1918), *A Yid oyfn yam* (*A Jew at Sea*, 1947), and *Amerike un Ikh* (1963) are among his volumes of poetry.

GLATSHTEYN, Yakov—see GLATSTEIN, Jacob.

GLATSTEIN, Jacob, 1896–1971. Yiddish poet, novelist, and critic. His book of verse *Yankev Glatshteyn* (1921), which inaugurated the introspectivist tendency in American Yiddish poetry, was followed by *Gedenklider* (1943) and *A Yid fun Lublin* (1966). He was one of the most richly inventive poets in Yiddish. He also wrote critical prose and travel narratives.

GNESSIN, Uri Nissan, 1881–1913. Hebrew author, one of the first to introduce a psychologically oriented prose style into Hebrew literature. He published poems, literary criticism, stories ("Hatsiddah," 1905; "Beinatayim," 1906; "Beterem," 1909; "Etsel", 1913), and translations.

GORDON, Judah Leib, 1831–92. Hebrew poet, writer, critic, and allegorist. Born in Vilna, Gordon was a major poet of the nineteenth century *Haskalah*. His poems—like "Kotso shel yod" ("The Point on the Top of the Yod," 1876) and "L'mi ani amel" ("For Whom Do I Labor?")—reflect his concern for the oppressed, and influenced the Hebrew revival movement.

GORELICK, Shemarya, 1877–1942. Yiddish essayist and literary critic. He was a cofounder (1908) and editor of the Vilna literary monthly *Literarishe Monatshriften*, which gave expression to the new national and romantic-symbolist trends in Yiddish literature. In 1933 he settled in Palestine and wrote for the Hebrew press. His essays were collected in five volumes (1908–24).

GRADE, Chaim, 1910–82. Yiddish poet and novelist. In the 1930s he became a leading figure in Young Vilna, a movement that tried to bring the mainstream of world literature to secular Yiddish culture. His work includes the poetry collections *Doyres* (*Generations*, 1945) and *Pleytim* (*Refugees*, 1947), stories in *Der shtumer minyan* (*The Silent Minyan*, 1976), and a novel, *Di agune* (*The Abandoned Wife*, 1961).

GREENBERG, Uri Zvi, 1896–1981. Yiddish and Hebrew poet, laureate of the Israel Prize for Hebrew literature (1957) and of three Bialik prizes of poetry. His poetry draws on biblical prophecy, kabbalistic symbolism, and Jewish Messianism. Among his Yiddish poetry is "In malkhus fun Tselem" ("In the Kingdom of the Cross," 1922); among his Hebrew poetry, "Rehovot hanahar" (1951). Greenberg was elected to the Knesset as a member of the Herut party in 1949.

GROSSMAN, David, 1953– . Israeli fiction writer. Author of *The Yellow Wind* (1987), *The Smile of the Lamb* (1983), and *See: Under Love* (English transl. 1989).

HADDAD, Ezra, 1903–72. Israeli Arabic scholar and leading educator among the Jewish community of Baghdad. He immigrated to Israel in 1951. Haddad published an Arabic translation of the travels of the medieval Spanish Jewish scholar, Benjamin of Tudela (Baghdad, 1945). In Israel he translated into Arabic stories by Agnon and other modern Hebrew novelists.

HALPERN, Moshe Leib, 1886–1932. Yiddish poet. He was the most independent poet of the literary group Di Yunge (1910–18). *In New York* (1919), which won him recognition as a major Yiddish poet, and *Die goldene pave* (*The Golden Peacock*, 1924) are among his volumes of poetry.

HARTMAN, Geoffrey, 1929– . American literary and cultural critic. He is the author of *The Unmediated Vision* (1966), *Beyond Formalism* (1970), *Criticism in the Wilderness* (1980), *Saving the Text* (1982), and *The Unremarkable Wordsworth* (1987) among other books, and the editor of many volumes, including *Midrash and Literature* (with Sanford Budick) and *Bitburg in Moral and Political Perspective* (1986).

HAZAZ, Hayim, 1898–1973. Hebrew writer. The stories he wrote after settling in Israel depicted the lives of groups of new immigrants, as in the volume *Hayoshevet bagannim* (1944), or in the epic novel *Ya'ish* (4 vols., 1947–52). Other works of his are the short story collection *Even sha'ot* (1973) and *Dlatot nehoshet* (*Gates of Bronze*, 1975).

HEINE, Heinrich, 1797–1856. German poet and essayist, and one of the greatest lyric poets in the German language. Some of his famous works are *Buch der Lieder* (1827), which includes the world-renowned "Lorelei"; the autobiographical *Reisebilder*, 4 vols. (1826–31); *Romanzero* (1851); and essays, which largely created a new literary genre, the feuilleton.

HESS, Moses, 1812–75. German socialist, a precursor of modern Zionism, and father of Zionist Socialism. Among his historical-philosophical works are *Die heilige Geschichte der Menschheit* (1837), *Die europaeische Trirarchie* (1841), and *Rom und Jerusalem, die letzte Nationalitaetsfrage* (1862; *Rome and Jerusalem*, 1918).

HIRSCH, Samson Raphael, 1808–88. Rabbi, writer, and leader and foremost exponent of Orthodoxy in Germany in the nineteenth century. Among his most significant works are *Neunzehn Briefe ueber Judentum* (*Nineteen Letters on Judaism*, 1836) and *Choreb, oder Versuche der Jissroels Pflichten in der Zerstreuung* (*Horeb—Essays on Israel's Duties in the Diaspora*, 1962).

HOWE, Irving, 1920–93. American literary and social critic. He wrote *Politics and the Novel* (1957) and was co-editor (with Eliezer Greenberg) of *A Treasury of Yiddish Stories* (1954), *A Treasury of Yiddish Poetry* (1969), and (with Ruth Wisse) *The Best of Sholom* [sic] *Aleichem* (1979). He also published *The World of Our Fathers* (1976) and *Celebrations and Attacks: Thirty Years of Literary and Cultural Commentary* (1979).

IBN EZRA, Moshe Ben Jacob, c. 1055–after 1135. Spanish Hebrew poet and philosopher. Concern for prosody is a hallmark of Ibn Ezra's poetry. His secular poems are pervaded by the joy of life, while his reflective poetry consists of meditations on life and death. His sacred poetry includes a corpus of *piyyutim* (liturgical hymns), of which the *selihot* (penitential prayers) are the most impressive.

IUSHKEVICH, Semyon Solomonovich, 1868–1927. Russian playwright and novelist. He wrote plays, including *Golod* (*Hunger*, 1905) and *Komedia o svadbe* (*The Comedy of Marriage*, 1911), as well as narrative works and stories. A fourteen-volume edition of his works appeared between 1914 and 1918.

KAFKA, Franz, 1883–1929. Czech-born German novelist whose work had an enormous impact on modern art and literature. He published several stories, among them "The Metamorphosis" (1916), "The Penal Colony" (1919), and "The Country Doctor" (1919). His most famous novels—*The Trial* (1925), *The Castle* (1930), and *Amerika* (1927)—were published posthumously.

KAHANA-CARMON, Amalia, 1923– . Israeli author most well known for her stream-of-consciousness fiction. Her works include the collection of short stories *Bi-khefifah ahat* (*Under One Roof*, 1966), the novel *V'hayare'ah be-Emek Ayalon* (*And the Moon in the Valley of Ayalon*, 1971), and a collection of three novellas, *Sadot magneti'im* (*Magnetic Fields*, 1977).

KATTAN, Na'im, 1928– . Canadian editor and journalist. He edited two collections of essays, *Les Juifs et la communauté française* (1965) and *Juifs et Canadiens* (1967), and is the author of *Adieu Babylone* (1975), which portrays the life of a young Baghdad Jew in the modern age. He has contributed to newspapers and periodicals in the Middle East, Europe, and Canada.

KAUFMANN, Walter, 1921–80. American philosopher, with main areas of interest in philosophy of religion, social philosophy, and the history of ideas since the nineteenth century. His best-known writings include *Nietzsche: Philosopher, Psychologist, Anti-Christ* (1950), *Critique of Religion and Philosophy* (1958), and *Hegel: Reinterpretation, Texts and Commentary* (1965).

KAVERIN, Benjamin Alexandrovich, 1902–1988. Soviet Russian writer. He was one of the few Russian writers of the detective story, including "Konets Khazy" ("The End of the Gang," 1926). He also wrote novels, like *Khudozhnik neizvesten* (1931; *The Unknown Artist*, 1947) and *Dva Kapitana* (1946; *Two Captains*, 1957).

KAZAKEVICH, Emmanuel Genrikhovich, 1913–62. Soviet Russian author. Much of his Yiddish verse is found in the anthology *Di Groyse Velt* (*The Great World*, 1939). Among his post-war novels in Russian are *Zvezda* (1947; *The Star*, 1950), *Vesna na Odere* (1949; *The Spring on the Oder*, 1953), and *Dom na ploshchadi* (1956; *The House on the Square*, 1960).

KAZIN, Alfred, 1915– . American author and critic. Among his published works are *On Native Grounds* (1942), a study of modern American prose literature; *Bright Book of Life: American Novelists and Storytellers from Hemingway to Mailer* (1973); critical articles and reviews, and the autobiographical volumes *Walker in the City* (1951), *Starting Out in the Thirties* (1965), and *New York Jew* (1978).

KLAUSNER, Joseph Gedaliah, 1874–1958. Literary critic, historian, and Zionist. In Odessa he was a member of Sefatenu Ittanu, a society for the revival of Hebrew as a spoken language. Later, in Israel, he was editor-in-chief of the *Encyclopaedia Hebraica* and author of *Historyah shel ha-sifrut ha-ivrit ha-hadashah*, 6 vols. (1930–50; *History of Modern Hebrew Literature*, 1932).

KLEINMAN, Moshe, 1870–1948. Hebrew and Yiddish author and editor. He began his journalistic career in *Hashiloah* in 1896. From 1923 until his death he was editor-in-chief of *Haolam*, central organ of the Zionist organization, moving to Berlin, London, and Jerusalem. He also published essays on Hebrew literature (*Demuyot ve-komot*, 1928) and a few monographs.

KOCH, Kenneth, 1925– . American poet. Koch's verse earned him recognition as one of the leaders of the "New York School," and influenced the formation of younger poets. Among his published volumes of poems are *Ko, or A Season on Earth* (1959), *Thank You, and Other Poems* (1962), *Art of Love* (1975), *On the Edge* (1986), and *Seasons on Earth* (1987).

KROJANKER, Gustav, 1891–1945. German author. His research on the role of Jews in German culture and literature resulted in *Juden in der deutschen Literatur* (1922). After settling in Palestine in 1932, he wrote essays on literature for the Hebrew press.

KURZWEIL, Baruch, 1907–72. Israeli literary critic, cultural historian, author, and educator. Among his main works are *Sifrutenu ha-hadasha—hemshekh o mahpekhah?* (*Our New Literature; Continuation or Revolution?*, 1965), *Bialik ve-Tchernikhovsky* (1961), and *Massot al sippurei S. Y. Agnon* (1966). See Notes on Contributors.

LACHOWER, Yeruham Fishel, 1883–1947. Critic and historian of modern Hebrew literature. As editor of the Jewish literary journals *He-tekufah* in Warsaw and *Moznayim* in Tel Aviv, he dealt with authors of the modern national renaissance. His work includes *Toldot ha-sifrut ha-ivrit ha-hadashah*, 4 vols. *(History of Modern Hebrew Literature*, 1947–48).

LAMDAN, Yitzhak, 1899–1954. Hebrew poet and editor. His poetic work, inspired by pioneer life in Palestine, also includes the long epic poem "Massadah" (1927). From 1934 on he published and edited his own literary monthly, *Gilyonot*.

LASKER-SCHUELER, Else, 1869–1945. German poet, known for her expressionism. Her early poems were published in *Styx* (1902). Her novel *Mein Herz* appeared in 1913, her lyrics on Jewish themes, *Hebraeische Balladen*, was also published in 1913; and her collected works appeared in three volumes between 1959 and 1962.

LAZARUS, Emma, 1849–87. American poet, best remembered for her sonnet, "The New Colossus," engraved on the Statue of Liberty. Among her works are *Songs of a Semite* (1882), a volume of prose poems, and a number of essays published in 1882 in defense of the Russian Jewish immigrants to America.

LEIVICK, H. (Leivick Halpern), 1886–1962. Yiddish poet and dramatist. His activities, in keeping with the revolutionary mood in Russia in the early 1900s, brought him to court and to prison, where he wrote *Di keytn fun Meshiekh* (*Messiah in Chains*, 1939). After escaping to America he continued writing poetry as well as plays, including *Der Goylem* (1921) and *Der nes in geto* (1940).

LEVI, Primo, 1919–87. Italian author. Levi's deportation to Auschwitz in 1944 is the subject of *Se questo e un uoma?* (1947; *If This is a Man*, 1959). In 1961 it reappeared as *Survival in Auschwitz: the Nazi Assault on Humanity*. He is also the author of *The Periodic Table* (1984) among other works.

LEVIN, Meyer, 1905–1981. American novelist. The author of one of the first English novels on kibbutz life, *Yehudah* (1931), Levin has written about both Israel (where he lived for several years) and the American Jewish community, in *The Old Bunch* (1937), based on his community in Chicago. His other works include *Settlers: A Novel* (1972), *Stronghold* (1965), and *Fanatic* (1964).

LEWISOHN, Ludwig, 1882–1955. American novelist and essayist. He published works of criticism, among them *The Spirit of Modern German Literature* (1916); impressions of his 1925 visit to Palestine (published in Israel in 1925, and translated into English as *The Answer: The Jew and the World* in 1934); and novels, some of which—like *The Last Days of Shylock* (1931) and *In a Summer Season* (1955)—are on Jewish themes.

MAILER, Norman, 1923– . American novelist and essayist. His novels include the bestselling *The Naked and the Dead* (1948), collections of essays including

Advertisements for Myself (1959), and *Cannibals and Christians* (1966); and documentaries such as *Armies in the Night* (1967). In 1980 he was awarded the Pulitzer Prize in fiction for *The Executioner's Song*.

MAIMONIDES, Moses ("Rambam," from the acronym Rabbi Moses ben Maimon), 1135–1204. Rabbinic authority, codifier, philosopher, and royal physician. His fame rests chiefly on the code of Jewish law—*Mishne Tora* (1180)—and the *Guide for the Perplexed* (1190), considered to be an outstanding philosophic work.

MALAMUD, Bernard, 1914–86. American novelist. His work includes the novels *The Assistant* (1957) and *Dubin's Lives* (1979), and the collections of short stories *The Magic Barrel* (1958) and *Idiots First* (1963). His novel *The Fixer* (1966) won the National Book Award and the Pulitzer Prize in 1967.

MANI-LEIB (Mani-Leib Brahinsky), 1883–1953. Yiddish poet who immigrated from Russia to the U.S. One of the New York poetry circle called *Di Yunge*. He was co-editor of *Insel*, one of the principal anthologies of *Die Yunge*, and author of *Lider un baladn* (*Songs and Ballads*, 2 vols. 1955) and *Sonetn* (*Sonnets*, 1961).

MEGED, Aharon, 1920– . Israeli writer and editor. In the 1950s he edited the journal *Ba sha'ar* in Tel Aviv and founded the bi-weekly literary magazine *Massa*. He wrote short stories, the first collection of which was *Ru'ah yamim* (1950); novels, including *Ha-hai al-ha-met* (1965) and *Al ezim ve-avanim* (*Just About Everything*, 1974); and plays.

MENDELE MOKHER SEFORIM (Shalom Abramovitch), 1835–1917. Hebrew and Yiddish writer and one of the founders of modern literary Yiddish. Among his most well-known works are *Dos klayne menshele* (*The Little Man*, 1864), *Dos vinshfingeril* (*The Magic Ring*, 1865), *Fishke der Krumer* (*Fishke the Lame*, 1869), *Di kliatshe* (*The Nag*, 1873), "Masot Binyamin hashlishi" ("The Travels and Adventures of Benjamin III," 1879). He also wrote literary and social criticism, satire, and works of popular science.

MIKHAEL, Murad, 1906–86. Iraqi poet and educator. He published his first collection of poetry-in-prose in Baghdad in 1931. After immigrating to Israel in 1949, he specialized in Arab education and wrote several textbooks.

MIKHAEL, Sami, 1926– . Israeli writer, born in Baghdad. After settling in Israel in 1949, he continued for a while to write in Arabic, but in 1974 he published his first Hebrew novel, which was followed by several novels and plays, often reflecting his Iraqi background. His best-known novel is *Hasut* (1977; *Refuge*, 1988).

MOLODOWSKY, Kadia, 1894–1975. Yiddish poet and novelist. *Kheshvendike Nekht* (1927) and *Likht fun Dornboym* (1965) are among her volumes of poetry. She also wrote the novel *Fun Lublin biz New York* (*From Lublin to New York*, 1942) and the short story collection *A shtub mit zibn fentster* (*A House with Seven Windows*, 1957).

MONTAIGNE, Michel de, 1533–92. French writer and philosopher. He is chiefly known for the *Essays*, begun in 1571, reflecting his humanistic skeptical philosophy and undermining existing theories. The *Essays* had an enormous impact on later writers.

NAHMAN (BEN SIMHAH) of BRATSLAV, 1771–1811. Hasidic religious leader in the Ukraine, known for his theological writings (*Likkutei Moharan*, 1806) and for his stories published in Yiddish and Hebrew (*The Tales of Rabbi Nahman*, 1956), which have been adapted and have influenced modern writers, among them I.L. Peretz and Martin Buber.

NAQQASH, Samir, 1937– . Israeli Arabic-prose writer. A graduate of the Hebrew University, he writes solely in Arabic, in which he has so far published nine volumes. His stories often reflect his Iraqi background.

NEMEROV, Howard, 1920– . American poet and critic. His verse collections include *The Image of the Law* (1947), *Guide to the Ruins* (1950), *Mirrors and Windows* (1958), and *Collected Poems* (1977). He is also the author of two plays, two novels, and a number of critical works.

NIGER, Samuel (Samuel Charney), 1883–1955. Yiddish literary critic, one of the most revered of his generation. In 1908 he founded, with S. Gorelick and A. Veiter, the *Literarishe Monatshriften* in Vilna. From 1920 on he wrote weekly reviews and articles in the New York Yiddish daily *Der Tog*. His posthumous works include *Bleter Geshikhte fun der Yiddisher Literatur* (1959).

OPATOSHU, Joseph, 1886–1954. Yiddish novelist and short-story writer. For forty years he contributed stories, sketches, and serials to the New York Yiddish daily *Der Tog*, ever since it was founded in 1914. He also wrote novels (*Farloyrene mentshn*, 1919) and historical novels (*Der Letster Oyfshtand*, translated as *The Last Revolt*, 1948–52).

OZ, Amos, 1939– . Israeli writer. His published books include *Artsot ha-tan* (1965; *Where Jackals Howl and Other Stories*, 1981), *Mikhael Shelli* (1968; *My Michael*, 1972), *Makom Akher* (*Elsewhere, Perhaps*, 1973), *Har ha'-etsah ha-ra'ah* (1976; *The Hill of Evil Counsel*, 1978), *Kufsah shehorah* (1987; *Black Box*, 1989), and *Lada'at isha* (*To Know a Woman*, 1989).

OZICK, Cynthia, 1928– . American novelist, essayist, and short-story writer. Her first full-length novel, *Trust* (1966) was followed by the collection of short stories *The Pagan Rabbi* (1971). Her other works include *Bloodshed and Three Novellas* (1976), *Levitation: Five Fictions* (1981), *Cannibal Galaxy* (1983), *The Messiah of Stockholm* (1987), and, most recently, *Metaphor and Memory: Essays* (1989) and *The Shawl* (1989). See Notes on Contributors.

PAGIS, Dan, 1930–86. Israeli poet. Born in Bukovina, he spent three years in a concentration camp, immigrating to Israel in 1946. A professor of medieval Hebrew literature at the Hebrew University, Pagis published many scholarly works as well as poetry. His books of poems include *The Shadow Dial* (1959), *Late Leisure* (1964), *Transformation* (1970), *Brain* (1975), *Twelve Faces* (1981), and *Points of Departure* (1981).

PASTERNAK, Boris, 1890–1960. Soviet-Russian poet and novelist. His novel, *Dr. Zhivago*, smuggled out of the U.S.S.R and published in Italy (1957), earned him a Nobel Prize in 1958, which he declined to accept for political reasons.

PERETZ, Isaac Leib, 1852–1915. Yiddish and Hebrew poet, dramatist, essayist, and fiction writer, and one of the founders of modern Yiddish literature. His two volumes of stories, *Khasidish* (Hasidic) and *Folkstimmlikhe geshikhten (Folktales,* 1909) were the major work of his career. His well-known plays are *Di Goldene keyt (The Golden Chain,* 1909) and *Baynakht oyfn alten mark (At Night in the Old Market,* 1907). Translations of his work are available in *The I.L. Peretz Reader* edited by Ruth Wisse (1990).

PINES, Shlomo, 1908– . Professor of general and Jewish philosophy at the Hebrew University. He published a new English translation of Maimonides's *Guide for the Perplexed* (1963) and *Scholasticism After Aquinas and the Teachings of Hasdai Crescas and His Predecessors* (1967).

PROUST, Marcel, 1871–1922. French novelist. His outstanding work, *A la recherche du temps perdu,* 15 vols. (1913–27; *Remembrance of Things Past,* 1922–32), had a major impact on Western modernist literature.

RABOY, Isaac, 1882–1944. American Yiddish novelist. He was a member of the literary group Di Yunge, in whose anthologies he published his first stories. His work includes the autobiography *Mayn Lebn* (2 vols., 1945–47) and the novels *Her Goldenbarg* (1923) and *Der yiddisher Cowboy* (1942).

RAHV, Philip, 1908–73. American editor and critic, one of the founders of *Partisan Review* and subsequently of *Modern Occasions.* Among the critical works he published are *Image and Idea* (1949), *Literature in America* (1957), and *Myth and the Powerhouse* (1965).

RAMBAM—see MAIMONIDES, Moses.

RASHI (Solomon ben Isaac), 1040–1105. Leading commentator on the Bible and Talmud. His comments, extending to most—if not all—the books of the Bible, are distinguished by an attempt to compromise between the literal and the midrashic interpretations. His commentaries center on meticulous analyses of the text's language.

RATOSH, Yonatan (Uriel Halperin), 1908–81. Israeli poet, translator, essayist, and founder of the Young Hebrews movement, later coined " the Canaanites." In his controversial writings he advocated a separation between the nation of the Hebrews and that of the Jewish people as it evolved in the Diaspora. His volumes of poetry include *Black Canopy* (1941) and *Who Walks in Darkness* (1965). See Notes on Contributors.

RAVITCH, Melekh (Zekharye Khone Bergner), 1893–1976. Yiddish poet and essayist. Among his works are *Nakete lider* (*Naked Songs*, 1921), influenced by expressionistic poetry, *Di fir zaytn fun mayn velt* (1929), and *Kontinentn un okeanen* (1937). Born in East Galicia, Ravitch lived for some time in Warsaw, finally making his home in Montreal.

ROLNICK, Joseph, 1879–1955. Yiddish poet. He broke with the tradition of didactic social poetry, paving the way for impressionism and symbolism. His poetry was published in collections of *Lider* (1915, 1926, 1935).

ROTH, Henry, 1906– . American novelist. His novel, *Call It Sleep* (1934), steeped in both Jewish and American culture, treats the theme of immigration and assimilation in a highly innovative, modernist style. His complete stories have been collected in *Shifting Landscape* (1987). His second novel, *Mercy of a Rude Stream*, was published in 1994.

ROTH, Joseph, 1894–1939. Austrian novelist. He worked as a journalist and published articles, short stories, and fourteen novels, among them *Hiob* (1930; *Job*, 1931), *Die Flucht ohne Ende* (1927), *Rechts und Links* (1929), and *Die Legende vom heiligen Trinker* (1939). His collected works were published in 1956.

ROTH, Philip, 1933– . American novelist. Controversial writer known for his comic and satirical treatment of American Jewish life and, more recently, the place of the artist in Jewish and modern society. His work includes the collection of short stories *Goodbye, Columbus* (1959), the novels *Letting Go* (1962), bestseller *Portnoy's Complaint* (1969), *Professor of Desire* (1977), *Counterlife* (1986), and *Deception* (1990), and the collection of essays, *Reading Myself and Others* (1975), and most recently *Operation Shylock* (1993).

ROSENZWEIG, Franz, 1886–1929. German Jewish theologian. His major work, *Der Stern der Erloesung* (*The Star of Redemption*, 1921) outlines a history of culture and proposes a theology of Judaism and Christianity. He translated Hebrew literary works into German (including the poems of Yehudah Halevi) and began a new translation of the Bible with Martin Buber.

RUBENSTEIN, Richard (1924–) American theologian. His works include *After Auschwitz: Radical Theology and Contemporary Judaism* (1966) and *The Age of Triage: Fear and Hope in an Overcrowded World* (1983).

RUKEYSER, Muriel, 1913–80. American poet and author of verse collections, including *Theory of Flight* (1935) and *Waterlily Fire* (1962), which show her preoccupation with social problems. Among her other works are books for children, a biography, and an Irish fantasy.

SAADIA (Ben Joseph) GAON, 882–942. The father of medieval Jewish philosophy. He edited the first prayer book, compiled the first Hebrew dictionary, and translated the Bible into Arabic. His major philosophical work is *Kitab al-Amanat wa-al l'tiqadat* (translated into English as *The Book of Beliefs and Opin-*

ions, 1948). He produced seminal studies on halakha, grammar, philology, philosophy, and liturgy.

SACHS, Nelly (Leonie), 1891–1970. German poet and Nobel Prize winner (1966). Known for her mystical and visionary poetry, mostly written after and influenced by the Holocaust. She was the author of several volumes of poetry, among them *In den Wohnungen des Todes* (1946), *Sternverdunkelung* (1958), *Und niemand weiss weiter* (1957) and *O The Chimneys* [English transl. Michael Hamburger] (1967).

SADAN, Dov, 1902–1990. Yiddish and Hebrew writer, critic, and scholar. The more than fifty published volumes of his work do not include even half of his total output, consisting of essays on folklore, humor, idioms, the Hebrew and Yiddish languages, and literature. Among his collections of Hebrew literary criticism are *Avnei Bohan* (1951), *Avnei Bedek* (1962), and *Avnei Gader* (1968).

SADEH, Pinchas, 1929– . Israeli writer, author of poems, stories, and literary articles. His work includes "Ha-hayim ke-mashal" ("Life as a Parable," 1966), the autobiographical story "Al mazzavo shel ha-adam" (1967), the novel *Massa dumah* (1951), poems, and children's books.

SALINGER, J.D. (Jerome David). 1919– . American author. Known for his celebrated first novel, *Catcher in the Rye* (1951), Salinger has subsequently published *Nine Stories* (1953) and *Franny and Zooey* (1961).

SANU', Ya'qub (James Sanua), 1839–1912. Egyptian playwright. One of the first authors of plays in spoken Arabic and one of the creators of satiric journalism in modern Egypt. When his antigovernmental articles and plays forced him to leave Egypt, he continued to edit periodicals from Paris, which were smuggled into Egypt.

SASSOON b. Salah, 1750–1830. The founder of the influential Sassoon family of Jewish merchants, philanthropists, and men of letters, originally from Baghdad. They had the reputation of being the merchant-princes of the Orient, "the Rothschilds of the East."

SCHNITZLER, Arthur, 1862–1931. Austrian playwright and author. Before World War I, his plays were among those most often performed on the German and Austrian stages. Among his plays are *Liebelei* (1895), *Der einsame Weg* (1904), *Zwischenspiel* (1906), and *Das weite Land* (1911). *Casanovas Heimfahrt* (1918) and *Fraeulein Else* (1929) are two of his novellas.

SCHOLEM, Gershom Gerhard, 1897–1982. Judaic scholar, authority on Kabbalah and Jewish mysticism. His work includes more than five hundred titles, among them his classic study of Hasidism, *Major Trends in Jewish Mysticism* (1941).

SCHWARTZ, Delmore, 1913–66. American poet, author, and critic. He was the editor of *Partisan Review* from 1943 to 1955 and a major contributor to the magazine *Commentary*. His most well-known collection of short stories is *In Dreams Begin Responsibilities* (1938). He also wrote a verse play and a collection of lyrics.

SCHWARTZ-BART, André, 1928– . French writer. Imprisoned in a German concentration camp, his book based on his experiences, *Les dernieres des justes* (1959; *The Last of the Just*, 1961), won the Prix Goncourt. He won the Jerusalem Prize for his subsequent book, co-authored with his wife Simone, *Un plat de porc aux bananes vertes* (*A Plate of Pork with Green Bananas*, 1967). His most recent book is *A Woman Named Solitude* (1973).

SHABTAI, Yaakov, 1934–81. Israeli novelist, story writer, and translator, known for his stream-of-consciousness technique. He was awarded the Kinor David Prize for his plays and the Bernstein Prize for the novel *Zikhron Dvarim* (1977; *Past Continuous*, 1983). His work also includes *Sof Davar* (1984; *Past Perfect*, 1987), published posthumously.

SHAHAR, David, 1926– . Israeli writer, who has made Jerusalem the setting of many of his works. Some of his collections of stories are *Al ha-halomot* (*On Dreams*, 1955), *Maggid ha-atidot* (*The Fortune Teller*, 1966), *Moto shel ha-elohim ha-katan* (*Death of the Little God*, 1970).

SHAMAS, Anton, 1950– . Palestinian-Israeli writer who has published his poetry and translations in both Arabic and Hebrew. Known primarily for his novel *Arabesques* (Hebrew 1986; Engl. 1988).

SHAMIR, Moshe, 1921– . Israeli author. The founder and editor of several literary magazines, he wrote realistic novels that reflect Israeli life, such as *Hu halakh ba-sadot* (*He Walked the Fields*, 1947) and *Ha-Gevul* (*The Border*, 1966), *Yonah Be-Hatser Zarah* (*Pigeon in a Strange Land*, 1975), historical novels, plays, short stories, essays, articles and literary sketches.

SHAPIRO, Karl Jay, 1913– . American poet and critic. He was the editor of the Chicago periodical *Poetry* between 1950 and 1955. The author of a number of critical works, he was awarded the Pulitzer Prize for the volume *V-Letter and Other Poems* (1944).

SHAPIRO, (Levi Joshua) LAMED, 1878–1948. Yiddish writer. He wrote stories, part of which were collected in the volume *Di yiddishe melukhe* (*The Jewish State*, 1919). Several of his stories were translated into English in *A Treasury of Yiddish Stories* (1954), edited by Irving Howe and Eliezer Greenberg.

SHAPIRO, Noah, 1866–1931. Hebrew poet and labor leader in *Eretz* Israel before the Second Aliyah. While his poetry was very popular, he also published articles on the affairs of the *Yishuv* in the Hebrew press.

SHA'UL, Anwar, 1904–84. Iraqi poet and journalist. He wrote poetry and fiction, publishing his own weekly in Baghdad, *Al-Hasid*, between 1929 and

1938. His work includes *Fi Ziham al-Madina* (*In the Tumult of the City*, 1955) and the volume of poems *Hamsat al-Zaman* (*Whispers of Time*, 1956). He settled in 1971 in Israel, where he published his collected poetry and his autobiography.

SHENHAR, Yitzhak, 1902–57. Hebrew author. He published poetry, fiction, plays, travel notes, and children's literature. His position in Israeli literature was established mainly through fiction and translations. Among his collections of stories are *Basar ve-dam* (1941) and *Yamim yedabru* (1945).

SHLONSKY, Abraham, 1900–73. Hebrew poet, editor, and translator. His vast poetic and literary output includes volumes of poetry like *Be'elleh ha-yamim* (1930) and *Sefer ha-sulamot* (1973), and translations of poetry, drama, novels, and short stories.

SHNEOUR, Zalman, 1887–1959. Hebrew and Yiddish poet and novelist. He was editor of and contributor to several Jewish literary journals in Europe and later in Israel. His first volume of verse, *Im sheki'at ha-hammah* (1906–7), marked the beginning of a vast poetic output. One of his best-known late works is the epic *Ba'al ha-parvah* published in the 1950s.

SHOFMAN, Gershon, 1880–1972. Hebrew writer. He wrote short stories, sketches, epigrammatic essays, and articles on literature and literary criticism, which he published in various Jewish periodicals in Europe and Israel. Awarded the Israel Prize for Literature in 1957, his collected writings first appeared in 1927–35 in four volumes.

SHOLEM ALEICHEM (Shalom Rabinovitch), 1859–1916. Extremely prolific and popular Yiddish author and humorist and one of the central figures in Yiddish literature. He wrote reports, articles, feuilletons, short stories, dramas, and novels. He created the memorable portraits of Menachem Mendl (published as a series of letters in 1892) and Tevye the Dairyman (*Tevye der milkhiger,* monologue, 1894). *The Best of Sholom* [sic] *Aleichem*, edited by Ruth Wisse and Irving Howe, was published in 1979.

SHOMER (Nahum Meyer Shaikevitch), 1849–1905. Yiddish novelist and dramatist. He achieved great mass appeal with his plays and his dime novels, first in Vilna and later in America. Of his more than one hundred novels and plays, at least a dozen have retained their popularity, among them *Di ungliklikhe libe* (1882), *Eyn ungerikhter glik* (1885), *Der yid un di grefin* (1892).

SHTEYNBARG, Eliezer, 1880–1932. Yiddish educator, writer, and master of the Yiddish fable. His fables were collected in the posthumous volume *Mesholim* (1932), which became a bestseller immediately upon publication.

SHTEYNBERG, Yaakov, 1887–1947. Hebrew poet, short-story writer, and essayist. He wrote his first short stories and novelettes in Yiddish, but in Palestine he started contributing regularly in Hebrew to *He po'el ha-tsa'ir, Moledet,* and *Davar.* From 1942 he was one of the editors of the literary periodical *Moznayim.*

SIMON, Akiba Ernst 1899–1988. Educator, religious thinker, and writer. In 1935 he joined the staff of the Hebrew University, where he taught philosophy and the history of education. Among his writings are *Hayim Nachman Bialik* (1935) and *Mishnato shel Pestalozzi* (1962). He coedited *Enziklopedya hinukhit,* 5 vols. *(Educational Encyclopedia,* 1961–66).

SINGER, Isaac Bashevis, 1904–91. Yiddish novelist, critic, and journalist, Nobel Laureate for literature 1978. His work includes the novels *Satan in Goray* (1935), *The Family Moskat* (1948), *The Manor* (1957), *The Magician of Lublin* (1960), and *Shosha* (1978), as well as short romances, novellas and short stories (*Gimpel the Fool and Other Stories,* 1957).

SINGER, Israel Joshua, 1893–1944. Yiddish novelist, playwright, and journalist, the older brother of Isaac Bashevis Singer. He published the short-story collections *Perl un Andere Dertseylungen* (1922) and *Oyf Fremder Erd* (1925), and fiction: *Yoshe Kalb* (1932), *Shtol un Ayzn* (1927; *Blood Harvest,* 1935), *Di Brider Ashkenazi* (1936; *The Brothers Ashkenazi,* 1936).

SOKOLOV, Nahum, 1859–1936. Hebrew writer, pioneer in modern Hebrew journalism, and president of the World Zionist Organization (WZO). As columnist of the newspaper *Ha-Zefirah* (1876), he created a vast reading public. As president of the WZO, he established the official Hebrew weekly *Haolam* (1907). His other publications include *History of Zionism 1600–1918,* 2 vols. (1919).

SONTAG, Susan, 1933– . American critic and author, most well known for her criticism. She has also published novels, among them *The Benefactor* (1963) and *Death Kit* (1967). Her essay collections include *Against Interpretation* (1966), *Styles of Radical Will* (1969), and *Illness as Metaphor* (1978).

SPINOZA, Baruch (Benedict) de, 1632–77. Dutch philosopher. His heretical views led to his excommunication from the Jewish community. His work includes *Principles of the Philosophy of René Descartes* (1663), *Tractatus Theologico-Politicus* (1670), and the *Ethics* (1674, published posthumously).

STEINER, George, 1929– . European literary critic with a distinguished literary career in England, Switzerland, and the United States. His works include *The Death of Tragedy* (1961), *Language and Silence* (1958), *After Babel* (1975), *In Bluebeard's Castle* (1971), and *Real Presences* (1989).

STERNHEIM, Carl, 1878–1942. German playwright. Known for his antibourgeois comedies such as *Buerger Schippel* (1913) and *Der Snob* (1914), and for essays containing anti-Semitic sentiments, such as *Berlin oder Juste Milieu* (1920).

STRAUSS, Leo, 1899–1973. American philosopher and political scientist. A native of Germany, his study of the reception and adaptation of Greek philosophy by medieval Jewish and Muslim writers constitutes an important part of his work. Among his other published books are *Spinoza's Critique of Religion* (Engl. trans., 1965) and *Persecution and the Art of Writing* (1952).

SVEVO, Italo (Ettore Schmitz), 1861–1928. Italian novelist. The author of the modernist novel *La Cosciena di Zeno* (1923; *Confessions of Zeno*, 1930), Svevo attracted the attention and support of James Joyce in Trieste. His collected works appeared in 1954.

TABIB, Mordecai, 1910–79. Hebrew writer. He published poems and prose in *Davar* and *Itim* and various Hebrew periodicals. Some of his books, such as *Keesev ha-sadeh* (1948), *Derekh shel afar* (1953), and *Ke-arar be-aravah* (1957), deal with the Yemenite community in Israel. *Massa la-arets ha-gedolah* (1968) contains stories and a poem.

TAMMUZ, Benjamin, 1919–89. Israeli writer and journalist. Former editor of the *Haaretz* weekend literary supplement and of *Art in Israel*, his work includes collections of short stories (*Holot ha-zahav*, 1950), the novels *Requiem le-Na'aman* (*A Requiem for Na'aman*, 1978), and *Pardes* (1971; *The Orchard: A Novella*, 1984), children's books, and translations of several literary works into Hebrew.

TCHERNICHOWSKY, Saul, 1875–1943. Hebrew poet. His work shows a tendency to break the restrictions of traditional Hebrew literature and to expand its content and form. He wrote verse, collected in volumes like *Hezionot u-manginot* (1898), *Shirim* (1910), and *Kokhevei shamayim rehokim* (1944), as well as stories, scholarly essays, and translations of several works from the Greek.

TRILLING, Lionel, 1905–75. American author, critic, and scholar. His critical work includes *Matthew Arnold* (1939), *The Liberal Imagination* (1950), *The Opposing Self* (1955), *Beyond Culture: Essays on Learning and Literature* (1965). In 1947 he published the novel *The Middle of the Journey*.

URIS, Leon, 1924– . American novelist. The author of one of the most popular bestsellers on Israel ever written, *Exodus* (1957), Uris also wrote a popular novel about the Warsaw ghetto uprising, *Mila 18* (1960). Among his other works are *Armaggedon* (1964), about the Berlin airlift, and *QBVII* (1970), about a Nazi doctor.

VEITER, A. (Eisik Meir Devenishski), 1878–1919. Yiddish writer and editor. He wrote plays, short stories, and essays. His plays include *Fartog* (1907), *In Fayer* (1910), and *Der Shtumer* (1912). Together with S. Gorelick and S. Niger, he edited and published in 1908 the *Literarishe Monatshriften*.

VOGEL, David—see FOGEL, David.

WASSERMANN, Jakob, 1873–1933. German novelist and essayist. Among his novels are *Die Juden von Zirndorf* (1897; *The Dark Pilgrimage*, 1933), *Christian*

Wahnschaffe (1919; in 1920 it became an American bestseller under the title *The World's Illusion*), *Der Fall Mauritius* (1928; *The Mauritius Case*, 1929), and *Doktor Kerkhoven* (1931).

WEININGER, Otto, 1880–1903. Austrian psychologist and philosopher. His major work, *Geschlecht und Charakter* (1902; *Sex and Character*, 1906) is a justification of misogyny and anti-Semitism.

WEINREICH, Max, 1894–1969. Yiddish linguist, historian, editor, and translator. He contributed to Jewish periodicals and taught Yiddish and literature in Vilna and the United States. Among his philological studies is *Geshikhte fun der yiddisher sprakhe* (1947; *History of the Yiddish Language*, 1980), while *Hitler's Professors* (1946) is an indictment of German scholarship during the Nazi regime.

WERFEL, Franz, 1890–1945. Austrian novelist, playwright, and poet. Among his novels are *Verdi: Roman der Oper* (1924; *Verdi: A Novel of the Opera*, 1925), *Das Lied von Bernadette* (1941; *The Song of Bernadette*, 1942), and *Stern der Ungeborenen* (1946; *Star of the Unborn*, 1946). His play *The Eternal Road* (1937) was set to music by Kurt Weill and staged in New York by Max Reinhardt.

WIENER, Meir, 1893–1941. Poet and literary critic who wrote in Hebrew, Yiddish, German and Russian. His prefaces to critical editions of Yiddish literary works were collected in *Tsu der geshikhte fun der yiddisher literatur in nayntsenten yorhundert*, 2 vols. (1945–46), and his book on Sholem Aleichem, *Vegn Sholem Aleichems humor*, was published in 1941.

WIESEL, Elie, 1928– . Romanian-born novelist and journalist. Having witnessed the horrors of Nazi concentration camps as a child, Wiesel has written many accounts of the Holocaust as well as other books dealing with Soviet Jewry, Israel, and Jewish spiritual life, among them *Night* (1960), *Dawn* (1961), *Town Beyond the Wall* (1964), *Gates of the Forest* (1966), *Legends of Our Time* (1968), *Beggar in Jerusalem* (1970), *Souls of Fire* (1972), and *Against Silence* (1985).

YEHOSHUA, Avraham B., 1936– . Israeli novelist and essayist. He published three volumes of stories—*Mot ha-zaken* (1962), *Mul ha-y'arot* (1968), and *Tishah sippurim* (1970)—and novels, including the bestseller *Ha-me'ahev* (*The Lover*, 1976), *Gerushim Meukharim* (*Late Divorce*, 1984), and *Molkho* (1987; *Five Seasons*, 1989).

YEHUDAH HALEVI, before 1075–after 1141. Hebrew poet and philosopher who lived in Spain. He composed both secular poetry—love poems, poems of eulogy and lament—and religious poetry—350 *piyyutim*, of which the *selihot* are among the greatest in Jewish religious poetry after the Psalms. His *Shirei Ziyyon* (*Poems of Zion*) are poems of longing for *Eretz* Israel.

YIZHAR, S. (Yizhar Smilansky), 1916– . Hebrew author, belonging to the first generation of native Israeli writers. His distinctive prose style, showing an awareness of the local landscape, influenced younger Hebrew writers. His works include the novel *Yemei ziklag* (1958), many short stories, novellas, and articles on political and public affairs.

ZACH, Natan, 1930– . Israeli poet. His published works include *Shirim rishonim* (1955), *B'mkom halom* (1966), *Beyt sefer l'rikudim* (1985), *Anti-mehikon* (1984) and *Shirim al kelev v'kalba* (1990). He translated Arabic folk songs together with Rashed Hussein (*Dekalim u-temarim*, 1967).

ZANGWILL, Israel, 1864–1926. English author. The world of East London Jewry served as his material for his "ghetto" novels: the internationally successful *Children of the Ghetto* (1895), *The King of the Schnorrers* (1894), *Ghetto Tragedies* (1899), *Ghetto Comedies* (1907), and *Dreams of the Ghetto* (1923). He also published several other novels and plays.

ZEITLIN, Aaron, 1898–1973. Hebrew and Yiddish writer. His Yiddish lyrics are collected in *Shotns oyfn shney* (1922) and *Metatron* (1922) and in the later *Gezamelte lider*, 3 vols. (vols. 1 and 2, 1947; vol. 3, 1957). In Hebrew he wrote essays and poems, and gave lectures during his frequent visits to Israel. He also wrote the drama *Yakob Frank* (1929) and the novel *Brenendige Erd* (*Burning Earth*, 1937).

ZEITLIN, Hillel, 1871–1942. Author and journalist. His writings include articles, monographs (on Spinoza, 1900; on Nietzsche, 1905), *Mahshavah ve-shirah*, 2 vols. (1911–12), *Al gevul shnei olamot* (1919), and writings on religious issues, including *Der alef-beys funem yudentum* (*The Alphabet of Judaism*, 1922). He translated the *Zohar* into Hebrew and wrote a commentary on it.

ZUNSER, Alikum, 1836–1913. Popular Yiddish poet and dramatist in Russia and eventually in New York. His poetic work includes *Shirim hadashim* (1872). In 1882 he composed songs for young immigrants to Palestine, "Shivas Tsion" and "Di Sokhe," the latter becoming his most popular song both in its Yiddish and in its Hebrew versions.

ZWEIG, Arnold, 1887–1968. German novelist and playwright. For a time the editor of the Zionist *Juedische Rundschau* and (with Leon Feuchtwanger) author of *Die Aufgabe des Judentums* (1933). Among his novels and plays are *Novellen um Claudia* (1912; *Claudia*, 1930), *Der Streit um den Sergeanten Grischa* (1927; *The Case of Sergeant Grischa*, 1928), and *Das Beil von Wandsbek* (1947; *The Axe of Wandsbek*, 1947).

ZWEIG, Stefan, 1881–1942. Austrian playwright, essayist, and biographer. He wrote biographies of Stendhal, Tolstoy, Marie Antoinette, Magellan, and Amerigo Vespucci, among others. His essay collections include *Erstes Erlebnis* (1911) and *Amok* (1922); among his short story collections are *Die Liebe der Erika Ewald* (1904) and *Kaleidoscope* (1934).

Index

Make books your companion
Let your bookshelf be your garden—
Judah Ibn Tibbon

to become a member –
to present a gift –

call 1 (800) 234-3151
or write:
The Jewish Publication Society
1930 Chestnut Street
Philadelphia, Pennsylvania 19103

A Jewish Tradition